The Indian Temple

THE INDIAN TEMPLE
– mirror of the world –

Bruno DAGENS

New Age Books
New Delhi (India)

Indira Gandhi National Centre for the Arts
New Delhi (India)

First English Edition: Delhi, 2016
Originally published in France under the title *Le Temple Indien Miroir du Monde*, Paris. 2009 (ISBN : 978-2-251-33831-6) by Sociéte d'édition Les Belles Lettres, 95 boulevard Raspail, 75006 PARIS, France.

ISBN: 978-81-7822-485-5

Published by
INDIRA GANDHI NATIONAL CENTRE FOR THE ARTS
Central Vista, Janpath, New Delhi 110051
Phone: 011-23388438, 23388241
Website: www.ignca.nic.in

and

NEW AGE BOOKS
A-44 Naraina Industrial Area, Phase-I
New Delhi (India)-110 028
E-mail: nab@newagebooksindia.com
Website: www.newagebooksindia.com

NAB Cataloging-in-Publication Data
THE INDIAN TEMPLE : *mirror of the world*
by Bruno Dagens
Includes Introduction, Glossary,
Bibliography and Index
ISBN 978-81-7822-485-5

Printed by
Replika Press Pvt. Ltd.

To Jacques DUMARÇAY
as a token of friendship

Foreword

IGNCA explores knowledge related to Indian Art and Culture in multiple dimensions and at different levels, through its various research programmes. These programmes are mainly carried out through five divisions known as Kalā Nidhi (Library & Information Division); Kalākośa (Research and Publication Division); Janapada Sampadā (Division for the Study of Diverse Living Traditions); Kalā Darśana (Division for Exhibition and Presentation); and Sūtradhāra (Division for Administration and Co-ordination). It also has a well-developed Media Unit for audio-visual documentation and film-making, as also a Cultural Informatics Lab for the production of interactive multimedia CDs, DVDs and developing a National Digital Data Bank on Culture.

In Kalākośa Division the main focus is on research and publications, carried out through its three fundamental programmes. Kalātattvakośa is the first, representing the intellectual vision in a series of multiple volumes shedding a fresh light on Indian thought system and the categories of knowledge. The second programme is Kalāmūlaśāstra devoted to the publication of critical editions with translations of the fundamental texts which are basic to the Indian artistic traditions and also primary texts that are specfic to a particular art. Kalāsamālocana is the third programme which comprises publication of critical writings on different facets of art and aesthetics. This series concentrates on the works of eminent scholars who have dwelt upon fundamental concepts, identified perennial sources and created bridges of communication while placing diverse traditions side by side. The criterion for selecting these publications is the value of the works for their cross-cultural perception, multi-disciplinary approach and inaccessibility for reasons of language or being out of print.

In this light, the publication of this volume titled "The Indian Temple - Mirror of the World" is a welcome addition to our Kalāsamālocana series. It is a manual on Indian temples that contains information related to the ideas behind the building of temples not only in India but also across the continent and, indeed, the globe. The Indian temple, representing the Universe, is an amalgam of consecrated time, space, elements and form. This has been analytically interpreted here according to Indian theology and as has been defined in the treatises on architecture. It also discusses the spread of the Indian temple all over the world, encountering various doctrines, especially in South-East Asia during ancient times and more recently on a much wider scale as a result of ever growing Indian Diaspora. In this way, Indian temples reflect the features of many other cultures while maintaining its basic characteristic that allowing the recognition of its unity.

We are grateful to Prof. Bruno Dagens for preparing the English version of his book which he had originally published in French and offering it to IGNCA for publication. Prof. Dagens has a long association with IGNCA. His critical edition along with its English translation of the well known treatise on architecture *Mayamatam* became a popular source book for both students and scholars working in the field of architecture and town planning, after its publication by IGNCA. I hope the present volume will receive an equally warm reception and we trust it will fulfill the quest of knowledge regarding the Indian temple not only of specialists but also of the common reader.

Dr. Sachchidanand Joshi
Member Secretary
IGNCA

Preface

The title of the present volume, "The Indian Temple - Mirror of the World" carries a multidimensional meaning of the Indian idea or thought that has given form to the Indian temple. The author, Prof. Bruno Dagens also has elaborted on this in detail. At the same time, it may not be out of place to refer here to one of the towering figures of classical India, Acharya Abhinavagupta, whose millennium year we are presently celebrating. His ideas were studied all over the sub-continent. The range of disciplines that he mastered and the erudite commentaries that he authored have remained unparalleled through the ages. According to his concept, the world is not a material reality but a reality in consciousness. *Ābhāsa* and *pratibimba* are the two important terms, the meanings of which may be given as 'appearance' and 'reflection' respectively. The meaning may be elaborated further by an example: when we see our face in a mirror, the position of the actual face remains as the archetype (*bimba*) and what is reflected in the mirror is appearance or reflection. For more clarity, the term *ābhāsa* may be distinguished from the term *vimarśa* meaning "thinking". When one imagines one's face in one's mind, that can be termed as *vimarśa* (just a thought), but when one sees the reflection in a mirror, it is *ābhāsa,* as it is an actual appearance. In this way, we see that *ābhāsa* (appearance) is objective but not material, as it is not a real object.

The world is *ābhāsa* projected or reflected in the mirror of cosmic consciousness. Abhinavagupta in the verses of his *Tantrāloka* (TA) explains this position with one of his favourite analogies, the analogy of the reflection in a mirror :

Just as earth, water etc. are reflected in a clean mirror without being mixed, so also the entire world of objects appears together in the one lord consciousness. (TA 3.4)

The lord appropriates the entire world to himself (reflecting the world) in the mirror of his consciousness, and in this way he has pure ubiquity. (TA 3.44)

This entire world of many-ness appears in the self (consciousness) like a reflection (pratibimba) and the self is the lord of the entire reflected world.(TA 3.268)

But in the case of the world being reflected in Śiva-consciousness, i.e. consciousness, as the Self or Śiva is the *bimba* (the world) that is reflected and consciousness is also the mirror in which the world is reflected. This is unlike the passive mirror which receives reflections from outside, as consciousness actively creates its own reflections. Therefore, consciousness is a creative mirror that creates reflections from within itself. Thus, the real reflector is consciousness. This theory teaches how to be aware in daily activities like talking, walking, tasting, touching, hearing or smelling. By practicing this, every action of an individual moves in the supreme consciousness.

The Indian temple emerges as one of the remarkable expressions of this very thought process. Prof. Degens has drawn on the tradition texts and treatises on architecture while divulging the idea behind the creation of the temple. His analysis of the origin of the temple followed by its spread all over india and around the globe is remarkable.

The Indian temple and the concepts related to it have been discussed in IGNCA's diverse programmes. For instance, in our series of key concepts, viz. Kalātattvakośa, the term *prāsāda* appears in the Volume V on Form/Shape: *Ākāra/Ākṛti.* Amongst many other meanings, the term *prāsāda* stands for both 'temple' and 'palace'. The term also represents Cosmic Puruṣa, the Cosmic Tree and the axis mundi. *Prāsāda* enshrines mantra, tantra, yoga and jñāna and is visualised not only as an abode of godhood, but as the manifestation of God. In the ultimate analysis, *prāsāda* is identical with supreme knowledge. The terms *mūrti, pratimā* and *vigraha* from the same volume enshrine in them further minute details related to the Indian temple. Under the programme of Fundamental Texts – the Kalāmūlaśāstra series – three texts related to temple have been published, viz. *Mayamatam, Śilpa Prakāśa* and *Śilpa Ratnakośa.* These have become source materials for the specialists working in the field of architecture.

In order to analyse the Indian temple in all its dimensions, viz. conceptual, literary, textual, historical, epigraphical, crafts traditions, ritual calendars, ritual treatises and performances, IGNCA also initiated two multidisciplinary projects, one in the South – the Bṛhadīśvara temple in Tanjavur and the other in the North – the Govindadeva temple at Vrindavana. Several publications have been published under these projects. Recently in 2014, IGNCA released an interactive multimedia DVD on the Bṛhadīśvara temple as a living tradition.

In the Kalāsamālocana series, IGNCA has brought out a number of publications dealing with temple architecture. What is most important here is to note that through the initiative of IGNCA a new line of scholars has emerged in whose studies a shift of emphasis and change of perspective on the study of the temple as an all encompassing entity is observed.

The inception of the present volume goes back to the year 2012 while meeting Prof. Bruno Dagens during the 15th World Sanskrit Conference held in New Delhi in January that year. Although Prof. Dagens' scholarship was known much earlier, especially since his monumental work on a seminal treatise on architecture, viz. *Mayamatam* was published by IGNCA in 1997, my first personal acquaintance with him took place at Helsinki, Finland in 2003. During the 11th World Sanskrit Conference held there, Prof. Dagens had chaired the first session in the

Tantra-Agama section and I had presented my paper on a tantra practiced in Kashmir.

During our discussion at the Delhi Conference, Prof. Dagens informed about his plans of preparing the English translation of his book on the Indian temple which had already been published in French. He also wanted to know if IGNCA would be interested in taking up that for publication. This was how it started. Thereafter, I worked out the modalities for taking it up as a publication project. It was fitting well into our Kalāsamālocana series focussing on analysis of arts. In due course Prof. Dagens submitted his translation and our work started in respect of making it worthy of publication and completing other necessary formalities. It is now heartening and deeply satisfying to see our efforts fructifying in presenting Prof. Bruno Dagens' work as a published volume under one of our prestigious publication series.

Advaitavadini Kaul
In charge Publications
IGNCA

Table of Contents

PART II: **USAGE OF TEMPLE**

List of figures

Introduction

The "Indian" temple is amongst those architectural creations which have spread all over the world in the wake of the religious ideologies which had given birth to them. Like the church, mosque, or "Greek" temple – all of which it met when travelling throughout the world – the temple has adapted itself to the various cultures which have adopted it or with which it has assimilated. All of them have interpreted it according to their own genius, to their own artistic taste or to their own technical options, while in most of the cases it has kept its distinctive basic characteristics.

Born out of necessity, this temple appeared in northern India most probably around the end of the 4th century B.C. or perhaps a little earlier but, in any case, it did so once the Indian religious tradition had experienced the fundamental change which brought it to 'devotion' (*bhakti*) and thus gave to the faithful the desire to be in close touch with the gods and to enter into dialogue with them. Speaking of dialogue, we naturally have in mind the *Bhagavad-Gītā*, a most magnificent presentation of that change to devotion. That conversation between Viṣṇu-Kṛṣṇa – a god turned into a man – and Arjuna – a king worried about existence – even if it ends with the divine manifestation of the god encompassing the whole cosmos, nevertheless remains a dialogue between two "terrestrial" beings.

Meant to lodge a god in the world of human beings and devised on the pattern of a human house, the temple developed and evolved at the pace of the doctrinal trends that it served and which it followed in their propagation across the world. Thus, it first spread over the whole Indian subcontinent, and then went further, especially towards South-East Asia and the Indonesian archipelago and, even if to a lesser extent, to the north and north-west fringes of India as well, and from there to Central Asia. Very recently, since the last one or two centuries, it marked the places where the Indian diaspora has settled throughout the world, be it in Europe, in North and South America, or in the West Indies, to say nothing of East Africa, islands of the Indian Ocean and of the South Seas, or Australia.

Like the similar religious creations already mentioned, the Indian temple had to meet the requirements of a wide set of doctrines. In this matter and as regards architecture, it is clear that the main ideological trends are often more perceptible than the sectarian views, even if the latter may be expressed through highly technical details such as perspective effects or orientation. This phenomenon gives to temple architecture a relative homogeneity which facilitates the setting-up of regional schools, centred more on aesthetic choices than on precise religious motives. Examples are numerous, the most obvious being found in South-East Asia. Cambodia, Java, or Champa all have simultaneously received Brahmanical and Buddhist faiths and have made them co-exist closely; as regards their architectural garb, they have hardly made it different, despite a few exceptions. In India, this homogeneity made the systematisation of temple architecture easier, through prescriptive theoretical treatises: these often claim to be universal and it is a fact that they hardly remain sectarian once they leave aside rites or iconography, to centre on the buildings.

Architectural Treatises

Indian temple architecture has been theorized long ago in treatises generally deemed as "technical treatises" (*śilpaśāstra*) or "housing treatises" (*vastu/vāstu-śāstra*). They reflect various regional schools and the best known of them are written in Sanskrit. Their content is often taken up by other treatises dealing with rites or even in broader works such as the religious and mythological encyclopaedias known as *Purāṇas.* Moreover one of the most ancient presentations of architecture is found in some chapters of *Bṛhatsaṃhitā*, an astrological treatise from the end of the 6th century A.D. The best known of treatises specializing in architecture come from South India, amongst which are *Mānasāra* (15th -16th c.), or *Mayamata* (ca. 10th c.).

All these texts are written in the same spirit underlying the same method. First of all, they claim to be of a divine origin which allows them to pose as being earlier than all human buildings and therefore never refer to an actual monument (in opposition with Vitruvius for instance). That is to say, they pretend to be normative while they are mainly descriptive and classificatory. Simultaneously, they deal with visible – thus mainly external – features of buildings far more than with their inner structure and with the problems that may arise in their construction: for instance, they make no mention of the corbelled construction technique used everywhere in the Indian world, or, elsewhere; they describe storied-buildings without ever clarifying if the storeys are real or false ones.

Their method is analytic. Whichever the construction, it is made up by combining various basic components which are potentially common to all types of buildings. The presentation of architecture starts with these components (basis, pillars, walls, etc., see below p.29$, Fig.6) then goes on to the various kinds of buildings in which composition these may enter (temples and sub-shrines, pavilions, halls, galleries, entrance pavilions, enclosure walls, as well as houses, palaces, etc.).

For each component, as for each kind of building, are proposed various typological classifications all marked by a strong hierarchical bias. At every stage each theorized model comprises a full set of variations starting from a basic type which is the smallest, simplest and most inferior one and going up to the biggest, most elaborate, etc., that is to say the most perfect one. All this, combined with a systematic use of proportional ratios, puts forward a modular architecture where all components are related to each other by such ratios.

To conclude, let us say that treatises offer a theory which is at the same time simplifying and unifying. Without entering into the extreme diversity of the real temples from which it has been extrapolated, this theory underscores the main features of their architectural arrangement and makes general and compelling rules of them. For instance, it lays down a full coordination of the temple compound (that is to say the "sanctuary", see below) from the sanctum to the outermost enclosure wall and it applies the principle of geometric precision to the whole extent of that compound, as big as it may be. This theory views only fully completed compositions. The most complete and the most perfect ensemble is supposed to be fully defined at the start and therefore to be the result of a full-fledged and unitary project. It results in treatises that do not consider the evolutional pattern shown by numerous temples, and especially the most important ones, which have grown together with their reputation through the ages. However, the hierarchical basis of the theory, according to which the most perfect temples are the biggest and the most complex ones, may be deemed as sufficient to vindicate the expansion of a successful temple.

This theorisation of architecture is ancient, most probably as ancient as the rites to be performed in the temple. It is in line with those technical manuals which at the foundation stage of Indian tradition were codifying the Vedic altar: we find the same concerns regarding geometric precision, balance of proportions, careful attention paid to building materials, as well as a special emphasis on the necessity to place the temple in the cosmos which is orientated and, henceforth, has for its centre the god to whom that temple is dedicated. Let us add that if architecture is the central topic dealt with by some treatises, it is also broached, at least regarding the temple and its annexes, in most of the general manuals devoted to public worship.

Such theoretical and normative presentations of the temple have travelled, and probably very early. They may paradoxically explain seemingly deviant architectural options followed sometimes in Indianized countries. They are of particular relevance for our studies as they are based on a rigorous analysis of architecture and as such are amongst the best tools for studying monuments found in the whole Indian world. While they contribute towards a clearer understanding of fundamentals forming the unity of the Indian temple, they allow us to better determine what may pertain to the native genius of the countries which have received it, as well as to the sectarian necessities of one or the other religious trend.

The present book has its origin in difficulties met when I was trying to integrate into a single discourse the countless architectural expressions of religious thought of Indian origin. This discourse was born from a constant and simultaneous association with monuments of ancient Cambodia and a Sanskrit treatise on architecture composed in South India; it had in mind reaching a better definition of the reciprocal contributions of Cambodian and Indian cultures in the establishment of monuments which appeared at the same time very homogeneous and born of a mixed parentage. I quickly discovered that I was to investigate the monuments of South-East Asia as well as their Indian counterparts about which one wonders if they were their models or their parallels. From a methodological point of view, this double investigation had to be based upon a functional definition of the Indian temple, freed from aesthetic and other contingencies.

It is while the investigation was in progress that I was struck by the omnipresence of that mirror which we shall use here as a medium in our presentation of the Indian temple. First, there is the temple reflecting mirror: it is as real as an ornamental pond or just suggested by an architectural '*mise en abyme*' and through it the temple becomes double or even multiplies endlessly in a movement far more significant than being a pure pleasure for the eyes. More important perhaps, it appeared that the temple itself was a mirror reflecting its own religious allegiance, as well as the numerous concepts which rule its terrestrial environment – either human or cosmic – and which govern its founding and its running, such as art, politics, society, economics, etc. What is more, this very mirror reflects tradition and thus puts the temple fully in line with Vedic practices, even if these were unaware of it, as they were not in need of terrestrial houses for the gods. The mirror is changing. Sometimes voluntarily deceptive, it is at any time liable to be 'mis-shapen' or more precisely to be 're-shaped' in order to better reflect the changes brought to its ruling concepts in the course of centuries.

We have already dealt with this mirror in a preliminary paper from which we shall borrow some parts. Here, however, the mirror will be used mainly as a tool to define first the temple and then its place in the Indian world. Let us however point out that the mirror also appears in some other contexts in the treatises dealing with architecture or ritual. For instance, it is told that altars for offerings must have their surfaces smooth 'as a mirror' (*darpaṇavat*, etc.). Elsewhere, the mirror is mentioned as a ritual instrument meant to receive the reflected image of a cult object, which image becomes a substitute for that object and is used for rites which may damage it: for instance, when a clay image is to be bathed with liquids. Lastly, the list of Goddess' attributes includes a mirror, as do some lists of 'eight lucky things' (*aṣṭamaṅgala*).

* * *

In the first part of the book, we shall delineate the religious and architectural nature of the temple. In order to define it more precisely as a dwelling, we define its inhabitant, the god, through the various cult objects used to shape him. Then, the monument itself is dealt with through the necessity which has given birth to it, that is to say through its function. Here our study starts from the core of the temple, that is, from the sanctum where the god is to be installed and to live. Thus, we first analyse the architecture of the 'temple' proper, namely the building, either simple or complex, worked out around that sanctum. Thereafter, going from the house of the god to the area on which it is settled and which it is generating, we shall first deal with the 'sanctuary' – the *temenos* according to Western classical tradition – that is, the bounded area surrounding the temple-house of the god, the area where possibly are to be found various annexes (sub-shrines, ancillary buildings, etc.). However, the territory of the god is far from being restricted by the outermost enclosure wall of his temple and we would have to look for the marks of its potential adequacy either to the city or the kingdom or even to the whole cosmos.

Throughout this centrifugal definition process appears a first set of images reflected by the temple through its architecture, its iconography, and its general arrangement. The most important of them is without any doubt that of the almighty eyes of the god reflected through the (sometimes multipolar) orientation of the inherently concentric composition of the temple and its surroundings. Other images concern the hierarchies which appear in and around the temple: the hierarchy of a pantheon which in each temple gets reorganized around its specific titular deity and the hierarchy of human society which is emerging from the general arrangement of the sanctuary.

The second part of the book aims at showing how the aforesaid reflected images as well as several others may express in a very tangible way the system of references which makes up the core of Indian tradition. First, we shall see how the temple is used to define and to characterize the god which lives in it. Then we shall look at the sometimes conflicting images of the social body and its hierarchies reflected in the temple: it will be seen how approaching the god is subject to rules which leave little importance to religious factors and mainly transpose to the temple the hierarchical pattern which was ruling social life of India up to the middle of the 20th century. We shall see also how the temple itself – together with the god – is given a place in that social hierarchy. However, it appears simultaneously that some ceremonies, including the yearly grand festival, involve the faithful in a devotion which seems to be collective and unifying and which flouts any respect of social rules, while at the same time allowing any devotee to extol his own social group. In this image of the social body, the King gets a pivotal role: he is the first of the temple patrons, but he uses the very same temple as a key instrument of power. This last observation leads us to the state temples, which may be deemed as the most political of all temples.

Further, we shall centre on the many-sided show that the temple puts on as well as on its performance, to which all temple components contribute. Starting with the idea that temples need to be beautiful, we try to determine the main fields where the show and some fundamentals of its performance may develop. In this process, we look at the tools of that performance through some examples dealing with the temple bestiary or with arrangements for effects of light as well as with the many sided '*mise en abyme*' of the temple. Then, looking at the adequacy of the temple to the universe, we shall see how the temple deals with space and, simultaneously, with time; on this last point, the Indian temple appears to be a very good time-keeper.

Thereafter, we shall also see how through their differences the numerous images mirrored in the temple reflect and define the various cultures where the Indian tradition has installed itself in South Asia and outside the sub-continent. First, we emphasize the continuity of the temple and the special case of Buddhism. Then we see how the diffusion of temples throughout India has been marked by complex movements in which politics as well as the geographical environment play their part. All is not clear in this process and some facts are more stated than explained; for instance, the regional differentiation of temple superstructures. Outside India we shall look at the vectors which have carried the temple throughout Asia and evoke some of the inventions which have marked its travels. We also evoke some other travels, imaginary as well as failed ones, or even just dreamt ones.

Our conclusion comprises a short presentation of the main stages in the gradual discovery of the Indian temple since classical antiquity up to global studies from the recent decades. Then some contemporaneous examples show that the use of the temple engenders interesting renewals in India.

* * *

Some more remarks. The first deals with the vocabulary we are using in this work. Our analysis results from a long-standing acquaintance with Sanskrit normative treatises and similar literature. However, we have done our best to use Sanskrit words only when they may support their English counterparts, especially when they pertain to the architectural vocabulary. We have explained elsewhere the reason for this option which is justified by the very common polysemy of technical Sanskrit terms in the field of architecture (see Dagens 1984b § 1.6). We shall not go back over that here and our short 'Glossary of Main Architectural Expressions' (below p.126$) briefly defines what is meant by the technical terms used in the book. On that point, let us underline that the study of Sanskrit architectural vocabulary in which we are engaged since the sixties was made greatly easier when the first edition of *Vocabulaire de l'Architecture* by Jean-Marie Pérouse de Montclos, was published in 1972.[1] Due to its normative scope and the clarity of the definitions it gives, this detailed and illustrated dictionary is a remarkable reference book and a fundamental tool even when dealing with languages other than French. We have borrowed several definitions from it as well as the very important technical distinction between the "temple", strictly speaking the building comprising the sanctum, and the "sanctuary" which is the bounded area corresponding to the estate of the god and which contains the temple and its various annexes and outbuildings.

To illustrate this book we have resorted mainly to line drawings, some of them being mere sketches, but all are to be seen only as examples. Thus doing, we have been able to confine this book to a size which is reasonable and, let us say, 'publishable'! However the bibliography lists several works where the reader can find, if necessary, images implicitly or explicitly referred to in the text. This bibliography includes several of my previous papers: I do apologize for that, which however allows me to avoid restating some results attained during the too long preparation of the present book.

Lastly we must add that this book owes a lot – and readers will see that this is an understatement - to Jacques DumarÁay,

1. For the full reference see Bibliography.

our long time friend to whom it is dedicated and with whom we have engaged for more than half a century a more or less continuous dialogue about architecture, temples, and many other topics. It owes a lot also to the generations of students with whom I have shared it for about twenty years. Many thanks to all of them.

This book was first published in French by "Les Belles-Lettres" Publisher (Paris, 2009). I am highly grateful to IGNCA authorities and especially to Dr. Advaitavadini Kaul, Co-ordinator, Kalāsamālocana Series and Head of Publication Unit, for having received it in their renowned Series as kindly as Dr. (Mrs.) Kapila Vatsyayana had done a little more than twenty years ago of my *Mayamata*, departure point of the present work. I particularly thank Dr. Advaitavadini Kaul for having taken good care of the editing of the book and for having committed Mr. Raghu Menon to revising my English version which he has so carefully and judiciously done.

PART I

FACTS FOR A DEFINITION

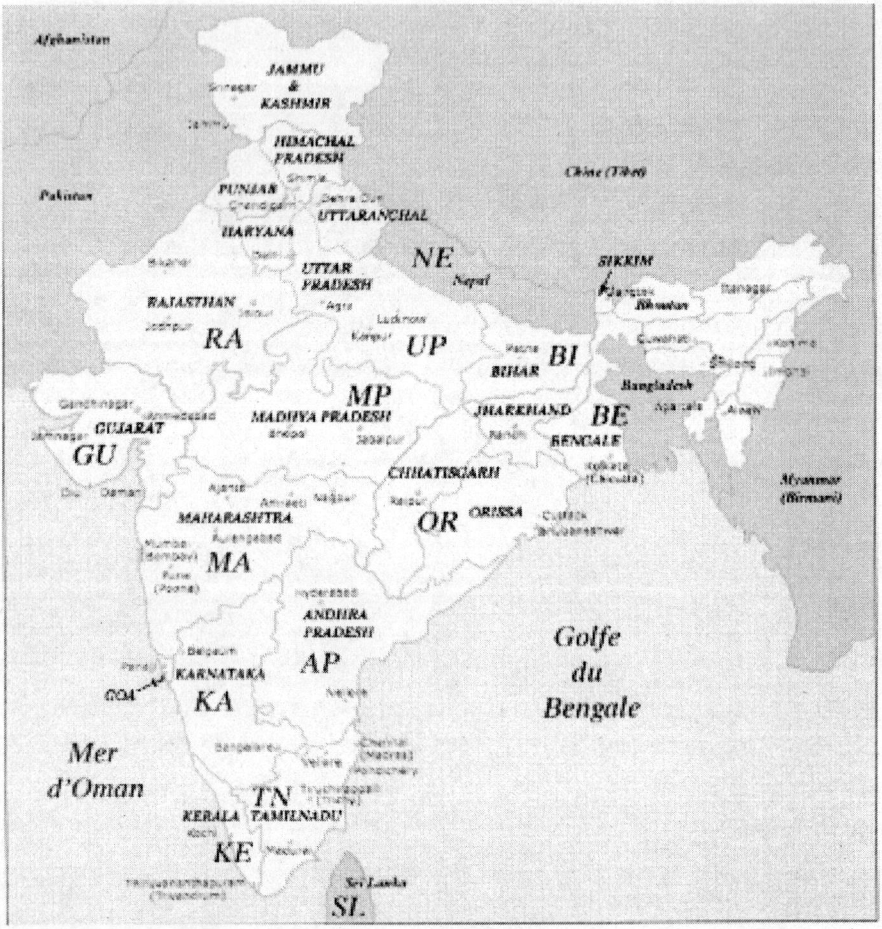
Afghanistan
JAMMU & KASHMIR
Srinagar
Jammu
HIMACHAL PRADESH
Shimla
Pakistan
PUNJAB
Chandigarh
Dehra Dun
UTTARANCHAL
HARYANA
China (Tibet)
Bikaner
Delhi
UTTAR PRADESH
NE
Nepal
SIKKIM
Gangtok
Itanagar
Bhoutan
RAJASTHAN
Jaipur
Agra
Jodhpur
Lucknow
RA
Kanpur
UP
Patna
BI
Guwahati
Kohima
Shillong
Imphal
BIHAR
Bangladesh
MP
Gandhinagar
Ahmedabad
MADHYA PRADESH
JHARKHAND
BE
Agartala
Aizawl
GUJARAT
Jamnagar
Bhopal
Jabalpur
Ranchi
BENGALE
GU
Kolkata (Calcutta)
CHHATISGARH
Myanmar (Birmanie)
Diu
Daman
Ajanta
Amravati
Nagpur
Raipur
MAHARASHTRA
OR
ORISSA
Cuttack
Bhubaneshwar
Aurangabad
Mumbai (Bombay)
MA
Pune (Poona)
Hyderabad
ANDHRA PRADESH
Golfe du Bengale
Belgaum
Panaji
AP
KARNATAKA
GOA
KA
Nellore
Mer d'Oman
Bangalore
Chennai (Madras)
Vellore
Pondichery
TN
Tiruchirappalli (Trichy)
KERALA
TAMILNADU
Kochi
KE
Madurai
Thiruvananthapuram (Trivandrum)
Sri Lanka
SL

Chapter I

The God at Home

When literally translated, the Sanskrit term "*devālaya*" often used to designate a temple makes it a "house for a god", that is to say a shelter – either building or cave – where lives the god to whom it is dedicated and from whom it gets its name. The 'god' is usually a divine entity taken as an individual, such as Śiva, Viṣṇu, or Gaṇeśa or else the "Goddess" (*devī*), under which name in India are conveniently grouped together the countless different appearances of the feminine form of the Supreme deity. To these main figures of the Brahmanical pantheon are to be added Buddha and Jina who, as far as we are concerned here, are to be seen as "gods" even if it may be surprising. Moreover, we have to recall that any Indian deity can get several names which may or may not correspond to specific forms of her. The god to whom a temple is dedicated can be as well a divine group of which the unity is often put forward by its name. Very often it is the pair formed by a god and his spouse: thus Someśvara that is to say "The Lord [Śiva] together with Umā [a name of Pārvatī]" or Lakṣmīnārāyaṇa ("Nārāyaṇa [= Viṣṇu] together with Lakṣmī"). There are also several triads. Some are family based such as Somāskanda ("[Śiva] together with Umā and Skanda [one of their two sons]"), but we meet also Śiva Trimūrti ("Śiva in his triple form", that is to say Śiva together with Brahmā and Viṣṇu [both of whom are considered as forms of Śiva]") or else a Buddhist triad well known especially in South-East Asia and comprising Buddha together with the bodhisattva

Avalokiteśvara and the goddess Prajñā Pāramitā (embodiment of the Perfect Science and often looked upon as the feminine counterpart of Avalokiteśvara). There are also several well-known divine series such as the seven or eight Mātṛkās ("Mothers"), the Navagrahas ("Nine astral deities"), or the Avatāras (Viṣṇu "Avatars" who are usually ten), etc.

The word "temple", used to define a building as a dwelling for a god, can properly speaking be applied to a "temple" that is to say the house of the Lord of a sanctuary as well as to a "chapel" that is to say a sub-shrine dependent on that "temple" and sheltering an attendant deity (*parivāra*) pertaining to the entourage of that Lord installed in that "temple". However, it may be emphasized that a deity is always the main god, the head of the pantheon at the level of her own house, even if this house is just a chapel depending on a main temple as the deity depends on the god of that main temple.

The God

The temple is the house of a god who is to be physically present in it. He does that in the guise of a cult object – image or symbol - which depicts him in some way or the other. He is the only divine figure of whom such 'physical' presence in the temple is necessary. His divine attendants are to surround him but this can remain purely 'virtual' and result from utterances of invocations or mantras during ceremonies. In other words, the physical presence of deities other than the main god is to be seen as an enrichment of the temple, such enrichment being by no means essential.

The Cult Object

The cult-object can be an 'image' or a 'symbol'. The image is that of a living being and is exhibited either in a naturalistic or monstrous manner. India has provided tremendous expansion to "phantasmic anatomy" which has led to an incomparable variety of divine images that fill temples and ornate their walls. Relieved from the strict limits dictated by nature itself, these images allow rendering of the most complex divine characteristics and to multiply the differentiated forms of a single divine entity (Gill 2000). However such potential (and definitely real) richness does not mean unrestrained fantasy. A god's image, whether sculpted or modelled in the round or in relief, or else engraved, painted, or just drawn, has to follow rigorous iconographic and iconometric rules which can allow only precise identification of the concerned god as well as, whenever necessary, the exact form which the image depicts.

Symbols are of two kinds which for greater convenience will be designated here as "definite" and "undefined". A "definite symbol" is something which has been specially made up and of which the value as a divine figure is based upon its adherence to rules, which for lack of anything better are to be called 'iconographic' and 'iconometric': they are as precise and imperative as those applying to images. In Hinduism the best known 'definite' symbol is the Liṅga, the phallic symbolic representation of Śiva and the form of that god most commonly found in the sanctum of his temples. Another definite symbol of Śiva is the trident (which is also seen in the hand of the god). As regards Viṣṅu the *śālagrāma* can be taken as a definite symbol closely parallel to the Liṅga, even if it is far less used. The term *śālagrāma* primarily designates a special kind of fossil shell (an 'ammonite') found in a river, but it exists in several varieties of this symbol; for instance, stone nodules bearing the mark of a shell (Joshi 1959). In a Buddhist context, the stūpa is the most definite symbol frequently used to display Buddha in a temple, even if it is first an architectural rendering of Buddha's funerary tumulus.

Amongst definite symbols are also found some man-made objects to which a precise divine identity is given through imposition of mantras. Such is the case of small offering altars often used to figure the Attendants deities all around the temple of their Lord (Dagens 1984b, § 5.13). Other definite symbols but more transitory ones are the "diagrams" (*maṇḍala*), of which the central case receives the mantra of the god while the surrounding ones are allocated to his Attendants; there is also the vase where a god is temporarily placed through a mantra during a rite or when he waits to be installed in an image. Lastly, the pedestal of a cult object can be a 'definite' symbol, at least in a Śaivite context: the pedestal of an iconic or symbolic representation of Śiva is considered as a symbol of Umā/Pārvatī his spouse and it is as such that it is to be installed and worshipped. In a very different field the five gross elements *bhūta* (*bhūta, mahābhūta*) can be seen as "definite" symbols as they represent Śiva in five important temples of South India: at Cidambaram it is Ether, at Kalahasti Air, at Tiruvannamalai Fire, in Jambukeśvara Temple (Srirangam) Water and lastly Earth in Ekāmbareśvara Temple (Kancipuram).

Contrasting with these perfectly codified representations, an 'undefined' symbol can be any material object; its value as a divine figure can be deemed as 'accidental' (even if lasting) and eventually it is the fruit of an act of faith and thus more or less unintentional. It results from the extraordinary look of the concerned entity, or from the exceptional circumstances of its finding, or from the fact that this finding has been announced by a premonitory vision; etc. As for their material nature, these undefined divine symbols may be objects made for any specific usage; thus, in village temples of Andhra Pradesh we have found a cart axle, a whip, a vase, or a carrying beam used to denote various Goddesses. However, such symbols are more often shapeless stones, but they may also be termite mounds or trees, to say nothing of geographical features such as that "mountain which is a Liṅga" (*liṅgaparvata*) standing in South Laos, near Vat Phu: located above an ancient Śiva temple, it is mentioned in an inscription as early as the 4th century A.D. (Coedés 1956).

Undefined symbols are often used to figure Śiva and then designated as "natural Liṅgas" or more literally "self-existing Liṅga" (*svāyambhūliṅga*) in contrast with "man-made Liṅgas" (*pauruṣaliṅga*) which are the "definite Liṅgas" already told about and which are to meet rigorous rules. Beside Śiva, many kinds of deities can be figured by undefined symbols, more particularly the countless village goddesses, which most of the time appear in their temples as mere shapeless stones, most often due to economic reasons.

In technical literature, a third category of divine figures is added between images and symbols. It is called "mixed" (*miśra*) or more explicitly "at the same time manifest and un-manifest" (*sakalaniṣkala*) and it combines both the others. The best known is the "Liṅga with face(s)" (*mukhaliṅga*), that is to say a Liṅga – symbol of Śiva – on which is (or are) applied from one to five faces of Śiva. Such an intermediary representation is very important at the level of theology as it shows Śiva when he changes from his un-manifest state to the manifest one, corresponding to the symbolic and to the iconic representation respectively. This being the case, the use of such 'mixed' figures do not seem to have any influence at the level of the worship nor regarding specific types of temple (see below p.20$).

The fine-looking aspect of images or definite symbols has nothing to do with their iconography. Of course, treatises rule that they are to be made "so that they will be beautiful" (*yathā śobham*) but they seem eager not to give the necessary rules for this purpose (p.95$). That is evidently out of the question with regard to undefined symbols, of which the appearance is dictated by chance.

In the Image of Man

Whichever the cult object, image or symbol, it symbolises a living being for which, somehow or other, Man is the archetype. As such, it possesses a "face" which in the case of a stone representation is to be marked according to the original setting of that stone in the ground (as the 'face' is its bottom part) (Dagens 1984b § 2.11). When a figure is defined as comprising several faces, one of them is deemed the main one. This face is normally in front of the door of the sanctum and its direction, which corresponds to that of the god's eyes, should be that of the temple's main axis. Let us add that this cult object, whatever its type, is most often of human size or even smaller and only rarely that of a colossus. By the same token its iconometry always stems from anthropometry.

That anthropomorphic characteristic of the cult object will be found again when we deal with the architecture sheltering that object. For instance, while numerous metaphors regarding the human body enter a temple description, it is often asserted that the temple is the body of the god while the cult object is his soul (for instance see the passage of *Sūkṣmāgama* quoted in Dagens 1996).

From Object to God: Installation and Worship

If we put aside undefined symbols about which treatises give conflicting rules, the object meant to be a representation of a god is not *de facto* that god. It will become that god thanks only to an "installation" ceremony (*pratiṣṭhā, sthāpana*), which turns it into a living being provided with a precise identity.[1] Once thus "installed" it *is* the god who is henceforth present in the temple. His presence must be maintained by a "daily worship" of which the interruption may cause his departure from the temple in such a way that a new installation ceremony will be necessary to bring him back to his house. However this "daily worship" is the only one which is absolutely compulsory, for it keeps the god alive by providing him with his daily subsistence. That does not, of course, prevent the temple from being the place and/or the centre of numerous ceremonies, either regular or periodic, or exceptional.

The necessary performance of worship in the temple has two main consequences on its architecture. First, several rites

1. About installation ceremonies see Barazer-Billoret 1993-94 (Śaivite tradition), Barazer-Billoret *et al.* 2004-2009 Vol. 2, p. 11-24 (*idem*), or else Bizot 1994 (recent or contemporaneous Buddhist practices in South-East Asia).

imply that the officiating priest (but only him) gets an easy access to the god: some of them are performed *in front* of him (invocation, food offerings, etc.) while others are done *on* him (sprinkling of liquids, clothing, placing of ornaments, etc.) and thus entails that the priest can at least enter the sanctum (even if it is not necessary that he can go around the god, see below p.24$). This access to the god is to be allowed for in the architectural project, as it creates constraints regarding the size of the sanctum and its door. Another constraint results from rites that are very important in Indian liturgy, the so-called 'baths' (*snāna*) offered to the god, who is then sprinkled with various liquids. However, the Indian theology of "rests" makes necessary the presence of a device to drain out of the temple building the liquids once they have "bathed" the god (for details see below p.23$) and such a device is also to be planned from the start of the building works. By the same token it happens, but more rarely, that another device brings running water above the cult object in order to make the bath easier or even continuous (*ibidem*).

Officiating Priest and Devotees

Any ceremony performed in the temple is entrusted to an officiating priest, a necessary middleman between god and the devotees. Expert in rites, he is most often designated as a "master" (*ācārya, guru, deśika,* etc.) and has been empowered to perform rites through a ceremony presided by his own master. He alone can approach the god and get physically in contact with him. From a more general point of view he is more or less the only one who can act in the temple. The necessity to perform a daily worship forces him to go to the temple everyday which is not the case for the ordinary faithful. Usually, a somewhat important temple is attended to by several priests; however, there is only one office and the multiplicity of empowered people mainly results in sharing the daily work and fees. A typical example is that of Cidambaram, the well-known Śiva temple: in this busy and important shrine, tasks and profit are shared amongst numerous hereditary priests (*dikṣitar*) who collectively rule its daily running thus shared (see Chockalingam 1981, p.535-536).

Devotees, above all, are spectators and occasionally patrons. If they wish to practise and express their devotion, they do that by visiting the temple in order to pray, to attend daily worship or other ceremonies, and if that is physically and socially not possible, to contemplate the god. However there is nothing compulsory in such a visit, which is in no way a requisite for worship or devotion. Towards the temple and the god, each devotee plays the part of the *yajamāna*, that is to say the patron of sacrifice in ancient Brahmanism and in thus doing he is supposed to bear the costs of building and running the temple as well as the expenses for the rites. However, such financial involvement is not a necessary part of devotion. The important change which has led to the invention of the temple has in the same way given the main place to personal devotion, or more precisely, to piety. Hence, it was no more sufficient to patronise a ceremony to obtain its fruit, and reciprocally it was no more indispensable to contribute to temple costs to enjoy the god's favour. Thus, the increase in the number of patrons goes together with an important alteration in their status: their generosity towards the god may remain purely symbolic and, in any case, it does not suffice to qualify for liberation. On the other hand, the real patron of a ceremony always enjoys a marked gratitude from temple authorities and fellow devotees.

From a practical point of view, all these devotees – so called patrons or true ones – do not play an active role in the worship and thus they do not enter the core of the divine house. They stay at the door, be it in a vestibule or the like, or outside. That does not mean that they are necessarily forbidden to go further inside the temple – even if this is often the case – but only that their approaching the god remains an exceptional and "passive" one. At the time of great festivals, crowds of devotees assemble in front of the house of the god or around it but not inside it. In this matter, the Indian temple strongly differs from churches or mosques, which are arranged as assembly halls. However, this is also a point where Buddhist practices diverge from the Brahmanical ones, as they imply that monks (and sometimes devotees) regularly or even daily assemble in front of Buddha's image or symbol. In architecture, that leads to a sanctum fulfilling a double function, house of the god and meeting place for faithful (or at least some of them). Lastly, we shall later see that any Indian temple which is more than just the basic model, most often comprises annexes (pavilions or galleries) which allow at least some of the faithful to stand under cover, close to the door of the sanctum.

The importance, numerically speaking, of the community of devotees regularly attending a temple is most variable. It can be a family group or a social one (sub-caste, caste, etc.) or else assemblies of the faithful from the village or the neighbourhood; but it may be also a more or less sectarian group assembling the full flock of the faithful of a particular deity. Lastly, and this primarily concerns places of pilgrimage, the community may theoretically assemble all Hindus (or all Jains, or all Buddhists). Whichever the case, it is evident that in India like elsewhere a group of the faithful may, at the same time, look "closed", but is "open" to others when it feels that it may consider them as its own.

'Minimal Project' for a Temple

A Basic Dwelling Unit

The facts collected up to now lead to a functional definition of the Indian temple which comprises the necessary and sufficient conditions for it being a temple. Such a definition can be deemed as the temple 'minimal project' and we shall put it like this:

> "An Indian temple is a dwelling meant for a god whose continuous presence is insured by a material representation as long as that last is regularly worshipped by an officiating priest; that priest acts on behalf and in the name of a community of which other members play a passive part of spectators and patrons".

Such a definition tallies with a basic dwelling unit meant for an individual who is to be the god. Represented by a static cult-object, he lives there where he is worshipped by another but definitely alive individual, namely the officiating priest. The inner arrangement of the dwelling comprises a few specifics: it must be wide enough to contain the god and it is to be provided with a device to drain out bathing produces. Its door should be big enough to allow the priest to enter the room. This door faces the god and through it the faithful can catch a glimpse of the god, at least theoretically. More important however, it is through this door that the eyes of the god and thus his power flash to the outside world.

Lastly, beyond these few necessary specifics, the temple is sponsored by a community, by some of its members, or by its chief and this for the glory of the god as well as for the fame of its patron(s), which are as many reasons to make it beautiful (below, p.95$). As has been already told when dealing with images, treatises insist upon such beauty without giving any hints about what it must be, most probably due to the fact that it pertains to a phenomenal realm which they ignore, unconcerned as they are about time and place. However, the same treatises simultaneously insist on the necessary balance between beautification of a temple and means of its patrons, which implies that such beautification, even if desirable and much sought-after, is in no way essential to the celebration of the god and the liberation of his devotees. This is well expressed in a verse quoted in a 17th century Śaivite compendium: "The devotee who builds a temple is to provide it with dimensions proportionate to his fortune; the temple could be small or big but the fruit would be the same for a poor man (in the first case) and for a wealthy one (in the other) (*Śaivāgamaparibhāṣāmañjaī*, 3.101, see Dagens 1979, p.124-125).

Universality of the Project

To say, as we have done, that the above definition is the temple's minimal project is no more than a statement of fact for in the core of almost all "Indian" temples – from the most basic ones to the greatest, and irrespective of time and place – is found a room corresponding to the minimal dwelling unit dealt with above. This room is basically fitted out to accommodate the god and to allow the priest to do his task. This 'sanctum' as we shall call it is most often designated in Sanskrit by an ambiguous compound (*garbhagṛha*) which means 'a house which is a matrix' as well as 'the house of an embryo' according to the sense given to word '*garbha*'. If these two renderings can be considered as mere synonyms, the ambiguity of the compound offers a fine example of the speculative strength often concealed in Sanskrit architectural vocabulary.

That the sanctum is the only indispensable part of the temple is well proved by the numerous temples which throughout India are no more than just four walls and a roof summarily encasing such a room, to say nothing of their rock counterparts which are no more than just a natural or artificial cave. As soon as a temple grows more sophisticated, its growth which can be significant mostly concerns the outer encasing of the room where the god lives: the room itself keeps its main characteristics such as simplicity of arrangement and moderate size, whatever are those of its encasing building.

This outward growth will often result in surrounding the sanctum with very thick walls out of proportion with the room they limit: see for instance the thickness of the walls around the sanctum of Śiva temple at Darasuram (below Fig.32). A marked increase in the size of the sanctum, in comparison with its usual moderate size, is most of the time due to a second function enriching the 'minimal program' as defined above (see below p.14$ insert about double function types of sanctum).

From Sanctum to Temple and from Temple to Sanctuary

Thus, the only necessary part of a temple is eventually an inner volume encased in a building. That building itself is usually lacking in respect of rock temples even if it may exist. Thus at Ellora, Cave No 29 comprises an underground 'edifice' cut out through the rock: it is provided with four doors and its outward faces are ornate like the façades of a man made open air temple (Rajan 1981 pl. CXLII). Usually that inner volume is the only room in a building (or in a main body) which itself is the 'temple'. Most of the time the functional steadiness characterising that room makes it totally disconnected from its encasing building (even if subtle plays of proportions may bring both together). That dichotomy is an essential particularity of Indian temple architecture where a building inner structure is most of the time totally different from what is suggested through the organization of its façades.

Very early, Indian architects freed themselves from the constraints imposed by the architectural encasing of a sanctum. Making the most of the various components of human houses clearly identified as early as Vedic times (Renou 1939), they have invented an architecture which is simultaneously fantastic and convincing. In doing so, they have followed the same step as their workmates, the sculptors, who were giving a perfectly human appearance to monstrous bodies having several heads and supernumerary limbs. This bringing together of the architects and sculptors, when dealing with the creation of the temple is not fortuitous for, in India as in South-East Asia, the architecture of the Indian temple is far more sculpted than built, which eventually gives a fair amount of leeway to invent new forms.

The temple which results from the architectural encasing of the sanctum is quite a complex building. Usually arranged around a single room, it often takes the shape of a tower. It can possibly comprise *several* sanctums which most of the time are organized into a hierarchy, as for instance the three sanctum main body of Candi Plaosan Kor A/1 temple (Indonesia, see Dumarçay 1981), or the numerous temples from Karṇataka and Andhra Pradesh which comprise three main bodies attached one to the other (*e. g.* Dagens 1984a Vol. 2, pl. VII), to say nothing of the Viṣṇu temples found in Tamil Nadu where three sanctums are placed one above the other (*e. g.* Vaikuṇṭhaperumāl at Kancipuram or Sundaravadaperumāl at Uttaramerur, see Meister & Dhaky 1983). The temple entrance often takes the shape of a porch or a vestibule; in front, it can be supplemented by one or two connected halls, each housed in a pavilion, while one or several chapels may be built against the back of the temple or as side parts of its main body.

Around that temple may be seen several separate structures. The first and more frequent is an enclosure wall which borders the sanctuary, that is to say the god's estate. The yard thus created between temple and wall may contain one or several chapels for attendant deities as well as various ancillary buildings. Sometimes, the sanctuary is arranged in concentric yards centred on the temple and separated from each other by intermediary walls. However, the temple and the sanctuary which encompasses it, whatever their size, are both designed and built with the sanctum as their central and only reference, for they are no more than its huge and complex extensions.

Temples without Architecture and Hypaethral Temples

Sometimes a god's house falls short of the most elementary architectural rendering of a temple plan. Such unquestioned divine houses, even if deprived of any architectural feature, may be considered as the most basic level of temples.

This category is most probably the oldest one, but it remains current nowadays and is even one of the most widespread, thanks to the worship of trees or more precisely of the deities inhabiting trees. André Bareau has supplied decades ago a convincing demonstration regarding how in the past the worship of an arboreal Yakṣiṇī had given rise to stories about the birth of the future Buddha at Lumbinī (Bareau 1987, also see Kosambi 1962, p.106-108). More recently, we have "visited" in an Andhra Pradesh village what was told to us to be the "temple" of the "Great Goddess" (*peddāmman*). As a matter of fact, that so-called temple was just a large stony stretch of ground where the village cows assembled each morning to go grazing. In its middle was stuck in the ground a shapeless piece of stone which 'was' the Great Goddess and was daily worshipped as such (Dagens 1984a Vol.I, p. 79 and 530). That summary arrangement could be seen as a country answer to the necessity of honouring the Goddess in a "temple". However, things could be more sophisticated, as the stamping of the place by cow hoofs is reminiscent of some well known purification rites. One of them is called appropriately "stamping by cows", another one "cow-fight" (Dagens & Barazer-Billoret 2000, p. 372-373), to say nothing of an "air bath" which is properly a dust bath performed by walking amidst a herd of cows raising clouds of dust (Brunner-Lachaux 1963, p. 40-41).

Not very different from this virtual temple are the numerous images installed on the roadside, especially at crossroads; without any doubt they are as much "temples", whatever their look, as stone statues or, as in Tamil Nadu, often crude clay images showing the "seven virgins" (*saptakanyā*) and about which D.D. Kosambi made interesting remarks regarding Mothers' worship (Kosambi 1962, p. 82 ff.).

Others, but a little more sophisticated, are those temples without architecture which we may call "enclosure-temples" and "platform-temples". In the first case a railing surrounds a sacred tree or some other cult object and thus marks the limit of the divine dwelling. That type appears at an early date as is shown by Buddhist reliefs staging the Bodhi tree; on a famous Bharhut panel the surrounding railing has become a true architectural structure and the "enclosure-temple" looks like a hypaethral building (*e. g.* Harle 1986 Fig.29). On the Brahmanical side, several ancient representations of a Liṅga surrounded by a railing are known, especially at Mathura (*e. g.* Kreisel 1986 Fig.1a and 1c) while the famous inscription of Ghosundi (Rajasthan 2nd c. B.C.) which mentions a "Nārāyaṇa garden" (*nārāyaṇa-vāṭikā*) may allude to a similar kind of "temple" (Sircar 1964, p. 91). More recent, the arrangement of the surroundings of some colossal Jaina statues (Karṇataka, 10th c. AD onwards) seems to follow the same pattern: see for instance the cloister-like structure with chapels which surrounds the Bāhubali-Gommata statue at Sravana Belgola (Sangave 1981).

Regarding "platform temples", they consist of a stone or brick-work platform on which is placed the cult-object. They are a very common feature in the Indian countryside and are used for various deities. In Andhra Pradesh we have seen them dedicated to Śiva, Viṣṇu, or Gaṇeśa as well as to various forms of the Goddess or to Nāgas. The oldest ones are shown again on Buddhist or Brahmanical reliefs: for instance at Amaravati in the first case (see Knox 1992, p. 95) and at Mathura in the other (Joshi 1973, Fig.181). Interestingly the "platform" of such temples is often ornamented by a railing-like motif which leads to a very illustrative semantic connection with the "enclosure-temples" previously dealt with. As a matter of fact two Sanskrit terms, *vedī* and *vedikā,* currently designate the "platform" and their use helps to show that these platforms are nothing more than a Vedic altar (*vedī*) adapted to a new religious context. This being the case, the same two words are also found in Buddhist texts (especially those written in Pāli) where they are applied to the railing surrounding the Bodhi tree or stūpa in the case of "enclosure-temples. Now, from a practical point of view it is often difficult on a bas-relief to distinguish a tree surrounded by a railing – thus an "enclosure-temple" – from a tree placed upon a platform of which the retaining wall is ornamented with a railing-like motif – thus a "platform-temple" (see for instance Knox 1992, p. 120). It is most probable that the shift in meaning from the massive platform-like altar to the lighter railing has occurred due to a mix-up in the identification of these two features. In any case, when placing the Bodhi-tree upon a platform, the idea was certainly to link its worship – and thus that of Buddha - with Vedic cult practices. Things are not different when dealing with Liṅgas placed on similar platforms.

As already seen, some of the "temples" we have just dealt with can be considered as hypaethral ones, thus the "enclosure-temple" of the Bodhi tree as shown on the Bharhut relief or that of the colossal Jain images from Karṇataka. To the same category we may add some Nepalese examples, such as the reclining Viṣṇu image installed in the midst of the ornamental pond of Buddhanalakantha at Khatmandu, or its replicas (Juramie 2001, p. 207-208). A more ambiguous case is presented by some Yoginīs' temples dated from the 10th-11th centuries and found in Orissa and Central India (see Dehejia 1986). From the best preserved examples it appears that they are arranged in a circular pattern materialised by a peripheral wall against the inner face of which are built 64 chapels (or niches) sheltering as many Yoginīs' images. In the centre a four pillar pavilion is occupied by a Śiva statue. At Ranipur where the god is dancing under the eyes of his 64 companions who look at him from the border wall; the whole gives a real impression of unity and the group made up by Śiva and the goddesses is – in spite of the space of ground separating them – as closely united as the pair formed elsewhere by Śiva and his spouse. However, if we see such temples as hypaethral ones, we may consider them as consisting of a wide sanctum bordered by the circular wall and where the divine inhabitants are each sheltered from rain and the like by the roofs of chapels or niches and by the central pavilion. Moreover, the sixty four Yoginīs together with their Lord are engaged in a cosmic performance which takes place right under the sky.

Chapter II

From the Sanctum to the Temple

The Sanctum

Basic Functional Layout

As we have seen, the sanctum – an inner volume – is just a room provided with an axial door. Most of the time it is square and bordered by bare walls, while being deprived of any post or pillar to support its ceiling. Its size and that of its door are sufficient to allow the priest entering it to perform his task. The god's representation is in line with the door which it faces and, usually, is placed in the centre of the room. The upper face of its pedestal constitutes a vat in which is collected the liquids poured over the god and it comprises a projecting spout to direct them to the floor; there, a duct bored in the wall takes them out of the building. Lastly, a sanctum can be provided with one or more windows (generally open-work ones) what means that it is not necessarily the "dark and mysterious" room often alluded to in the West and of which the origin is to be sought in the early Western descriptions of rock caves of the Bombay region, the first Indian "sanctums" ever seen by Europeans (Mitter 1977).

This basic layout is found in every temple. It can be modified in all its parts but, with a few exceptions, that does not disrupt its main characteristics. These changes intend to adapt it to various contingencies regarding the god himself (personality, requisites of his worship or specifics of his representation) as well as the architectural context (structure of the building encasing the sanctum, existing exterior constraints). The main exceptions ensue from taking into account some exceptional specificity of the cult object as, for instance, the very big size of a Liṅga leading to the establishment of an upper floor in the sanctum from which water could be easily poured on its head (see below p.24$). Elsewhere it may be necessary to arrange a sanctum fit for a double function (see below) or else to adapt the temple to some theological speculations as in the case of Buddhist temples with a central newel found in Burma at Pagan (Pichard 1985 et Duchemin 2001).

Sanctum with a Double Function

The most common double function sanctum is found in Buddhist temples where it simultaneously houses a representation of the Buddha and an assembly of monks (possibly with lay devotees). The Buddha's image is placed at the back of the sanctum made long enough to seat the assembly in front of that representation. In the earliest monuments (ca 2nd-1st c. B.C.), Buddha is represented by a stūpa which explains the apsidal plan of the sanctum of the rock-temples found in Western India, the apsidal plan of which was kept even when a statue replaced the stūpa (Dehejia 1972). The general pattern lasts till date in the Buddhist countries of Theravāda persuasion (Sri Lanka and South-East Asia) but with an oblong plan without apse (or, rarely, a square plan, see for instance the Hāta-da-ge at Polonnaruwa in Sri Lanka).

The "pseudo-library" created by the architects of ancient Cambodia is another case of a building encasing a double function sanctum. That oblong type of building which is a very common annexe of Brahmanical or Buddhist temples is used at the same time as a dwelling for a deity (or a divine series) – installed in the back part of its only room - and as a sacrificial hall occupying the front part of the same room. In a Brahmanical context the cult-object usually figures the Navagrahas'series of astral deities, while in a Buddhist sanctuary it is most often Avalokiteśvara or Vajrapāṇi (see Dagens 2003, p.193).

Another creation of Ancient Cambodia seems to pertain to the same category. It concerns the entrance-pavilions of which the central passage is at the same time a sanctum which explains that it is closed by a door at both its extremities (see Dagens 1994 and, below, p; 114-115$ and Fig.59).

Obvious Constraints

To make an actual building rendering the temple basics is subject to obvious constraints, which however are never explicitly mentioned in the Indian architectural treatises. They may concern materials as well as the arrangement of the sanctum and of its ceiling or roofing, and they have repercussions on the whole building.

First, in the whole Indian world and in a systemic way, any building encasing a sanctum – that is to say, any temple – is constructed with heavy, massive, and long-lasting materials such as stone (dressed and bonded) or fired bricks (bound with mortar). When it is stone, it is used not only for walls and corbelled roofing, but also for beams and ceiling. On the contrary, wood is a very sparingly used material with a few regional exceptions that are easily understood, as they mainly concern Kerala and Nepal. Elsewhere, wood is sometimes used for making a ceiling (but this feature is often in stone). When it is given some architectonic role it can be counter-productive. Thus in Cambodia around the 11th c. stone beams were often hollowed out in order to be filled with wooden beams supposed to reinforce them; however due to rot, or insects the fast deterioration of these wooden pieces directly led to the breaking of the stone beams which had been weakened by their hollowing. This bias for heavy materials is not explained nor even mentioned in theoretical treatises. It is probably linked to a strong will to provide the god with a non ephemeral house, suitably convenient for his permanent sojourn thereafter. This being the case, it is somewhat illogical to notice that very often the façade ornamentation of these massive stone or brick temples evokes a light wooden construction (see below p.30$).

Another constraint stems from the interior arrangement of the sanctum and more precisely concerns its "covering".[1] As already told, the sanctum is usually devoid of pillars and other posts which would bear that covering, and which therefore has to lean on top of surrounding walls only. To obtain this result, architects from India and South-East Asia have made use of various processes, most of them related to corbelling techniques: corbelled vaults and similar devices for roofs and tower-like superstructures or ceilings with stacked beams and central coffers. Thus it systematically avoided resorting to carpentry work roofs or brick or stone true barrel vaults, or cupolas in respect of temple buildings. In Kerala the use of wood allows carpentry work roofs but such a roof is then built right above a corbelled device which it does not replace but just supplements (p.112-113$ and Fig.57; Sarkar 1978, *passim*). As for temples with barrel vaults or cupola roofs, the only ones to be found are in areas and from periods where Iranian and/or Moslem influence was significant (for instance, North-Western areas as well as Punjab and Kashmir up to 8th-9th c., Bengal in 17th-18th c.). Accordingly, everywhere in India, the ancillary buildings and galleries are very commonly roofed with barrel vaults or cupolas contrary to the temple they are surrounding and to its chapels or sub-shrines.

Interior Volume Delimitation

- Walls, Partitions, and Materials

The sanctum inner walls are either the interior face of the façade wall of the building encasing the sanctum or that of a

1. Let us elucidate that the "covering" there is what bounds an interior volume towards the top, while the "roofing" closes the top of a building, the first often being just the intrados of the second.

partition wall separating the sanctum from a surrounding ambulatory. They are rarely ornamented and where it exists their ornamentation is sober, unlike that of the façades of the temple and of pavilions, galleries, etc. That ornamentation is mostly architectural (pilasters, moulded cornices and niche-frames, etc.). It may also include reliefs or paintings displaying attendant deities of the god or illustrating his feats. In some cases it comprises one or several images which, in one way or another, duplicate the representation of the god standing in the sanctum. Thus, in several South and West Indian Śaivite temples from the second half of the 1st millennium A.D., a Śiva *image* is placed against the back wall of the sanctum, beyond the central Liṅga, according to an arrangement which can be interpreted in various ways (see Dagens & Barazer-Billoret 2000, Vol. I: XLVI ff.). On the Vaishnavite side, the sanctum of the central tower of Prasat Kravanh (Angkor) was housing a Viṣṇu statue and on its walls are seen relief images of three different forms of the same god (the same arrangement may be seen in another Cambodian temple of the same period but the wall images are then paintings).

Lastly, there are only few cases where a row of pillars border the sanctum instead of walls and thus makes the temple a true open building (even if, as already mentioned, the ornamentation of the temple façade often tends to suggest that). However, a fine example of such a composition is the kiosk-like four pillared chapel dedicated to Vṛṣa – Śiva's bull mount – which is seen in front of temples of Śiva such as at Thanjavur (Pichard 1995 ph. 68-69). It is interesting to note that technical literature sometimes rules that such a Vṛṣa chapel is to be in the form of a pavilion (*maṇḍapākāra*), i.e. a type of building which theoretically at least is hypostyle (Dagens 1984b § 5.14).

- *Covering the Sanctum*[2]

The sanctum is topped either by just the intrados of the roofing of the building or in a more sophisticated way by a flat ceiling which comes to shelter the god's figure from dust and dirt falling from this roofing. However, the presence of such a ceiling is far from being general and often it is not easy to understand why it exists or why it is not there. Thus in Indonesia amongst the 240 identical chapels surrounding Candi Sewu main temple, some were arranged to get a ceiling and others not (Dumarçay 1981). Sometimes the ceiling is replaced by just an inner cloth canopy fastened to the corners of the room (especially in 7th c. temples in Cambodia). There are also simpler devices such as a wood and fabric canopy covering the centre of the room and held by four posts surrounding the god's pedestal; in some 7th c. Cambodian temples such a canopy is rendered in stone and thus made everlasting (Fig.1)!

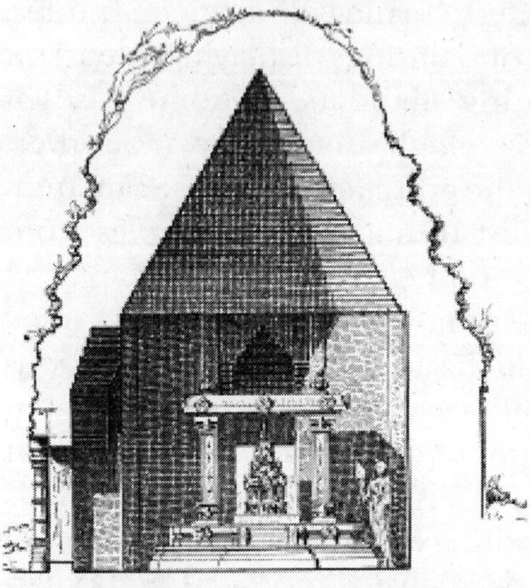

Fig.1. Sambor Prei Kuk: Temple S2 (Cambodia, 7th c. A.D.), (cross section, PARMENTIER 1927). Inside the sanctum, a stone-built canopy was sheltering the cult-object.

If the ceiling is far from being a constant feature of the sanctum, a detail however shows clearly that it has, or more

2. It is most often difficult to examine the intrados of roofings; moreover, they are often not mentioned in written descriptions and rarely pictured in photos. Section drawings are not always reliable (see below about ceilings). We have used the extensive documentation collected by Klaus Fischer (1974).

probably, had some importance. On temple façades at the level of the entablature, a frieze is often made visible, decorated with butts of beams as regularly spaced as would have been the beams of a ceiling, of which the materiality is thus evoked by a purely decorative device. What is really interesting is that the connection of the ceiling and such decorative butts is semantically emphasized by the use of the same word – *prastara* – to designate a ceiling *and* the entablature to which pertains the butt frieze.

Made in wood or stone, a sanctum ceiling is often borne by four beams crossing each other at right angles and thus forming a nine coffer pattern. When it is in stone, such an arrangement can be genuine or false. In the second case, beams are simply sculpted on the slabs making the ceiling, slabs which the beams are supposed to bear. Being a mere decoration without any architectonic function, they are given the dimensions of the wooden beams they are just feigning; however they make the whole ceiling heavier and that limits their use to rather small sanctums (*e. g.* Dagens 1984a, Vol. II Fig.450 where the ceiling is that of a pavilion).

When there is just a change in the material, the wooden arrangement being literally rendered in stone, things are rather different. First the beams are to play a load-bearing part for which the stone is not the appropriate material. In order that stone beams get sufficient bending strength, their section is to be far more sizeable than that of similar wooden beams; all the more since their weight – which increases together with their section and their length/span – is

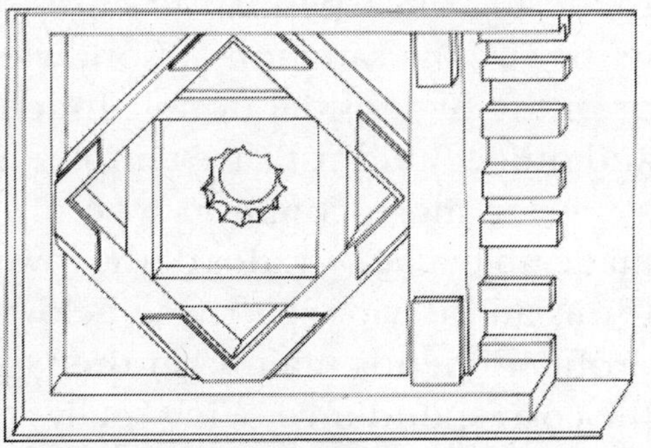

Fig.2. Foladi (Bamiyan area, Afghanistan, 5th-6th c. A.D.): Ceiling with a central coffer cut in the natural ceiling of a cave temple (DUMARÇAY 1996).

to be added to that of the slabs they bear. A weight and span limit is quickly reached beyond which the arrangement is no more usable. That explains why Indian architects have resorted to a different technique for arranging the stone ceiling: beams are stacked in the corners which results at one point in creating a central coffer and on the other by the beams being shorter than the width of the room (see Fig.2). This type may be called "ceiling with corner corbellings" or "ceiling with central coffer" (or "lantern ceiling", see its German name, "Laternendecke"). Nowadays wooden examples are seen in Kailash area of North-West Pakistan and stone ones all over India from Kashmir to South India (Fischer 1974, p. 40 ff.). The pattern has been faithfully reproduced in the Buddhist cave temples of Afghanistan (Fig.2), and went from them to Chinese Turkestan, up to Dunhuang where oversimplified representations of it are painted on the ceiling of some caves.

The covering of the sanctum may also be concave: this is the case for early rock temples where such covering reproduces the intrados of carpentry work with screeds and which are amongst the outstanding creations of Indian architect-cum-sculptors. They are found in the earliest known cave-temples (3rd c. B.C., caves of Barabar in Bihar) without however detailed rendering of carpentry work as is the case a few centuries later in the circular sanctum of Kondivte or Guntupalle cave-temples or in the big apsidal double-function sanctum of Karla, Bhaja and other Buddhist cave-temples in Maharashtra.[3]

A far more common type of covering for the sanctum is made up by the intrados of the tower-like superstructures which forms an interior shaft (see below, p.37-44$); its precise inner profile depends mainly on the type of superstructure without the correspondence being really constant as is clearly shown by

3. See Mitra 1980 ph. 105 (Kondivte) and Fig.14 and ph. 134 (Guntupale/Gunthapalli); about Kondivte see also a fine engraving by Thomas Daniell (from J. Wales, reproduced in Archer 1980, Fig.140); about big apsidal halls see Dehejia 1972.

the variations met in some big Javanese sanctuaries (see for instance at Candi Sewu, Dumarçay 1981).

Plan of Sanctum

The square type of sanctum is by far the most frequently found and it can serve for any specific god. However, a sanctum may also be oblong (extending length-wise or width-wise), cruciform, circular, elliptic or apsidal, as well as polygonal (octagonal or pentagonal) or even stellate. The full set exists as early as the beginning of the Christian era, apart from stellate and pentagonal plans which appeared later and were just regional or even local singularities. The universality of the square plan as well as the diversity of options also applies to the external plan of the building, housing the sanctum, without being a necessary correspondence between the interior plan of the sanctum and exterior plan of the temple. Moreover, plans are not always as geometrically rigorous as is implied by their designation (or asserted by the often falsely regular look of plans as published in books): thus a "square" plan can in fact be trapezoid (e.g. main sanctum of Shore Temple at Mahabalipuram), some "orthogonal" layouts do not comprise any right angle (e.g., most of temples built in Jayavarman VII's time in Ancient Cambodia) and some "circular" sanctums are just roughly rounded (see Lomas Rishi cave-temple at Barabar or the central sanctum of Bayon at Angkor).

The precise reason for using a particular type of plan is not always obvious. For instance, all patterns are used for Śiva temples, other than the pentagonal one. Besides, when looking, for instance, at the numerous Sūrya temples built in Gujarat during the 8th-10th centuries A.D., it appears that their respective sanctums are square or oblong (length-wise as well width-wise) without the choice of one or the other form being deemed as more or less logical (Nanavati & Dhaky, *passim*).

Thus, there are some steady correspondences between the gods or at least the iconographical forms of some of them and the specific types of sanctums. Thus, a width-wise oblong sanctum is often used for installing widespread statues or steles such as those figuring Durgā fighting the Buffalo, Viṣṇu sleeping on the Serpent, or Buddha lying on his deathbed, or the Seven Mothers seated on a line, just to mention some obvious examples. From a more general point of view it appears that this width-wise extending plan is more or less compulsory as regards temples and chapels of the Goddess, whichever is the form of her image. Interestingly, the importance of this rule is underlined by the fact that usually this form of the sanctum is displayed by the same width-wise extending shape being given to the whole building and, more than that, even when just the sanctum is in square form. We shall see below that the whole composition is liable to be no more than a mere appearance: a visual effect makes a square-plan temple look like a width-wise extending one, which itself suggests that it encases a similarly width-wise extending sanctum while this is also actually a square-plan!

Another type of correspondence results in that temples dedicated to Gaṇeśa as well as some other deities connected to elephant (see for instance Śāṣṭṛ) are often provided with an apsidal sanctum or at least given an apsidal outside-plan, the metaphorical designation of such apsidal plan being "elephant back" (*gajapṛṣṭha*). Therefore, the seemingly earliest temples that followed an apsidal plan are those Buddhist cave-temples where a stūpa housed in the back of the room justified the choice of an apsidal form. Lastly we can mention the curious case of a technical text which rules first that Gaṇeśa is to get an "elephant back" temple, and that for Skanda is to be a "cock temple" (*kukkuṭālaya*), which last remains mysterious in spite of the well-known connection between Skanda and the cock (especially in early times) (*Dīptāgama* 11.44 or 74.43).

From a general point of view, it appears that regional traditions most probably play an important part in the form of the sanctum. Thus, in Ancient Cambodia where there is obviously a general tendency to simplify the Indian model, whichever the concerned field, sanctums are very systematically square, and rarely oblong, the few exceptions being two temples with octagonal sanctums at Sambor Prei Kuk (7th c. A.D.) and the roughly rounded sanctum of Bayon Temple (end of 12th c. A.D.). In the same way the very few known stellate sanctums were all built at the same place (Baudh) in Orissa and at the same time (ca 10th c. A.D.); similarly, the numerous sanctums with a pentagonal plan or/and a central newel are all Buddhist and found only in Burma (Pichard 1985).

Entrance to the Sanctum

- Door and Doors

While most of the time the sanctum has an only door, it can however be provided with several, in which case the door which is facing the god is seen as the main entrance to the room. It does happen that the door is not in the front of the god but such exceptions are very few and may be considered as resulting from specific circumstances as would be, for instance, a change in the religious persuasion ruling the temple (see below p. 78-79$) or more simply a topographical constraint of the site (e.g. Dagens 1984a, Vol. 1 p. 270-271, regarding a temple of Āñjaneya-Hanuman where the god faces south as specific for him while the door is on the western side due to a local topographical constraint).

The only door (or the main one) opens right away on to the outside or on to a porch, or a front pavilion, or else on to a corridor linking the sanctum to such a pavilion. Its orientation usually rules that of the whole compound centred on the sanctum. However, if the middle of that door is in line with those of the sanctum and of the cult object, various and often speculative reasons prevent their coincidence to be rigorous, the main one being a general principle according to which axis are not to coincide. Treatises are rarely straight on this point but it is obvious in the way they back with precise figures their rules about the position of the door, foundation deposits, etc.

In the same line are also found precise rules for throwing off centre the cult-object position in the sanctum (see below p.22-23$)

The size of the door is to be proportional to the sanctum but not necessarily to the cult-object. In fact, the latter is often set in place prior to the building of the sanctum walls, especially when the door would have been too narrow to allow the image into the room. This case is expressly considered by treatises and well testified by numerous monuments in India and in South-East Asia; furthermore, it is referred to in Śūdraka's *Clay Cart* (*Mṛcchakaṭikā*), one of the most famous Sanskrit plays where a character, talking about the mother of the heroine, exclaims:

> "Oh! How great is the expanse of the belly of this ugly she-ghoul! What, then, was the beautiful entrance of this house constructed after she was set here, as is done with a (huge) idol of Śiva?"[4]

Recently (2003) a huge stone image of Āñjaneya-Hanuman was installed in a temple once its base had been built, and the sanctum walls were not built until afterwards, so that the temple was completed and inaugurated only four years later (see below, p. 122$).

Provided with two leaves which open on to the inside, the door of the sanctum is to be closed at night and during slack periods during daytime. In the morning it is opened with rites comprising mainly invocations to the several deities who rule its leaves, door-jambs and other parts of its frame, etc. and who are not physically represented (Dagens & Barazer-Billoret 2000, p. 31 and 409-410; see also below, p.96$). Beyond the door is usually found a curtain which allows the god's figure to be hidden at some stages of the worship while the sanctum is kept open. Such curtain is also drawn to avoid pollution of that figure by impure eyes (*e. g. Dīptāgama*, 94.290).

---

4. Mṛcchakaṭikā IV.29. M.R. Kale translation (Kale 1972, p. 168-169).

Usually the exterior frame of the door is ornamented and it is, most often, the only decorated part of the temple (p. 96$). As early as the Gupta period, it was given its usual form of a set of several decorative frames fitting into each other and combining vegetal and animate patterns. This arrangement suggests a light construction which would be in front of the door, a sort of porch with a lintel borne by two small columns. In South-East Asia a strong emphasis is laid on porch elements – decorative lintel and columns – which get a conspicuous position around a classical door-frame sculpted on the outside face of the fixed stone frame of the bay.

- *Door(s) and False-Doors*

A sanctum with several entrances is a common feature of South-East Asian temples. It is also found in India (even for cave temples, see at Elephanta or Ellora for instance, Rajan 1981). The arrangement is real or simply suggested according to the nature of secondary entrances which may correspond to open bays or comprise just a frame filled up with the sculpted image of a closed double leaf door. Such "false-doors" are common is Cambodia where frame and leaves are sculpted in a very realistic way; in most of the cases they are provided with a threshold, sometimes with entrance steps and even with a porch, all features which tend to make them convincing. In India the emphasis is laid on the frame and it is not easy to determine if it is of a false-door or of just a niche. This being the case, several examples of typical false-doors are found, especially in Madhya Pradesh and Kerala. Amongst them the false-doors of the Lakṣmaṇa Temple at Sirpur (Madhya Pradesh) are very similar to those found in Cambodia, even if there is no break in the mouldings of the base below these supposed doors which makes them quite improbable (Harle 1986: Fig.154). In the same way, false-doors found in Kerala temples are above a unbroken moulded base; however, their mock door leaves are generally carved with great care, sometimes without even omitting the rabbet-bar covering the gap between the two leaves (*e. g.* Sarkar 1978: Pl. 40-B or 68-B).

When a temple gets several "entrances" they usually correspond with four cardinal doors or with one real door and three others which are false. Most often, this pattern is found with a square sanctum, but it may also be seen with a circular or oblong one. Some variations are interesting. For instance, the Śiva Temple (so called Mundeśvari Temple) at Ramgad (Madhya Pradesh) is octagonal and comprises one door on each of its eastern and western sides and a window on the southern and northern ones (Meister & Dhaky 1988, p. 118 ff., Fig.48). In Cambodia the so-called libraries get a door on their western extremity and a false door on the eastern one, while in Burma pentagonal and octagonal sanctums usually have as many doors as sides.

The arrangement with several entrances does not seem to have any connection with a particular deity. It has been considered significant that a four faced Mukhaliṅga was found installed in a four door sanctum; however that very same type of Liṅga is often found in temples with a lone door and it is such a Mukhaliṅga which is housed in the octagonal Mundeśvari Temple at Ramgad, just talked about. By the same token we may mention the main sanctum of Ādinātha Jain Temple at Ranakpur which comprises four entrances and contains a four faced stele. Thus, there does not seem to be any specific rule in that matter.

From a more general point of view, the raison d'être of multiple entrance arrangement is not very obvious, leaving aside a few exceptions. For example, in Burma it is clearly the fruit of the development of the temple type: the five or eight sanctums of the original pattern have been combined into one, without changing the corresponding numbers of images and doors. Elsewhere, we may eventually hesitate between two explanations which are not mutually exclusive, one of which falls within the province of architecture and the other within that of theology. In the first case, the four entrance arrangement would express a concern for architectural regularity and symmetry which is very common in South-East Asia, where it corresponds to an obvious tendency to stage the temple as a performance. In the second, we may say that multiplying the entrances is a fine expression of the god having the power which pervades all directions, even if his eyes stare at only one of them.

Orientation

Since the Vedic period, the Indian world has been definitely set according to directions. At that time, the cardinal pattern was already established as regards sacrifice and its relation with the cosmos. Thus, East is "in front" (*pūrva*), for the priest faces the rising sun; South is "to the right" (*dakṣiṇa*), while North can be "to the left" (*vāma*) while it is most often "above" (*uttara*); lastly, West is "behind" (*paścima*).

Installed in his temple, a god usually faces a point of the compass (even if a close investigation shows a small difference). As already stated, his eyes are in line with the sanctum door and thus the general orientation of the sanctuary is set, whatever its size. Things are different however as regards chapels of attendant deities: their orientation depends on that of the main temple and their position in relation to it. More than that, a change in this field can express a change in the status of the concerned Attendant. Therefore, in South India a Goddess' chapel is usually amongst the annexes of a Śiva temple and its normal position is to be to the North of the Śiva's temple while facing it, that is to say facing the South (see for instance at Thanjavur). A change arose around the 12th-13th c. A.D. Thereafter, a new chapel often appears in Śiva's sanctuaries, dedicated to the Goddess but quite different from those built previously. Being far bigger, it is built like a genuine secondary temple, provided with its own enclosure wall and entrance pavilion. That new ensemble remains located inside Śiva's sanctuary (but is often in its 2nd enclosure). Like before, it kept its place to the North of Śiva's temple, but with an important change in its orientation, for now it no more faced the South (that is *towards* Śiva's temple) but the East (*like* Śiva's temple). This change corresponds to an architectural staging of the growth of the power of the Goddess, a well known phenomenon of the 12th c. A.D. Being Śiva's spouse, she remained associated with Him but as she had become more or less his equal she acquired a bigger chapel, as well as a 'private' enclosure, and also the same cardinal orientation as that of Śiva's temple. A very good example is given by the Goddess Temple built around the 13th c. in the second enclosure of Śiva Airavateśvara Temple at Darasuram (Fig.3). However, this phenomenon has been a general one and reached beyond the boundaries of Śaivism, which explains why similar architectural evidence is presented with the type and importance of the Goddess' Temple in several sanctuaries of Viṣṇu, such as at Srirangam for instance.

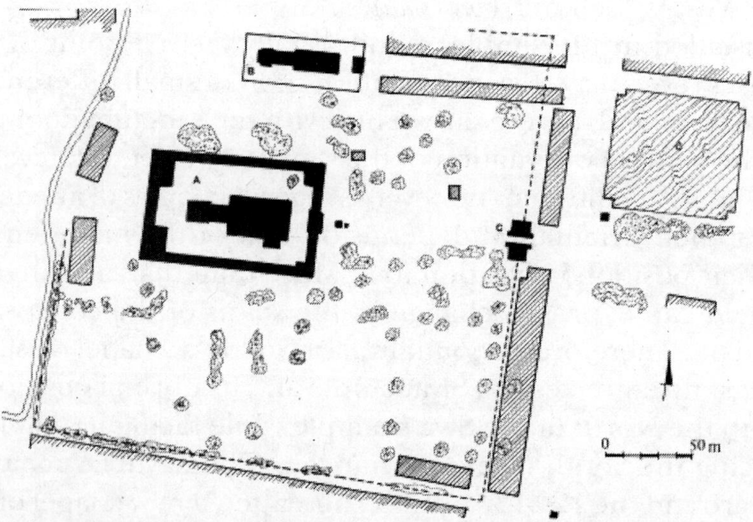

*Fig.3. Darasuram (Tamil Nadu): Sanctuary of Śiva (general map, Dumarçay 2001). The Goddess temple (**B**) surrounded by an oblong enclosure and facing east is located to the north of Śiva's temple and outside its first enclosure (**A**), in an area which probably pertains or was planned to pertain to the Śiva temple's second enclosure, of which the only surviving element is its eastern entrance pavilion (**C**); its wall itself (marked here by a dotted line) perhaps was never built.*

Facing East may be deemed as the default orientation for a temple; it is more or less the standard one for Śiva's temples as well as for Buddha's ones. However various factors play a part in the choice of the main direction of a temple-to-be. They are related to the god himself, or to the general arrangement of the sanctuary or to elements exterior to the temple. Some deities are systematically facing directions other than East. This is the case of Āñjaneya-Hanuman, the monkey god, whose temples or chapels always face South, or of Vīrabhadra, a form of Śiva for whom they face North. Things are more complex for Viṣṇu: the rules given by treatises as well as what is seen in Indian or South-East Asian temples show an obvious balance between West and East.

Several constraints external to a temple and not directly related to its main god can *disorientate* the sanctum. They are linked to topographical factors such as the wish to get the best from a limited space like a rocky spur (Prah Vihear Temple in Cambodia) or the necessity of adapting a new foundation to existing buildings. For instance, the huge compound of Prah Khan of Kompong Svay is centred on a two enclosure temple and bordered by a square moat which is 3 kilometres wide; it has been established with an orientation which is at an angle of 25 degrees to the East-West line, most probably in order to adapt to the local river and stream system. At P'imai (Thailand) the whole concentric compound - from the central temple to the outermost walls of the ancient city is orientated towards South-South-East - most probably to be in line with the Angkor Road, the road leading to the capital city of the Khmer kingdom (Pichard 1976).

Adaptation to topography also can emphasize some specific links between a temple and its natural surroundings. We present here two interesting and apparently contradictory examples which we have come across in Andhra Pradesh, one being a few kilometres from the other on the banks of the Krishnā River, one of the biggest of India and a major element of religious geography of the area. Both cases concern a Śiva temple which is facing West (instead of the more usual eastward orientation). In the first case a Śiva Siddheśvara Temple is built on the *eastern* bank of the river and it faces *west*, which thus underlines the directing role of the river. A little upstream, another Śiva temple called "Śiva Rāmatīrtha" (lit. "Śiva of the holy place [founded by] Rāma") stands on the *western* bank of the same Krishnā River but has its back to it and faces *west*, where there is a spring supplying water to an artificial pond located in front of the temple. Obviously this spring has taken over the directing role from the Krishnā River and it was most probably at the origin of the holy place which, as very frequently in South India, is said to have been established by Rāma when he was going to Laṅka, looking for Sītā.

Several factors can be involved simultaneously. For instance, at Narttamalai (Tamil Nadu), the Śiva Vijayacolīśvara Temple (10th c. A.D.) is built upon a flat space located on the side of a rocky hill between a steep slope to the East and a vertical cliff to the West. The temple itself faces west towards the cliff, at the bottom of which two cave-sanctums had previously been excavated; on the back of the temple is found the only entrance pavilion, located just at the top of the inaccessible slope. This apparently useless building was most probably intended to indicate from faraway that there was a shrine; however it also could have been to "rectify", at least visually, the apparently unusual orientation of the temple (which orientation is most probably connected to the existence of the two ancient cave temples).

It is often difficult to explain why a temple is not in line with a cardinal pattern. Thus, the main axis of the big Śaivite shrine at Tiruvannamalai is at an angle of 13 degrees to the east-west line: it can be due to an astronomical reason (reckoning of the east-west line with a gnomon in February or October, see L'Hernault *et al.* 1990, p. 59-60) or to the existence of some spring or stream which was part of the sacred place at the time of the first establishment of the temple, neither proposition being truly satisfactory. A similar deviation of the main axis occurs at Bṛhadīśvara Temple at Thanjavur and it can be the result of some gnomonic reckoning or the adding of this state temple in an already existing and perhaps crowded city (Pichard 1995, p. 24); the second hypothesis can be favoured by the fact that, twenty years later, the new state temple built at Gangaikondacolapuram in an area apparently devoid of any previous installations strictly follows a cardinal pattern. Another interesting case is that of Angkor Wat: this state temple built in the 12th c. at Angkor and dedicated to Viṣṇu is facing west while all the preceding state temples established in the same capital were dedicated to Śiva and face east (the only one built later than Angkor Wat was also facing east but dedicated to Buddha). The western orientation of Angkor Wat was connected by 20th century scholars with the funerary function which was then supposed to be that of Cambodian state temples. At present the two most acceptable hypotheses would be that of an orientation related to the dedication of the temple to Viṣṇu (see above) or else to the practical necessity to find enough place for such a big religious composition.

Inner Arrangement of the Sanctum

The arrangement of the sanctum is very simple, apart from the device(s) connected with the bathing rites. The ground is bare of any pillar base or the like and the only piece of "furniture" is the cult object usually placed upon a pedestal and accompanied by some accessories (lamps, small table, canopy and the like). Beside the rare images set on the walls (see above), there can be some secondary free-standing ones (favourite attendant deity, movable image of the main god, etc); they are usually few even if sometimes a sanctum may look overcrowded as, for instance, that of the "Vaithal Deul" Goddess' temple at Bhubaneswar (Orissa) where about fifteen attendant deities surround the main goddess, Cāmuṇḍā *alias* Kāpālinī.

- Pedestal and Placing the Main God

Most often the pedestal takes up a good part of the room floor (a ninth of it according to several treatises). Usually made in stone and decorated with mouldings, its shape is sometimes related to that of the sanctum (thus the stellate sanctum of Baudh temples contain a Liṅga set on a stellate pedestal). Square pedestals are the most common, apart from images of widthwise spread or group representations which have oblong ones; there are also circular ones, without there being any precise relation between a particular type and a specific deity. For instance the Liṅgas are provided with a square or circular pedestal without clear reason for the choice of one or the other form.

A central position seems to be the basic principle when the sanctum is square or circular and when the cult-object is a Liṅga. A shift to the back of the room is common when the sanctum is oblong and occurs quite often when the cult object is a statue. Therefore, as regards the "central" position, technical treatises always rule that there must be a slight distance between the geometric centre of the room and that of the cult object, the shift being most generally towards the North-East when the temple entrance faces East (see *Mayamata* 33.37-40a and Dagens 1984b § 4.7). In practice, it has been shown that the shift to the North noticed in the main sanctum of the Phnom Bakheng state temple at Angkor, involves the whole temple including its five step pyramid (Dumarçay 1972 p. 13).

- Draining away Bathing Liquids

In India, a device to drain away the liquids poured on the god out of the sanctum and the temple is found from the Gupta period (3rd-4th c. A.D.) and perhaps even earlier (Dhaky 1982), while in South-East Asia it is a regular feature in Cambodia as early as the 7th c. A.D. (Parmentier 1927). As mentioned before, such a device is necessary for the bathing liquids become "leftovers" (or "rests") immediately after flowing on the god and, as such, become polluting and even dangerous as is the case of any leftovers of a meal or offering according to an ancient Indian tradition (Malamoud 1972). Such an idea leads to many questions which have given rise to a sophisticated casuistry (what to do with the leftovers of the food? who can eat them? etc.). The topic has been developed about *nirmālya*, that is to say the remains of garlands (*mālā*) and other offerings (food, flowers, liquids for bath, etc.) made to the god at the time of worship (Brunner 1969). Regarding Śiva, such remains are to be given to one of his attendants, Caṇḍa/Caṇḍeśvara, who will eat or drink them: his chapel is conveniently placed to the north of Śiva's temple and near the gargoyle that carries the bathing liquids outside. For other gods and goddesses, generally it is difficult to know who is to receive the food offering remains; but it seems that, as usual, pattern of Śiva's followed. Thus we learn that it is some "Tejaścaṇḍeśa for Sūrya, "Tejas" being an alternative name for Sūrya (*Sūkṣmāgama*, chapter 6), while for the Goddess, if it may be a female deity said to be "She who bears the *nirmālya* (*Nirmālyadhāriṇī*)" (*ibidem*, chapter 54), there is also a certain "Caṇḍeśī" (eg. Dhaky 1970 regarding a Goddess' temple in Rajasthan).

In this regard, what is most important for us here is not to know who receives these remains, but the fact that they are to be taken out of the temple and, being liquids, they are also to disappear into the ground. From a practical point of view, the bathing liquids once collected in the vat on top of the pedestal and sent to the ground through the spout of that pedestal, are then led through a duct outside the temple building. Discharging out from there through a gargoyle, they flow into the ground and disappear unless they go through another duct which crosses the temple's enclosure(s) before reaching the exterior area. There are many variations in the general arrangement of the device, but the care brought to organize that draining even in the most difficult circumstances (see for instance in complex cave temples) shows the great importance given to it. Another mark of this importance is the careful attention required regarding the watertight character of the vat formed on top of the pedestal: a special "eight ingredient mortar" (*aṣṭabandhana*) is used to preserve it, and if decayed, that mortar is to be immediately replaced during an elaborate ceremony described in all temple ritual treatises (*e.g. Dīptāgama*, chapt.83).

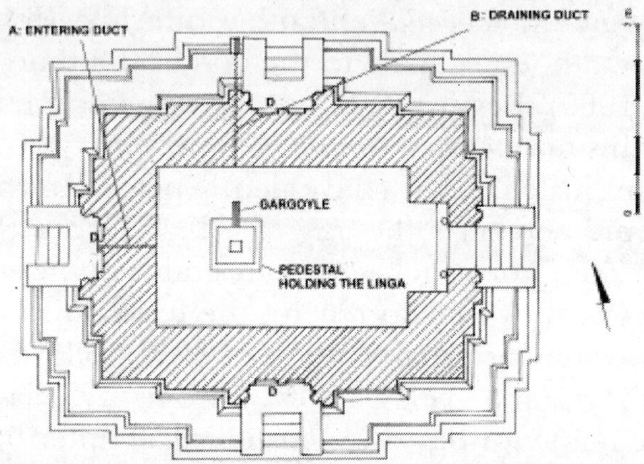

Fig.4. Devices for bringing in and draining out lustral liquids in the Śiva temple at Vat Phu (Laos, beginning of 11th c.) (Dumarçay 1998). Spring water enters the sanctum through duct "A"; then, once it has bathed the Liṅga it is drained out through duct "B". "D" indicates the three false-doors (each provided with steps).

- *Bringing inside Bathing Liquids*

Some temples also comprise a device meant to facilitate the offering of a bath to the god, especially when this bath concerns a huge cult-object or when it is planned to make it continuous. For instance, in Indonesia some Buddhist temples comprise in the sanctum a wall built at the back of the statue and provided with steps which allow the priest to reach the top of the image to pour liquids on it (Dumarçay 1982, Fig.19). Elsewhere, in South India (Andhra Pradesh, Tamil Nadu and Orissa), some Śaivite temples contain a very high Liṅga in their sanctum. In order to allow the pouring of liquids on the head of that Liṅga, the sanctum has been provided with an upper storey; its floor is pierced in the centre by a hole through which rises the top of the Liṅga, and it is made accessible allowing the priest to perform easily the bathing rite (Pichard *et al.* p. 35).

Some of these ritual baths are said to be continuous. In such cases, it is usual to arrange a wooden tripod supporting a vase above the cult-object, of which the pierced bottom lets liquids flow slowly but continuously (*e. g. Dīptāgama*, Vol. III p. 35 and 462-465). However, more sophisticated devices may be arranged by making use of a spring or a stream to provide a continuous flow. One of the most creative devices of the kind is found in South Laos at Vat Phu (Fig.4). On the slope of "the mountain which is a Liṅga" (Liṅgaparvata, see above), a Śiva temple has been built at the same level where there was a spring. This spring's water (which in fact gushes from the Liṅga which is the mountain!) has been harnessed and led to a duct bored through the back wall of the temple: thus it enters the sanctum, bathes the Liṅga from above and leaves the room through the usual way. A similar device can be seen in the Śiva Temple at Tadpatri (Andhra Pradesh, 16th c., Michell 1989, p.395). At Mahānandin (Andhra Pradesh, ca 11th c.) a stream that flows under a Śiva temple is made to flood its sanctum.

- Turning around the God in the Sanctum?

The "turning around" (*pradakṣiṇa*, lit. '[turning around persons or things so as to place them] on one's right') is the most common personal token of respect presented to a god or one's master (the same word *pradakṣiṇa* also designates a procession moving around the temple and, then, any procession). Technical treatises mention it as a rite performed around the temple, i.e. outside the sanctum. In some Śaivite works it is even ruled that it has to be performed without stepping across the duct (*somasūtra*) draining the bathing liquids from the temple through the courtyard: to avoid that, one is to go up to the duct, then to turn back and go again to the duct, but by the other side, or else to move away from the temple building in order to bypass the crossing (e.g. *Dīptāgama*, 99.6-7). An existing ambulatory, set around the sanctum (but inside the temple building) could be a device to allow such turning around near the god, while outside the sanctum; however, we have not found in treatises any hint about the ritual use of such ambulatories (see below). In any case, performing such rites inside the sanctum itself would be difficult and, in many temples, physically not possible due to several factors (cluttered sanctum, pedestal set against the back-wall, protruding pedestal spout, etc.).

As a matter of fact, proper exceptions to this turn-around in the sanctum seem to concern stūpas used as cult objects set in a sanctum. In this case, it is noticeable that there is always a free space around the stūpa and one may think that the custom of going respectfully around Buddha's relics embedded in a stūpa built in the open air has been also kept for any replica housed in a sanctum as a figure of the Buddha.

Encasing the Sanctum

Prototype and Developments

A temple building can be no more than a simple functional encasing of the room we have just described. From a statistical point of view it can even be said that this kind of temple is the most common. It can be considered as the prototype from which the temple may develop in various ways, keeping in mind that "prototype" and "development" are used here without any chronological prejudice.

Whichever they are, temple developments always are in embryo in the minimal programme, of which they amplify the practical rendering; for instance, in order to make performing of worship easier, to arrange for attendance of devotees, or else to multiply the number of divine beings physically present in the temple through images set all around the main god, in or outside the sanctum. All such developments express the devotion and commitment of the community and they tend to glorify the god as well as the community itself, and the temple's patrons.

In spite of the wide extent and the complexity they can give to the temple, such developments however remain "secondary", as is well demonstrated by the numerous temples which are in perfect working order in spite of their obvious unfinished condition: tower-like superstructure not built, crude wall surfaces, just rough outside ornamentation, toothing-stones for yet incomplete foreparts and other outbuildings, etc. Whatever importance is given to arrangements made outside the sanctum, that is the only self-sufficient part of the temple: once the god has been ritually installed in it, that sanctum *is* the temple, regardless of the stage of completion reached of the building encasing it.

Three Categories of Temple Developments

Three main categories of temple development can be considered, which are more or less independent of each other. The first one concerns the encasing of the sanctum in a building, while the second one is characterised by the adding to that building of secondary elements which are materially linked to it. The third category deals with the organization and arrangement of the plot of ground allocated to the god around the temple.

The first two of these categories result in the house of the god, the temple, that is to say a simple or intricate building which houses the sanctum where is installed the god and which may comprise one or two secondary bodies. The third one is the making up around that temple of the "sanctuary", that is the estate which is physically bordered and is the property of the god.

In the following chapters we shall detail the potential results of each of these three kinds of development, all of which have to be concentric around the sanctum simultaneously and in line with the axis of its main entrance. Here we will describe them only in broad outline.

The architectural envelopment of that interior volume which is the sanctum can be defined as an encasing with several interlinked aspects. In the first place, the planned building is established on a support which can be a relatively complex base or a genuine stepped pyramid. Then, the sanctum is to be closed by walls which can be split in two in order to form an in-work ambulatory; this walled ensemble is to be covered and roofed; then, its façades are to be arranged and, if necessary, outwork foreparts are built back on to them, for instance to provide the entrance with a porch.

This building, whatever its size and complexity, may be supplemented by a secondary body (sometimes two) which is built in front of it and attached to it (directly or through a corridor). This secondary body is in line with the (main) entrance of the sanctum and the eyes of the god. It is usually a pavilion which – open or closed – is bigger than the sanctum, of which it is a nearby annexe, often used to keep paraphernalia needed for worship and ceremonies. It is also used by devotees who find a shelter just in front of the dwelling of the god. Usually there is one such pavilion only, but it is not rare to find two of them (but never more); if two, they are built on the same axis but are not necessarily similar in type (close or open, etc.) or in size.

The organisation of the space surrounding the temple itself consists of its delimitation as well as the establishment of various annexes. The limits of the god's estate are delineated by the building of an enclosure wall provided with one or several entrances; the space thus delimited can be sub-divided by inner concentric walls which delineate as many concentric yards. The single or several enclosures thus determined are procession paths around the temple and the god it houses. It is also there that are to be found various kinds of annexes. Some of them, closely linked to worship in the sanctum, are placed on the axis of the last one (flag pole for the standard of the god, altar for offerings, image of the mount of the god). Others are either separate buildings or found located inside galleries built against the enclosure wall(s) or else inside big pavilions built in the yard(s). In the first place, these annexes are shrines for the main attendant deities attached to the god (and amongst whose are his spouse and also his mount, already mentioned). Then are found various ancillary buildings (treasury, kitchen, granary and other storehouses, offices, etc.), as well as pavilions intended for some specific ceremonies (e.g. dance pavilion) or for the use of devotees. Lastly, there are to be facilities for supplying and keeping the necessary water to be used by the temple and often by the surrounding village. Such facilities usually comprise at least a well and a reservoir while, in Cambodia, the reservoir is supplemented or most often replaced by a surrounding moat, an utilitarian facility as well as metaphor of an ocean surrounding the axis mundi, that is to say the temple (below p. 54$)

Initial Project and History

Dealing with the organisation of the plot of ground allocated to the god, the third category of developments may easily lead to an overlapping of several divine dwellings which combine with various procession walkways as well as socially organised areas, all these being parts of a multipolar hierarchy and located inside the closed estate of the god, Lord of the temple. Most of the developments included in this category are not necessarily parts of the initial project. As a matter of fact, they pertain more often to the temple's history than to its foundation pattern.

The architectural project which is drafted before building a temple must at least concern the installation of a building sheltering the representation of the god on the plot of land allotted for that. The project may or may not be ambitious, which is demonstrated by whether the temple is planned as a basic construction or as a sophisticated complex with several bodies. In the same way, the planned organisation of temple surroundings may comprise just the building of an enclosure wall or include the construction of numerous and elaborate annexes. Thus, at Candi Sewu, the initial project comprised the building of more than two hundred chapels surrounding the main temple in regular rows. At Angkor Wat, it included the building of a huge three level pyramid (on which were to be the temple proper as well as a full arrangement of galleries and of some other annexes) and that pyramid was planned since the start to be surrounded at quite a distance by an enclosure wall and a wide moat.

When brought to completion, the initial project succeeds in establishing the theoretically complete and perfect monument which its designer had in mind. However, these alleged qualities of completeness and perfection can only concern the main central body of the building encasing the sanctum, for it is the only part of the whole which cannot be "developed" again (unless it is destroyed and rebuilt from the start). However, it will always be possible to later on build against it a secondary body, and there is no limit on the number of annexes that can be added in the enclosures surrounding the temple. The organisation and the arrangement of the estate can be completed in several ways including adding of new annexes; thus a new enclosure wall may be built: if it is an intermediary one it creates a new sub-division in the estate, but if, to the contrary, the new wall is exterior to the previous composition it will mark an increase in the size of the same estate. In some cases, however, this new wall is built near the temple in order *to reduce* the size of the estate (e.g. Bayon Temple at Angkor, see p. 48-49$).

No matter where they are and no matter what their respective causes, these developments which are planned once the initial project of the temple has been carried out, mark the entry of that temple in history. When adding new constructions or altering old ones, the changes in tastes, customs, or techniques are to be taken into account, which is sufficient to require the use of new options and which often results in giving a heterogeneous look to the new composition thus created.

In the same way, new developments take into account the changes in religious practices, and sometimes even those in religious persuasion, which could have possibly led to change of practices. It may be sometimes just a shift with limited consequences – for instance, when Śiva-Vīrabhadra takes the place of Śiva as Lord of a temple. In some cases, however, there is a reversal of hierarchy: that happens in former Śiva's sanctuaries - where Skanda, son of Śiva and one of his attendant deities – has taken over the Lordship. Then his "chapel" becomes the main 'temple' to the detriment of Śiva's temple, which results in the religious and practical decentring of the sanctuary (L'Hernault 1978). Things go further when there is a change from a major religious current to another with a real disruption of ritual practices. That happened at Angkor Wat in the 15th or 16th century when that sanctuary was converted from Brahmanism to Theravādin Buddhism. The centre of religious practices which was located in the main sanctum on the top floor of the pyramid was transferred to the first floor, at a crossing of galleries more convenient for ritual practices as performed by a Buddhist monastic community of Theravādin persuasion. Simultaneously the four cardinal doors of the ancient Brahmanical sanctum were definitely closed, and the central body of the temple was converted into a massive and blind tower which could be seen as an avatar of the stūpa set on a magnificent pyramid.

Chapter III

The God's House

Prolegomena

The sanctum is the only room – or at least the main one– of the edifice in which it is encased and of which it occupies the ground floor, and is also its only habitable part. Exceptions correspond to temples comprising several sanctums one above the other, to say nothing of that sanctum provided with an inner upper floor and previously dealt with. The ground floor itself rests on a base which may or may not be raised, and it is surmounted by the various parts of the roofing. This last is often a kind of tower which dominates the fore-parts and other secondary bodies of the temple but which, however, can be lower than some annexes in the temple compound, particularly its entrance-pavilions.

Constraints

Building an edifice around the sanctum is subject to various constraints. The first of them is related to materials, ceiling or orientation as well as the suitability of the plan for the god or his image; these have been already dealt with. Other constraints concern the outer form of the building. Some are directly connected with the decorative option chosen for the arrangement of façades and they depend strongly on the region and the period. Others go hand in hand with the creation of perspective effects while yet others are aimed to distort physical reality in order to assert the majesty of the god and the appropriateness of the temple to him. These also are related to regional traditions and to the options of the day; however the personal selection and options of the architect are perhaps more important. It is not uncommon that implementation of such constraints – whichever their type – goes to illustrate in a very subtle way the importance given to appearance and to false (or mock) architecture, both being typical of master builders of the Indian world.

Fig.5. An ascetic's hut as shown on one of the Sanchi gateways (Madhya Pradesh, 1st c. B.C., author's photo). At the top of the roof is seen a finial (most probably a terracotta one) making the top watertight.

From a technical point of view the main problem is that of the roofing. The option for a heavy material and thus for corbelling could render obsolete the basic notions linked to a light architecture featuring carpentry work: it is the case of the "roof" and of the kind of finial which tops it and of which it is an integral part. As a matter of fact, the finial closes the roof at the very point where the rafters converge, and thus it saves the roof-trussing from rainwater leaks (Fig.5).

Real carpentry-work roofs are useless due to the implementation of heavy material corbelling. However, Indian builders when they have theorized the temple have very often decided to keep an *image* of such a roof as a major part of the temple and they have kept, by the same token, the finial which tops that roof. However in some regions – North India and South-East Asia – and perhaps due to an "aesthetic" option, the image of the roof itself has been suppressed, but the finial has been kept most probably as a "ritualistic" option, and in spite of the fact that it could look as an integral part of the suppressed roof. As a matter of fact, whether that finial tops a roof or not, it is set in place in the course of a crucial ceremony, for it marks the completion of the temple building work. At that time a sacred deposit is placed under it, symmetric to the foundation deposit set under the temple base at the beginning of the work. More than that, the bottom of the finial is often provided with a tenon which seals a small aperture let through the top of the roofing (whichever it is): this last point confirms that symbolically the finial placing makes the building watertight for good and thus signifies that the construction work is definitely complete.

The Norm

- Theorizing the Façades

Fifteen centuries ago, authors of technical treatises have theorized the arrangement of temple façades. Doing so, they have defined six different levels of elevation (Fig. 6). The first one – the "base" – corresponds to the basis of the building; above it are the "level of pillars" and then the "entablature" which, as far as a temple is concerned, make an inseparable pair "dressing" the elevation of the ground-floor, that is, the sanctum. The three other upper levels correspond to the roofing of the temple; they are the "attic" (4th level, also called "neck" or "intermediary level"), above which is the "roof" (5th level) and on top the "finial", the sixth and last level of which the importance has been already stressed.

These levels are horizontal and purely decorative divisions, of which the position on the elevation of a façade does not necessarily tally with that of the structural division which each of them displays. Similarly the "level of pillars" in spite of its name does not necessarily include pillars or pilasters or anything of the sort which may suggest a hypostyle composition; as a matter of fact it often looks as just a bare wall.

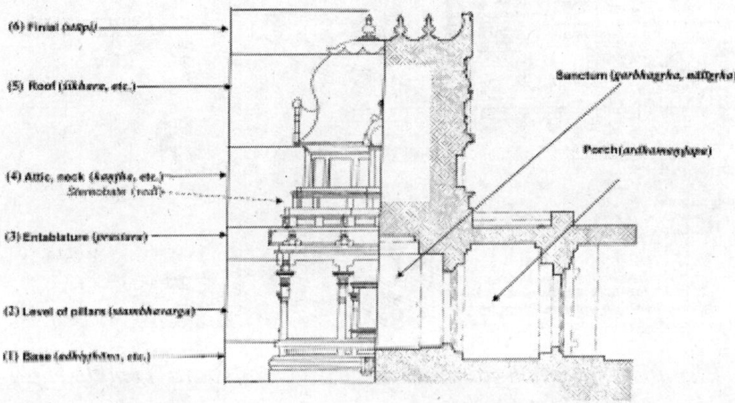

Fig.6. The temple six levels of elevation (according to Mayamata nomenclature; drawing based upon DUMARÇAY *&* L'HERNAULT *1975). The drawing shows the Śiva Viraṭṭāneśvara Temple at Tiruttani (Tamil Nadu, 9th c.), an apsidal building. On its ridge piece are seen several finiuls as if it was elongated in plan. The apsidal shape is found only at attic and roof levels while the base, level of pillars and entablature follow an orthogonal pattern. Level of pillars is decorated with pilasters.*

These levels appear on various categories of edifices. However, as the temple constitutes the most perfect category, it comprises all the six levels listed above. On the contrary its annexes do not usually show the complete set, except the entrance pavilions which are said to be "in form of a temple" (see below, p.59$) and the chapels which are a variety of temple. Thus, the pavilions (*maṇḍapa*) - certainly the most frequently found type of edifice amongst temple annexes - are theoretically provided with the first three levels (starting from the base) (below, p.44$), while the "halls" (*sabhā*) get four of them (lacking the entablature and attic) (Fig.8).

The façade of a small sized temple comprises all the six levels, each of them appearing only once. As regards bigger temples,

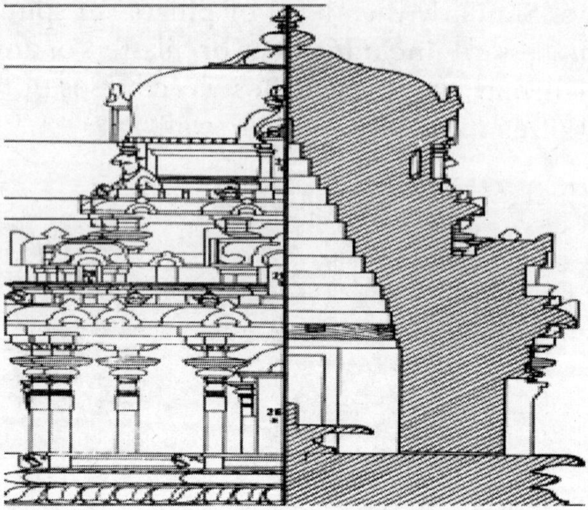

Fig. 7. Elevation of a two-storey temple (Śiva Coḷīśvara Temple Kilaiyur, Tamil Nadu, end 9th c.-beg. 10th c.; drawing adapted from LEGRAND *1987). The second storey (levels 2b and 3b) is partly hidden by aedicules which surround it and which stand on a peripheral platform at the top of the ground floor entablature (3a). Like for the temple seen in Fig.6, the decorative horizontal division of the façades does not tally with the inner structure of the edifice.*

as soon as it is technically necessary to increase the height of their corbelled roofing superstructure (see below), the façade of that additional height is covered with one or more of the pair – i.e. level of pillars and entablature – which covers the ground floor (Fig.7 and below). Thus the tower-like superstructure above the ground floor which surrounds the corbelling inner shaft is covered by horizontal divisions piled one of the top of the other with a progressive decrease in their width and height: they look like several storeys surmounting the ground-floor (see below). This pattern concerns all temple superstructures, even if it does so with important variations in detail that makes it necessary to distinguish three main types amongst them.

- *Norm and Structure: From "Attic" to Superstructure*

As set forth in treatises, the norm apparently deals only with the façade arrangement. However, even without making any mention of structural problems, it obviously takes them into account or at least does that for some of them and particularly those adopting the heavy material option for roofing the edifice. It is most probably there that are to be found the whys and wherefores of the presence of the called "attic" or "neck" amongst the set of levels of elevation. This element is indicated in Sanskrit only metaphorically through various terms meaning "neck", due to the fact that it is always recessed in relation to the "entablature" which is below it and the "roof" which is above it. It corresponds to a sort of drum, of which the structural purpose would be to reduce the extent of the roof base: if it was not there, this base would have been the same as that of the ground floor. By the interplay of proportions, such reduction occurs for the height of the roof as well as for its width; it thus allows for the necessary lightening of the "roof", a massive element which its weight makes incapable of spanning more than a very narrow area. The famous Draupadī Ratha at Mahabalipuram is a good counter-example: it is a temple without an attic and its existence as a stone edifice has been made possible only through its nature of sculpted monolith (Fig.8): the absence of an attic results in an enormous roof which would have been inconceivable in a stone-masonry building. As a matter of fact that sculpted temple has the shape of a *sabhā*, a sort of edifice of which the only stone-built examples are this monolithic one and the small corner stonework aedicules often topping the entablature. When found amongst temple annexes, an edifice provided with the formal characteristics of such a *sabhā* always comprises a real carpentry work roof (see for instance the Kānakasabhā and other well known *sabhās* built in the courtyard of Śiva's temple at Cidambaram).

Fig. 8. Draupadī Ratha at Mahabalipuram (rear view, author's photo). This temple dedicated to the Goddess is a hewn rock monolith; it had a four level elevation (base, level of pillars, roof and finial [that last has disappeared]). The façade seen here comprises a niche cum false door while the corners of the roof are adorned with foliage scrolls as a part of temple festive setting (p.104-105$).

Any widening of a space to be roofed with a corbelled structure automatically results in an increase in the height of this structure. We have already seen how that increase is visually dealt with on the façades by multiplying the pair of levels making up the ground floor façade. The result of such an option is a more or less pyramidal superstructure. Being a perfectly coherent encasing for the corbelling shaft, it allows keeping the pair made up by attic and roof within reasonable dimensions; in the present case, a reasonable weight for that pair is processed in stone or brick work. We shall see later that the ultimate result of combining the attic and roof is to top the temple by its own image (p.35-37$).

Two Main Decorative Options

In order to cover the façades of the massive and heavy structure which the temple is, architects of the Indian world have resorted to two main decorative options which are based on the will to represent two different and even strictly contradictory structures.

- *False Reversion to a Wooden Architecture?*

According to one of these two options, the general appearance of the temple is to be in conformity with its heavy structure and thus it looks like a stone-work (or brick-work) edifice where closed parts of façades are far more important than the open ones (Fig.9). To the contrary, according to the second option (Fig.10), the decorative setting of façades gives to the temple the look of a light hypostyle wooden structure which would be bordered by 'porticoes', in other words it would be wide open. Such a suggested open appearance has nothing to do with the real structure which is closed and massive: 'colonnades' and 'porticoes' are just rows of pilasters set against walls while the 'open' intercolumniations are no more than these solid walls. As for the other elements – "pillars" shafts, bell and bracket capitals, entablature, etc. – they are all hewn out of stone or bricks, sometimes moulded out of stucco, but they invariably resemble wooden models with great accuracy even in the most minute detail; that is made possible by the change of materials and the subsequent giving up of initial architectonic constraints.

On the façades, this pseudo-hypostyle structure can be displayed flat like a theatre scenery or it can be provided with articulated recesses and projections, of which the angles are accentuated by pilasters. That second solution creates an impression of flexibility more appropriate for the light buildings which are imitated than for the heavy structures which are thus decorated.

Fig. 9. Stone-work like façade: Śiva Mallikārjuna Temple (Aihole, Karnataka, 7th c. A.D.) (MICHELL 1975).

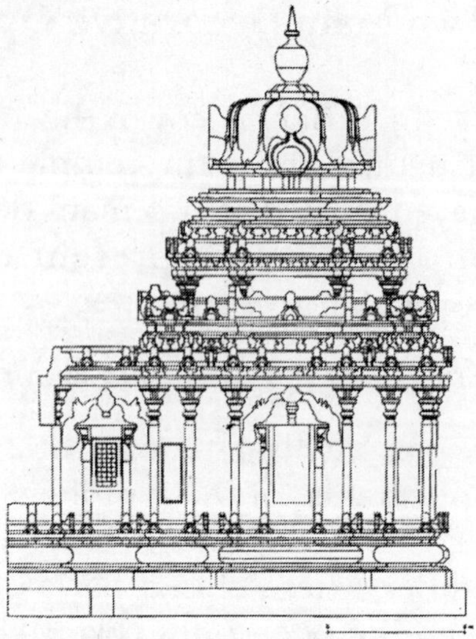

Fig. 10. Pseudo-hypostyle façade: Śiva Bhujaṅgeśvara Temple (Saṅgameśvara, Andhra Pradesh, 8th-9th c. A.D.) (DAGENS 1984a).

- *Geographical Distribution of the Two Options*

The pseudo-hypostyle option is a typical feature of South Indian temples from the 7th c. A.D. till the present. Its oldest known examples pertain to the Pallava (Tamil Nadu) and Cālukya (Karnataka and Andhra Pradesh) schools, but it survives in all the later schools of the area (Rāṣṭrakūṭa, Cola and Pāṇḍya, then Vijayanagar, to mention only the main ones). Its northernmost main manifestation, the Kailāsanātha Rock Temple at Ellora, dates from the second part of the 8th century, when the Rāṣṭrakūṭa dynasty was in possession of a big part of Peninsular India which resulted in transferring South Indian cultural elements to the north. Outside India, this pseudo-hypostyle option has been exported to South-East Asia where however it has been strongly modified. Thus in Cambodia, the Indian model has virtually lost its so-called hypostyle appearance; pilasters vanished or became just vertical bands decorated with plain or historiated foliage-scrolls. In the same way, the attic-roof pair vanished after some time and its disappearance was made up with an enlargement of the finial. Nowadays, this so-called hypostyle option follows the recent implantation of the Tamil diaspora in South-East Asia and elsewhere in the world.

The second option is characteristic of North Indian temple architecture but is found in the South down to the Cālukya region centred on the Krishnā, where it has developed concurrently with the pseudo-hypostyle one in such a way that they sometimes coexist in the same monumental grouping. Besides that, a kind of 'contamination' occurred between both the options in their meeting area, an interesting proof of their purely decorative nature; this phenomenon is common in the Vijayanagar period but it was already perceptible some centuries earlier as, for instance, in Andhra Pradesh during the 9th-10th centuries (e.g. Pratakota temples, Dagens 1984a).

Perspective and Other Effects

Whichever the chosen option, it is often subject to adjustments connected with the pursuit of perspective and other similar effects. Regarding proper perspective effects, they are commonly used to amplify the dimensions of an edifice in the whole Indian world. As early as the end of 7th century A.D., the technique was well established in South India; from there it went to Indonesia (middle of 8th c.), then to Cambodia (beginning of 9th c.) and lastly to Burma (11th c.?), being at each stage revived and rethought (Dumarçay 1983).

In these various countries, architects have made use of various processes (*ibid.*). Most often the true perspective is forced, in order to increase the distance which it indicates: thus the lower part of some architectural element is not figured, which gives the impression that it is hidden (Fig.11); sometimes dimensions which are theoretically constant – such as the width and the height of the steps of a stairway for instance - are gradually decreased in order to suggest that the viewpoint is farther than it really is: consequently, the structure on which this point stands appears proportionally bigger. As we shall see later, the use of such effects goes further than just a visual exercise and sometimes concerns the definition of the temple's god (see p.74$).

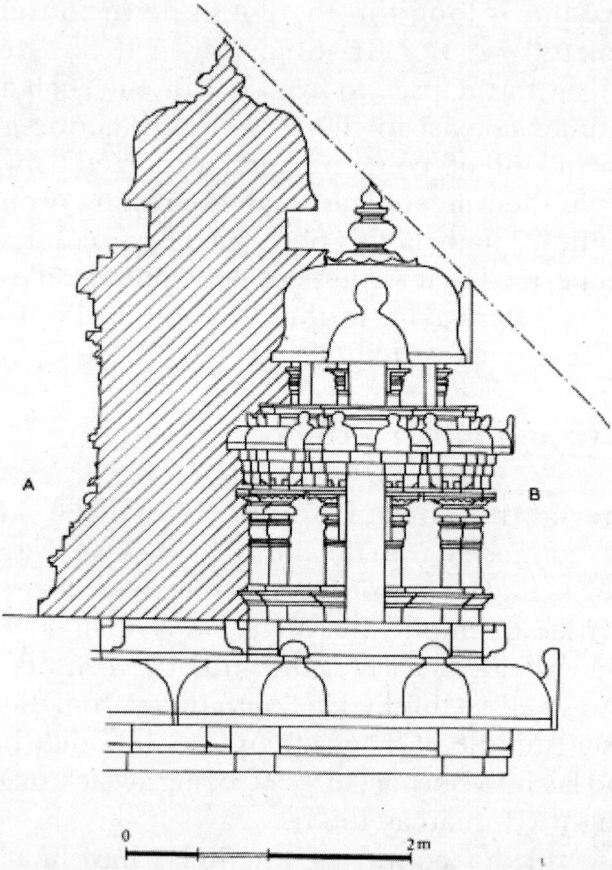

*Fig.11. Perspective effects on the superstructure of Śiva Temple at Darasuram (*Dumarçay *2001). Here, an aedicule stands on an entablature and its lower part has been suppressed to suggest that it was hidden by the rim of the entablature cornice. Inevitably the spectator mentally restores the missing part (shaded area) and thus sees the aedicule as bigger than it really is.*

While using these perspective effects to visually modify the dimensions of an edifice, Indian architects have also resorted to optical effects for changing its form – most specially its plan. In that field, the most common process, a very simple one, is to use the roof of the edifice to visually transform its plan. The basic principle is the well known fact that a roof provided with a centred plan easily gives the impression that an edifice is perfectly square or circular even when in fact it is slightly elongated (oblong or elliptic); in the same way, a roof comprising a ridge piece – either a double slope roof or a wagon-roof – looks oblong or elliptic even when it is square or circular. In India this disguising technique is often applied to Goddess' temples for which a theorised tradition prescribes a width-wise oblong sanctum. That oblong shape is very often suggested just by a two slope roof provided with a ridge piece above a temple which has an outside and inside square plan. The same process has been used, it seems, for the famous Viṣṇu temple at Srirangam in South India (Fig.62, p.119$): its double hipped wagon-roof suggests a width-wise extended sanctum as it suits the image of a reclining Viṣṇu which it houses, while this sanctum is actually circular. In Cambodia several pseudo-libraries from the end of the 12th century are of square plan but provided with a wagon-roof which makes them look oblong.

Colouring the Temple

At present, renovation of a temple in South India often leads to the colouring of its façades and also of its entrance pavilions, with special emphasis on the colouring of the images occupying the façades of the tower-like superstructures. Some ancient evidences show that this is not a recent practice (see for instance the 16th century Western travelogues mentioning temples with coloured façades at Vijayanagar). However it seems that its usage varies from region to region. If expressive polychromatism is a common feature in Tamil Nadu, plain whitewash is very common in Andhra Pradesh. As regards North India it seems that there is a quest for simplicity with plain coloured temples, often toned down red and sometimes with two tone effects (see at Mathura for instance). However, it is to be conceded that in any case the monsoon rains make such colouring rather temporary which necessitates its frequent renewal.

Ground Floor Arrangement

Arranged around the volume made up by the sanctum, the ground floor is limited by a wall, of which the thickness is sizeable whenever the monument is important, but can be split in two by creating an inner void which may or may not be accessible.

The outside plan of the building can follow any of the various shapes listed above for the sanctum plan. However, the arrangement of façades modifies the detail of the layout most often and it can obliterate its main lines so much that the not-uncommon conformity with the inside plan of the sanctum vanishes: that phenomenon strengthens the impression that the outside look of the temple is no more than the outcome of only disguising façades. The most important modifications result from the setting up of more or less developed foreparts or of more complex structures built against the main body.

Foreparts

Foreparts are used to enlarge or beautify the real or false entrances to the sanctum but they can also serve as chapels or pseudo-chapels.

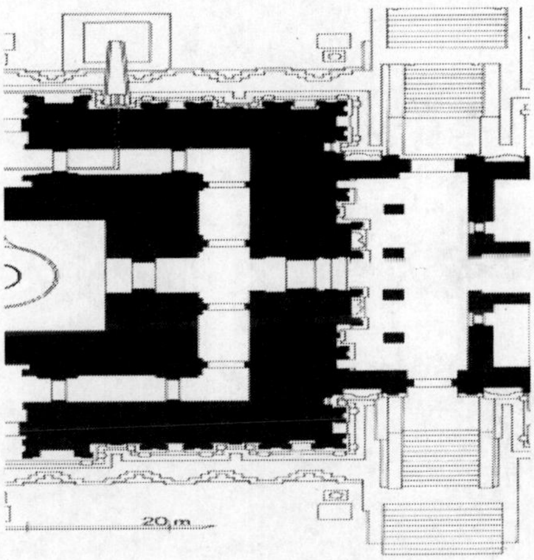

Fig. 12. Ground floor with an in-work ambulatory: Śiva Rājarājeśvara Temple (Thanjavur, Tamil Nadu, beg. 11th c.). South, west, and north entrances are just above a drop. To the north the drain duct is following a zig-zag line (PICHARD 1995).

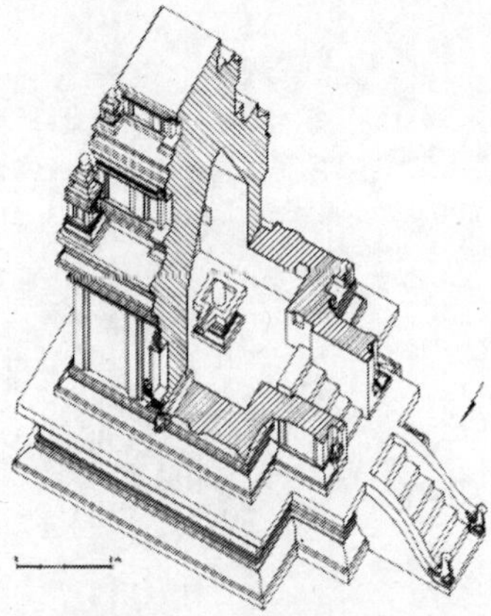

Fig. 13. Simple type of sanctum set upon a high base: Candi Arjuna (Java, 8th c.) (DUMARÇAY 1986).

- Entrance Foreparts

Adding a forepart to make a porch or a vestibule in front of the sanctum main door is the most common modification made to the outside plan of the temple (and usually the only one). While it highlights the entrance to the sanctum, that element serves sometimes as a shelter to those who stand near that door or as a chapel for the mount of the god which normally faces the one directly in line with the sanctum (see for instance the Bull in Śiva's temples). The adding of such foreparts to the lateral and back sides of the temple, whether they are open or blind, is less common and is always combined with that of a forepart on the main façade. However such multiplying of foreparts is often a result of a trend to homogenize the four façades, a trend which is common as regards the upper parts of a temple and which would be then made perceptible even at the ground floor level (see above).

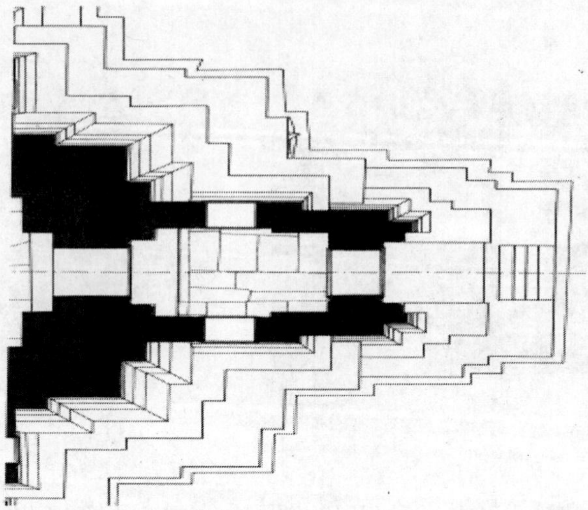

Fig.14. Porch with a double forepart: Buddha Vimaya Temple at P'imai (Thailand, end of 11th c.: northern side of main temple) (PICHARD 1976). The double forepart perceptible from outside is just an illusion: the porch comprises one room only; inside, its ground is flat and the progressive slope suggested by the façade arrangement does not exist.

Wherever a porch opening is made straight towards the outside or a vestibule linking the sanctum with a pavilion is made, the entrance forepart is provided with a flat roof or a curved two-slope one: in the second case its gable takes the shape of a historiated pediment. Architects of ancient Cambodia have created a façade arrangement suggesting that two foreparts are piled one against the other, while actually there is only one room inside: see for instance at P'imai (Fig.14) where the two rooms suggested with different ground levels materialize as a single room with a flat floor.

Similar arrangements can also be found on lateral and back façades of the ground floor: they correspond to secondary entrances to the sanctum, entrances which can be real (as in P'imai) or false (as most often in Cambodia, see for instance Thommanon temple at Angkor, 12th c.). Whichever the case, they can be similar to those found on the main façade or no more than just a sculpted and often slightly projecting décor.

- *Chapel or Pseudo-Chapel Foreparts*

Foreparts being chapels (or pseudo-chapels) also are a very important feature in the organization of façades following the pseudo-hypostyle option. Each of them looks like a projection built against the main body at its corners and in the middle of its facades, where there is no entrance arrangement.

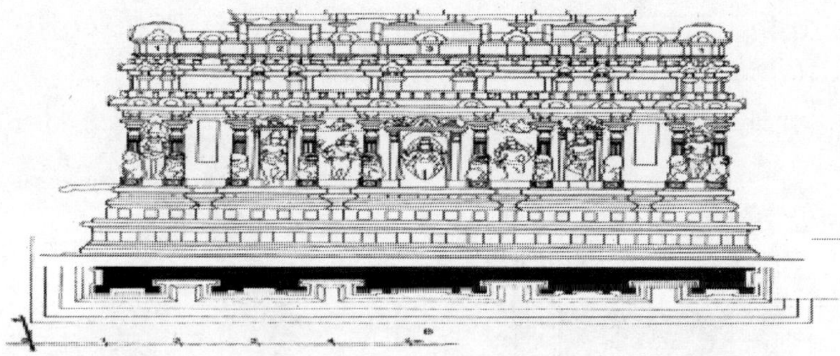

Fig.15. Foreparts being chapels or pseudo-chapels. A: Śiva Kailāsanātha Temple (Kancipuram, Tamil Nadu, 8th c.): At each corner and in the centre of façades a prominent projecting forepart encloses a sanctum sheltering an image; the main sanctum contains a huge Liṅga and the inner ambulatory comprises stairs leading to an upper level. B: Śiva Kailāsanātha Temple (Tirupattur, Tamil Nadu, 8th c., PICHARD 1995): The façade is arranged with five vertical projecting elements, each topped by a square or oblong aedicule with a centred roof (at the corners) or a wagon roof (elsewhere).

Rising vertically, such foreparts are topped above the entablature of the ground floor by aedicules which partly hide the lower part of the second floor, or more precisely, the first false floor (Fig.15B). Sometimes they constitute real chapels and encase a sanctum (see for instance Kailāsanātha Temple at Kancipuram, Tamil Nadu, Fig.15A), but most often the presence of a sanctum is only suggested: the forepart is then a solid feature but its façade comprises a niche with an image; the frame of the niche suggests the existence of a door and the image thus looks as being inside a sanctum and seen through its door (Fig.15B).

Outwork Ambulatory and other Outwork Features

An outwork ambulatory is occasionally built at ground floor level, all around the main body of the edifice and against it. Outwardly bordered by a light wall, it is covered by a slightly sloping lean-to roof or by a flat one (Fig.16); it may comprise axial windows (*e.g.* the so called Pārvatī Temple at Nachna, Madhya Pradesh, 6th c.) or just loopholes such as on the Śiva Temple at Tirupattur (Fig.16) or Śiva Vijayacolīśvara at Narttamalai (Meister & Dhaky 1983 Vol. I Fig.66).

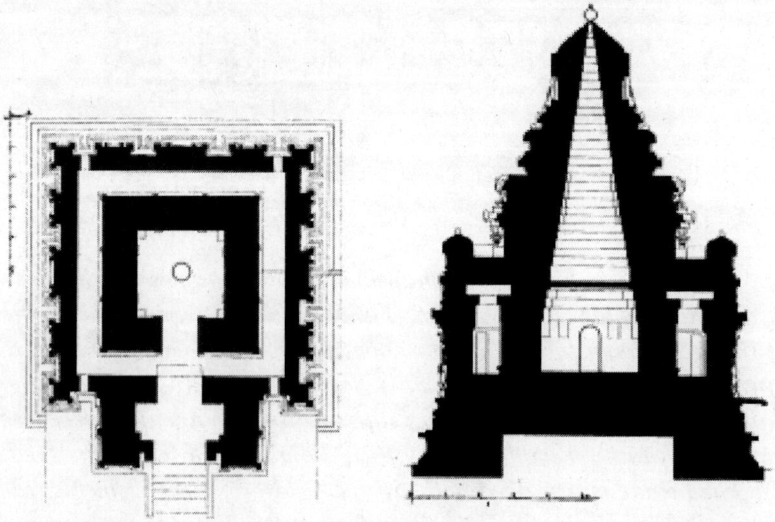

Fig.16. Outwork ambulatory lighted by loopholes: Plan and cross section of Śiva Kailāsanātha Temple (Tirupattur, Tamil Nadu, 8th c.) (PICHARD 1995). The suggested outside passageway around the 2nd floor is not accessible.

The concordance in the plan between the outside of the whole building and its main body is general, with a few exceptions: for instance, at the Narttamalai temple where the circular body comprises on its outer face four vertical elements, the whole being surrounded by a square plan ambulatory aisle. In Kerala the outwork ambulatory is often roofed by the eaves of the all-encompassing carpentry work roof and closed on the outside by a thin stone wall or a wooden partition with latticed windows (see below p.112-113$ and Fig.57).

An interesting variation on the surrounding ambulatory arrangement is found in what we call the 'temple with a surrounding pavilion'. The main body of this temple towers above a pavilion in the back part of which it stands; such an arrangement results in creating on one part an ambulatory like passage along the lateral and back faces of the main body and on the other a large hypostyle and flat roofed hall in front of that body; this hall plays the part usually allotted to the "pavilion built in front of the sanctum door" (Fig.17 and below, p. 45$).

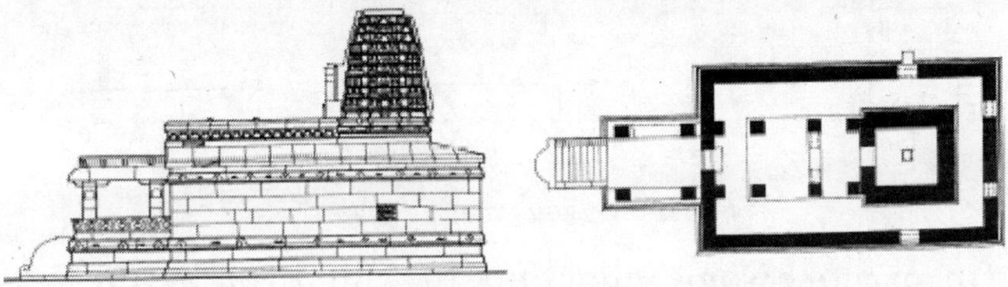

Fig.17. Temple with a surrounding pavilion: Plan and cross section of the Śiva temple known as Huccimalli (Aihole, Karnataka, 7th-8th C.) (MICHELL 1975).

That arrangement is mainly seen in Karnataka (Michell 1975) and Andhra Pradesh (Dagens 1984a) with some interesting variations (see for instance the apsidal plan of the so-called 'Durga' temple at Aihole). However, examples are also found elsewhere, as for instance in Madhya Pradesh with the Kaṇḍarīya Mahādeva temple at Khajuraho: there the structure encasing the aisle around the main body extends in such a way that this aisle is continued on both sides of the main entrance corridor.

Temple Roofing

Generalities

According to the theoretical pattern of a *prāsāda* the roofing corresponds to the three upper elevation levels. However, whenever the edifice is large, this group of levels is raised by a tower-like superstructure of which the façades are covered by one or several repetitions of the pair made up by the level of pillars and entablature making many upper storeys. This roofing is wholly built with heavy materials, which means that the "roof" is a false-roof, the 'attic' a false inhabitable level and, most of the time, the storey(s) false-storey(s).

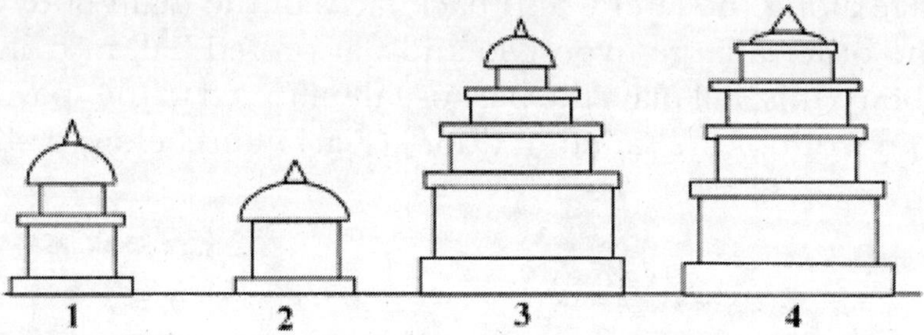

Fig.18. Various roofing options.

In practice some elements provided for by the basic theoretical pattern may be omitted and this results in four options (Fig.18): a basic type in conformity with theoretical pattern (No 1), a variation of type No 1 without attic (No 2, Fig.8), an enlargement of the basic type by inserting a superstructure between the entablature of the ground floor and attic (No 3) and a variation of type No 3 with omission of the attic-roof pair and enlargement of the finial (No 4).

To these four main options can be added, first, a type comprising an all-encompassing carpentry roof and where the finial tops that carpentry-roof which itself covers a massive false roof in masonry. Typical to Kerala, this type is seldom found elsewhere but similar arrangements are mentioned in Java (see for instance Candi Sambisari, Śaivite temple from middle of 9th c., Dumarçay 1993, Pl. XLIII). There is also the "flat roof" which – apart from perhaps very few exceptions – points to a rudimentary, or unfinished, or ruined edifice (see Insert).

Flat Roof Temples?

Flat roof is the minimal roofing, being that of the prototype for which span constraints are limited and for which the main purpose is to close the sanctum upward. In that case the flat roof is made up with stone slabs (covered with a mortar layer) or with stone or brick work supported by beams; its downward side is the ceiling of the sanctum while its upward one is often slightly rounded to make rainwater flow easier and is sometimes bordered by a dripstone shaped cornice.

However as soon as temples became more elaborate, what looks as a flat-roof is most often a horizontal area just ready to support a more complex roofing structure which has not been built or which has disappeared. In some cases the temple is obviously incomplete or ruined, but things may look less clear: this especially is the case of the earliest built temples that are preserved (Sanchi), which has led to the hypothesis that they were "flat roof temples" and that the earliest form of Indian temple was a flat-roofed one.

From this hypothesis are derived some theories using the allegedly vouched for precedence for flat roofs to prove that the Indian temple originated in caves or dolmens. However, and without questioning the possibility of such origins, it is to be emphasized that – as has been shown long ago by Odette Viennot – most of examples (if not all of them) chosen to back up these theories concern temples of which the flat roof is "accidental" being just the basis of a disappeared roofing arrangement or of a planned but not built arrangement (Viennot 1968).

Under these conditions it seems better to say that whichever was the model of the earliest Indian temples, there have always been temples more or less carefully built, bearing in mind that what we call "prototype" is ageless. In the same way it is to be reminded that nowadays temples are still being built of which the walls are just stone vertical slabs driven into the ground and supporting a "flat roof" made of horizontal slabs, thus apparently not very different from a dolmen: we noted fine examples of such temples in Andhra Pradesh. However it must be recalled that the "dolmen" itself, referred to as a prototype of supposed flat roof temples, is not a flat roof building but just the inner walls and ceiling of a room which is to be fully covered by a tumulus.

Horizontal Layout of Roofing

The plan of the temple roofing is not always similar all along its full height; changes normally may occur at the foot and/or at the top of the attic, or at the top of the superstructure when it is devoid of attic and roof. Exceptionally, a break can be perceptible at half-height of the superstructure (see below about Gangaikondacolapuram) but never at its foot which necessarily follows the layout of the ground floor plan. Whichever level it occurs, a break always results in a multiplication of the sides of the plan figure – for instance from square to octagon – or in the change from a polygonal to a circular plan. In most of the cases, the ground floor and superstructure are of square plan, while the attic is octagonal and the roof and finial circular. However, such breaks do not disrupt the consistency of the elevation, which is marked by the more or less a simplified repetition of some of the ground plan detail modulations in the topmost parts of the edifice.

Roof and Finial

The earliest built temples were provided with a real carpentry work roof as is shown by the few exploitable examples such as the apsidal temple at Sonkh (Haertel 1993) or the elliptic one at Besnagar, as well as by the rock hewn copies found at Barabar and some other sites. The shift to the heavy material option had however started very early, which made "real" roofs becoming exceptional. Stone or brick masonry roofing reproduced real roofs, probably pertaining to the civilian or domestic architecture of the time, and a corpus of such disguised forms was then established which has changed little up to now. It combines roofs which are centred, or two or four sloped, or hipped. It is worth noting the great success achieved by slopes with curved profiles, supposed to imitate screed roofing with a wide set of contour variations. Another point is the importance given to false dormer-windows: on centred roofs they emphasize the main directions and sometimes intermediary ones, but they are also found on wagon-roofs. Lastly it is to be noted that the flexibility of disguised architecture allows for creating forms which are seldom conceivable in real architecture, such as the stūpa-like or liṅga-like roofs found in Indonesia (p.73$).

The change from light to heavy material came together with a change in the constraints regarding the use of materials and related to the variation of technical properties between real and false roofs. Stone or brick false roofs offer a great flexibility for imitation of curved forms as well as placing false dormer-windows and other secondary elements, all of which being just sculpted ornaments, while their placing on "real" roofs needs complex arrangements of carpentry work. On the other hand, a false roof – whether hollow or solid – is heavy and, more than that, not homogeneous if it is of masonry as is most often the case. The span of all these false roofs is far shorter than that of the real structures they imitate and that results in a decrease in the area covered without intermediary support and also a reduction in the projection of all overhanging elements (cornices, eaves, etc.).

Due to their homogeneity, big monoliths may be used to allow for an increase of the span, but that quickly brings an overweight problem. Various processes used to tone down the technical inconveniences due to material have already been mentioned, such as the placing of an attic or/and a pyramidal superstructure using the corbelling technique. This being the case, there is no solution as regards eaves of which the overhanging is to always remain a slight one in disguised architecture. As regards struts (see Hoyśalas' monuments for instance) and other similar devices supposed to "support" the ends of "rafters", they are like those rafters with disguised elements playing just a decorative part, contrary to what is seen in Nepal, one of the few areas where wood is systematically used (p. 112-113$ and Fig.58).

Lastly we may remind that finial is always kept even when the roof is omitted. In this case, a link element is generally inserted between the top of the superstructure and the finial in order to facilitate their assembly: it is generally a wide ribbed and flattened round piece which is in the form of a myrobolan fruit (*amalaka*) in Orissa and North India or of a lotus (especially in Cambodia).

Attic and Summit Aedicule

We have already underlined the technical function played by the attic in the lightening of a temple's upper parts. Therefore, this level is without any doubt a fine example of the ability to imitate in stonework a model of light architecture, a model which most probably never did exist. As regards shapes, the attic together with the roof and finial constitute a sort of aedicule which tops the edifice. This similarity is often emphasized by the placing of niches for images (or of false doors) on the attic, above which the false dormer windows of the roof are made like forepart gables; in the same way, the moulded stereobate on which rises the same attic looks like the base of the edifice it figures. Lastly the recessed position of the attic leaves around it a kind of peripheral platform at the corners of which are often placed images of the god's mount. Such composition is found together with various types of roofs: centred, two-sloped or hipped ones.

The reason why the elevation of the set that the attic, roof and finial make up has been arranged since long to look like an aedicule placed on the top of the temple is not clear, apart from the fact that this process is part of the general trend to decorate the temple with its own image. As long ago proposed by Stella Kramrisch (1946, Vol. I, p.194), this composition – she called it "higher temple" – beyond being a decorative element can be seen as a vertical projection of the temple reduced to the bare minimum (in our terminology 'to its prototype'), the roof and finial being those of the temple while the attic and its stereobate

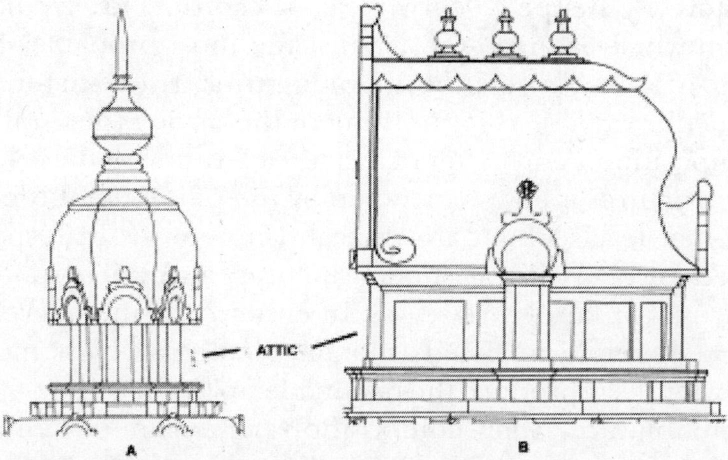

Fig. 19. Summit Aedicule (Dumarçay & L'Hernault 1975). A: Octagonal summit aedicule (Śiva temple known as Shore Temple, Mahabalipuram, Tamil Nadu). B: Apsidal summit aedicule (Śiva Vīraṭṭaneśvara Temple, Tiruttani, Tamil Nadu).

would represent the temple walls and base. The strange thing is that Indian treatises consider these three levels – attic, roof and finial – as separate entities and they never do establish between them the relation on which Stella Kramrisch based her proposal, and which is obvious even to the least well-informed observer. Lastly, we shall see below that this summit aedicule constructed on the temple may be an important feature in the general composition of the sanctuary built around the temple (below, p.103$).

Superstructure: General Features

Here we shall apply the term "superstructure" to very different realities: on one side a tower of which the massive structure overshadows the ground floor of the temple and, on the other, a roofing of which the proportions are functional and well in harmony with those of the other parts of the edifice.

On the basis of the arrangement of their elevation we have split Indian temple superstructures in three main types – 'with false-storeys', 'stepped', 'curvilinear' – according to a typological division which is in no way against the most probable shared origin of the three types, nor against the existence of intermediary types, to say nothing of the obvious general unity of composition. As a matter of fact, the elevation of these Indian superstructures is always made up by the piling up of repeated horizontal levels which are thin and numerous in respect of stepped and curvilinear superstructures, and thicker and less numerous for false-storey types. In either case, these levels can be most generally analysed as binary elements which, more or less obviously, reproduce the pair made up by the levels of pillars and entablature. Such compositions underline a deliberate prejudice in favour of horizontality which well shows that, contrary to the Western cathedral spire, the Indian temple superstructure does not mark a shift from horizontal to vertical even if some decorative arrangements may suggest it: therefore, the division in vertical bands of curvilinear superstructure elevation or the creation of vertical directrix by the superposition of corner *pieces d'accent* and other ornamental elements placed on the top of entablatures of Cambodian false-storey superstructures.

The plan and surface area of the bottom of the superstructure are the same as those of the ground-floor and it is only above that the plan modifications already stated may occur. Like for the ground floor, the detailed lay-out of the plan is dictated by various secondary elements which "dress" the elevation and which generally underline the individuality of each of the horizontal levels making up the superstructure. However, the regular repetition of such elements at each of these levels can bring out vertical lines starting from the ground floor. This is often the case when such secondary elements are in vertical continuation of those which modify and define the ground floor plan. Sometimes, as already said, such an arrangement is used to create perspective effects which stretch height-wise from the superstructure and/or alleviate its fundamental horizontality.

Aedicules and 'Piéces d'accent'

Aedicules are found on any type of superstructure but they are typical of false-storey types and more specifically of those following the pseudo-hypostyle option. Allowing for a few exceptions they represent a basic "temple" of which the elevation comprises only four levels: the base (more or less visible), level of pillars, roof and finial. However on curvilinear and stepped superstructures their roofing is either curvilinear or stepped and their finial is in the form of a flattened and ribbed bulb.

As regards false-storey superstructures, aedicules may be square and provided with a centred roof with straight or curved slopes, or either square or oblong but provided with a two sloped roof; some have an apsidal plan and a corresponding hipped-roof (they are then most often seen face on but sometimes in profile as, for instance, at Gangaikondacholapuram). These various types are often connected one to the other by gallery-like elements provided with a two curved slopes. Aedicules are placed at the corners of the edifice and between these (however I do not know of any temple with aedicules between corners and without aedicules at these same corners). The corner aedicules systematically are of square plan and provided with a centred roof while those with two sloped roof or apsidal plan are always on the façades between corners.

As regards false-storey superstructures, aedicules are installed on the peripheral platform created by the recessed position of a false-storey, above the entablature of the ground floor (as regards the first false-storey), or on the underlying false-storey (as regards the second false-storey onward); their number and their arrangement vary according to several factors (size of the false-storey, its vertical position on the elevation, etc.); however, the composition is always symmetrical in relation to the centre of the concerned façade; it is the same for all the façades of the concerned (false) storey, even if some adjustments may be seen on the main façade or when the building is of oblong plan.

The precise composition is always imposed by the plan of the peripheral platform mentioned earlier. Each aedicule tops one of the real or false foreparts or projecting elements which punctuate the ground floor façade (for the first false-storey) or the underlying false-storey (in other cases) (see for instance Fig.15).

It has been proposed that technically aedicules were acting as a counterbalance to avoid an inward fall of the inner walls of the corbelling shaft (Hoeckveld-Meijer 1981). That hypothesis is possible but it must not conceal the importance of their decorative and symbolic functions. They play an important part in the setting of perspective effects (Fig.7) and in the ornamentation of the temple with its own image. In the field of symbols, they are involved in the accommodating and multiplying of the divine inhabitants of the temple (see p.72$)°; moreover, surrounding the core of the temple they represent circles of chapels similar to the virtual circles of deities which surround the main god when the "five circles worship" >> (*pañcāvaraṇapūja*) is performed. In the same way, the miniature galleries which generally link all the aedicules located on the same storey are perfect images of the concentric enclosures surrounding the temple.

Piéces d'accent are characteristic of Cambodian superstructures from the last quarter of the 10th century onwards. Their pediment is bordered by a more or less ogival arcature of scroll foliage and comprises an image of a deity or just a foliage decorative motif. Being at right angle when they crown an angle and flat or slightly rounded in other cases, they underline the modulations of the façades of the lower level. They may also play an important part in visually giving a curvilinear profile to a false-storey elevation (Fig.27 and p.42$). Like aedicules, they are involved in the multiplying of the divine population of a temple and they often seem an alternative to the presence of façade divine images on its superstructure.

(False-) Storey Superstructure

"False-storey" superstructure comprises one or more storeys which generally are false, hence the name given to it by archaeologists. There is no precise corresponding name in the

Indian traditional treatises which mention the real or false nature of "storeys". The elevation of each of these storeys – false or real – comprises the same arrangement as the ground-floor, however with simplification of details and some progressive decrease in dimensions. Each of them is thus smaller than the one it is topping which, all around, creates a peripheral platform where are often placed decorative elements (aedicules, *piéces d'accent*) or statues. The recessed position of the storeys gives to the superstructure the profile of a stepped pyramid on the top, on which is found the composition comprising the attic, roof and finial or just an enlarged finial.

The prototypes of false-storey superstructure are perhaps to be seen in the northern area (Madhya Pradesh and Uttar Pradesh) where later the curvilinear type prevailed. However, the bad condition of the preserved monuments makes corroboration very doubtful (see for instance temple N.45 at Sanchi). Later, this false-storey superstructure is found in India and South-East Asia (Cambodia and Thailand, Champa, Indonesia). In India it is the only one used in Tamil Nadu since the first temples were built there at the beginning of the 7th century. It is also found during the same period in Karnataka and Andhra Pradesh but here curvilinear and stepped types were concurrently used. A few examples are found northwards in Western India that are very close to their South Indian equivalents (see for instance the Kailāsanātha rock temple at Ellora). Lastly the type is found in Nepal, but there the roofs and false-storey eaves are wooden carpentry works (Fig.58, p.113$).

Regional variations are numerous and involve decorative options, false-storey proportions, presence of real and habitable storeys, presence and arrangement of aedicules and/or *piéces d'accent*, to say nothing of the divine faces featured on some 12th-13th c. Cambodian tower-like superstructure (Fig.21).

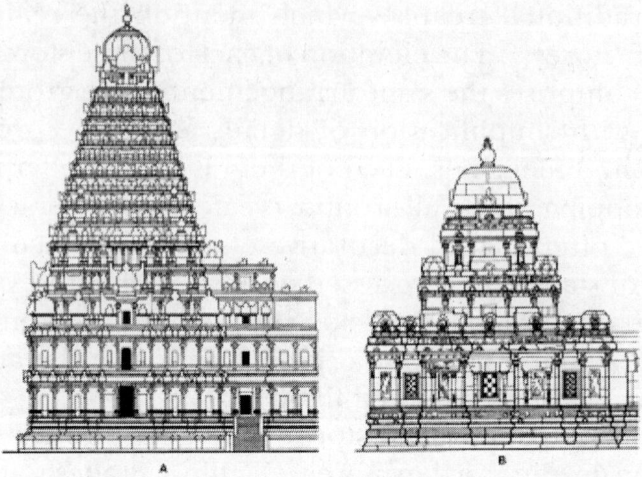

Fig.20. False-storey superstructures in South India A: Tamil Nadu: Śiva Rājarājeśvara Temple at Thanjavur (PICHARD 1995). B: Karnataka: Śiva Saṅgameúvara Temple at Pattadakal (MICHELL 1975).

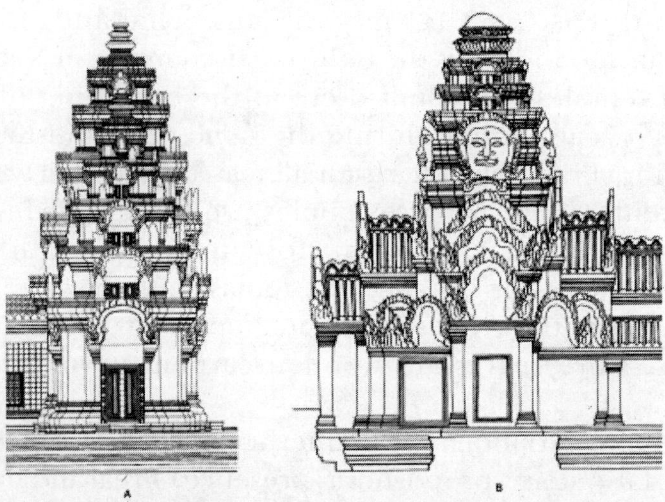

Fig.21. False-storey superstructures in Cambodia A. Śiva Temple at Banteay Srei (10th c.) (DUMARÇAY 1988). B. Tower No. 37 of the Bayon (Buddhist state temple, end of 12th c.) (DUMARÇAY & ROYÈRE 2001). In both cases, the topping aedicule is replaced by an enlarged finial with a lotiform base; false-storeys are provided with a false door (on the Bayon tower this door is sometimes hidden by the human face).

In a general way the number of storeys is in relation with the size of the edifice and the height of its superstructure, but important differences appear from one region to another and even within the same region. Temples in Karnataka (e.g. Pattadakal, Fig.20B) are characterized by the small number and the important relative height of their false-storeys, while in Tamil Nadu generally their number is higher and their height smaller. However the Śiva Rājarājeśvara Temples at Thanjavur and Gangaikondacolapuram, which are of the same size and have been built at a close interval in the same cultural and political context, have superstructures which comprise thirteen false-storeys at Thanjavur and only seven at Gangaikondacolapuram.

The façades of a false-storey superstructure generally follow the same decorative option as those of the corresponding ground floor. Some arrangements go together with the pseudo-hypostyle option: presence of a topping aedicule at the summit, aedicules of the false-storeys linked by miniature galleries, presence of rounded dripstone-like cornices at the entablature of each storey, and, in a very few cases, existence of some habitable storeys. On the contrary, the non-hypostyle massive option most often goes together with an enlarged finial, as well as with stringcourse-like entablature cornices and frequent replacement of aedicules by *piéces d'accent.*

In accordance with the chosen decorative option, the walls of each storey may or may not bear pilasters which mark the corners, as well as the real or supposed modulations of the plan. A middle false door on false-storeys goes together with the massive option and it is generally topped by a pediment which hides a part of the entablature. In other cases this potential entrance to the main body is replaced by the false door of an elongated aedicule occupying the middle of the façade of the concerned false-storey. The entablature of false-storeys can be quite complex, from a simple horizontal stringcourse to a straight or curved cornice; if the roof is of real carpentry work, the eaves-like cornice is straight and strongly projecting: in Nepal it often looks like a lean-to roof.

Stepped Superstructure

A stepped superstructure is made up by the superposing of thin binary elements, each comprising a recessed lower part and a projecting upper one. Typologically speaking this superstructure looks like an intermediary between the false-storey type (storeys here being simplified and multiplied) and the curvilinear one (horizontal lines here being more important but rendered in a very simplified manner). The general outline remains that of a truncated pyramid topped either by an attic-roof-finial composition (see below about Gop temple) or by an enlarged finial.

Fig.22. Stepped superstructure: Śiva Temple at Pratakota, Andhra Pradesh 11th c. (DAGENS 1984a). The façades of the ground floor follow the non hypostyle massive option; the finial has accidentally disappeared.

This type is well known in Central and Western India and even more in non-Tamil South India (Andhra Pradesh and Karnataka, Dagens 1984a and Michell 1995 [especially p.29, Fig.4]). In South-East Asia only a few examples are found (concurrently with false-storey ones) and all at the early beginning of so-called Preangkorean period (7th c. A.D.: Sambor Prei Kuk or Phnom Bayang, see Parmentier 1927); thereafter the type disappeared from Cambodia.

The plan is square or oblong (with the exception of two octagonal chapels at Sambor Prei Kuk); steps are either rectilinear or provided with projections corresponding to those of the ground floor which are most often slightly protruding.

The main façade of the superstructure is usually arranged as the others, but is sometimes partially hidden by the roofing of the entrance forepart. The ground floor elevation of the temple generally follows the non-hypostyle option but the hypostyle option may be also found on ancient or recent temples. The outside wall-iconography of the temple is limited: besides the images on the ground floor façade niches and those on the pediment of the entrance forepart, only small images are found placed on the pediment of the false-dormers windows set on the cornices of steps and on the roof.

The material used most of the time is the stone, bricks being rare. Generally, each part of a binary step corresponds to a stone-course of the inner corbelled shaft of the superstructure. The upper and projecting part of the step is usually given a shape which faithfully conforms to the ground floor entablature cornice. The lower and recessed part is vertical and its height is inferior or similar to that of the upper one; it is either continuous or divided by small pilasters or similar jutting elements which are regularly spaced. Sometimes such jutting elements display a row of beam butts with very small spaces between them; in this case the recessed lower step element can be very much thinner than the upper projecting one which then occupies several stone courses. A fine example is found on the temple of Gop (ca. 7th c.) in Gujarat: its superstructure comprises two steps only, each with a high and oblique slope which supports large false dormer-windows, while the slim recessed lower part is ornamented with a row of beam butts (Fig.23). The Gop roofing arrangement could be an image of a carpentry work composition comprising pagoda-like superposed roofs, or else an original and very coherent type of heavy material roofing: a faithful rendering of the progressive inner corbelling with decorative eaves sheltering very short vertical "façades" and a small terrace-like bordering area marking the base of each step.

Fig. 23. Stepped superstructure: Gop temple (NANAVATI & DHAKY 1969). The cornice of both steps supports big false dormer-windows; at its base can be seen a row of beam butts; projections are limited. The false roof is small, circular and curved.

Some other temples of the same region combine the Gop temple's roofing arrangement with corner aedicules (see for instance temple No. 1 at Sonkhamsari) which results in what looks like a clumsy assembly of heterogeneous forms, but the numerous examples of it would be surprising for just a result of clumsiness (*cf.* Nanavati & Dhaky 1969).

Curvilinear Superstructure: Main Features and Geographical Distribution

The general outline of a curvilinear superstructure is convex with variations between a continuous curve starting above the ground floor entablature (Karnataka, Gujarat, Andhra-Pradesh) and a vertical rise with a strong bent at the top (Orissa).

The horizontal levels are thin or even very thin and they are brought together in relatively complex subsets. At the top there is often an enlarged finial and, more rarely, a "roof". The general impression is often that of a massive tower out of proportion

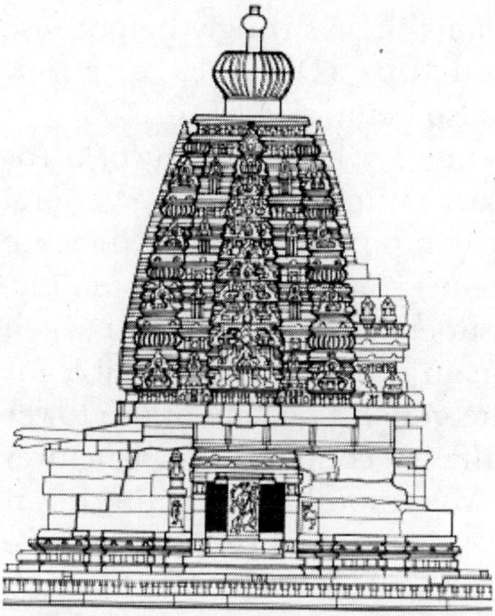

Fig.24. Curvilinear superstructure (Karnataka): Galaganātha Temple at Pattadakal (MICHELL 1975).

Fig.25. Curvilinear superstructure (Orissa): Brahmeúvara Temple at Bhubaneshwar(Author's photo.).

with the ground floor which it overshadows and sometimes seems to encompass: this is in full opposition with false-storeys which are no more than simplified repetitions of a ground floor bigger than each of them, as well as with stepped superstructure which is as different from its ground floor as may be a roof from the walls bearing it.

The main characteristic of curvilinear elevation is the importance given to vertical directrix lines rising from the ground floor to the base of the finial. The profile is determined by the outward alignment of the projecting parts of horizontal levels, their recessed parts looking hollowed out in the volume of the tower. From a practical viewpoint, several unfinished monuments show a tower-like superstructure which is fully assembled without any horizontal projection: it already possesses its general outline and needs just to have its ornamentation sculpted, that is to say, hollowed out (Nanavati & Dhaky 1969).

Lastly, in 18th century Bengal were built some temples of which the curvilinear superstructures were influenced by Western Gothic architecture which explains their strongly height-wise elongated forms with pointed tops (Datta 1975, about Bhāndīśvara temples, 1754; see also below, Fig.61, p.119$).

Some possible secondary elements which are outworks (or supposed to be so) take their part in underlining the general verticalness of these curvilinear compositions. When they are really outworks and thus modify the ground plan of the temple, each of them is provided with a superstructure of its own which generally is a reduction of the main one against which it leans or in which it is engaged. On the general outline of the tower this results in the curved lines of these secondary superstructures meeting those of the central one with smooth joins, toning down the horizontality which the decor may suggest (see for instance Kaṇḍarīya Mahādeva Temple at Khajuraho, Fig.20). In some cases such additions do not modify the ground plan as they concern just the superstructure, the secondary superstructures being then engaged in the main one (*e. g.* Temple No 1 at Miyani, Nanavati & Dhaky 1969, pl.51).

The curvilinear option is notably ignored in the southernmost regions of Peninsular India (Tamil Nadu and Kerala). Elsewhere it appears under the guise of regional types the most characteristic of them being found in Karnataka, in Orissa, in Central India and in Gujarat with frequent interferences.[1] In South-East Asia it is truly found only in Burma in the Pagan period where it has been obviously borrowed from Orissa and where it is used to roof Buddhist temples concurrently with the stūpa (Fig.26).

In Cambodia and Thailand things are more complex. First, it appears that at the end of the 11th c. at P'imai and, more clearly, some decades later at Angkor Wat in the first half of 12th

1. Karnataka: Michell 1975; Orissa: Donaldson 1985-87; Central India: Viennot 1976; Gujarat: (Nanavati & Dhaky 1969).

Fig.26. Pagan, Temple No 664 (Burma, 13th c.). (Pichard 1992-2001, Vol. 3) Curvilinear superstructure is here combined with a stepped (or false-storey?) composition and corner aedicules.

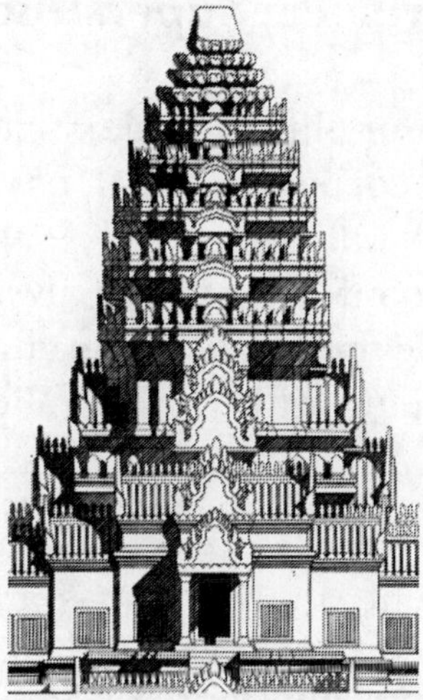

Fig.27. Angkor Wat. Central tower (12th c.) (Nafilyan 1969). Piéces d'accent *are mollifying horizontal lines; in the centre of façades, arches mark the position of the false doors (at the bottom of the drawing the building seen in the foreground is the entrance pavilion of the 1st enclosure).*

c., 'piéces d'accent' have been used to give a curvilinear general profile to false-storey compositions (Fig.27). Such visual conversion is probably due to an effort to adapt to Indian forms different from those which up to then had more or less been followed with freedom. One may assume that this was due to an influence coming from Orissa and reaching Cambodia, perhaps through Burma. One and a half centuries later, at Sukhotai Thai architects drawing their inspiration from Angkor Wat have created the '*prang*', a Buddhist monument born from the blending of the stūpa and the Khmer temple in order to adapt that temple to a new religious context, that of Theravāda Buddhism, where the stūpa plays an important part.

Curvilinear Superstructure: Structure and Organization

Curvilinear superstructure is a perfectly coherent encasing for a corbelling shaft, of which the regular and slightly concave inner walls get progressively closer to join at the top. However, that conformity is not always as clear; for instance, in the temples where the inside of the curvilinear tower is filled up with masonry made up with rubble (Viennot 1976).

Analysis of Curvilinear Superstructures (Fig.28)

The analysis of a panel's arrangement is often complex, especially with regard to the recessed ones: generally they are narrow and more or less hidden by projecting panels when it is not by outwork structures. We have already mentioned that these recesses sometimes are hollowed once the stonework has been assembled and are not visible on unfinished temples. Another difficulty lies in the marked projection of the central panel which dwarfs the adjoining recesses.

The main feature of façade organisation in horizontal levels is the presence of vertical groups of projecting elements which on the corner panels are regularly separated by flat ribbed bulbs. The analysis is to begin with that of recessed intermediary panels; these last are the only visible parts of the façade of the tower main body; the projecting central panel corresponds to aedicules and/or foreparts leaning on the façade and the corner panels to square aedicules; the presence of these corner aedicules is very often emphasized by their ribbed bulb finial, the image of the one which tops most curvilinear superstructures

The layout of the central projecting panel is more complex, even if the piling up of elongated aedicules of progressively decreasing size is visible. The importance given to the central false dormer window is striking; such an element is of a big size and made more conspicuous by the two half-gables which surround it below, the whole taking the form of an entrance forepart set on the long side of an oblong edifice.

A curvilinear superstructure normally is built above a ground floor provided with a centred plan (square or stellate). The few examples of an oblong plan are to our knowledge found only in Orissa and are combined with a wagon-roof: all of them seem to correspond to Goddess' temples for which we have seen that an oblong width-wise plan may be deemed as canonical (Vaithal Deul, etc., see Donaldson 1985). The presence of a roof is in itself noteworthy as a curvilinear superstructure normally corresponds only with an enlarged finial.

Fig. 28. Superstructure of Śiva Jambuliṅga Temple at Pattadakal (Michell 1975).

Regarding the arrangement of curvilinear superstructure façades, the main point is that it comprises elongated vertical panels of which the number is variable but in any case uneven; these are alternatively projecting and recessing and are symmetrically organized in relation to the central one which normally is the most important. A simple composition quite commonly found, especially in Karnataka (see for instance Fig.28), comprises five panels bordered by curved lines; the central panel projects more than the others and its top is pointed; the corner panels are also projecting and their width is roughly the same from bottom to top; in between, the intermediary panels are recessing and slightly narrower.

The marked projection of the central panel is emphasized by its central part being made up of jutting elements piled one upon the other and corresponding to similar variations of the ground floor layout. Thus, the central panel appears to comprise several sub-panels and its emphasis results in decreasing the importance of the corner panels and dwarfing of the intermediary recessed ones.

Without going into details [see insert], let us say the three projecting panels just mentioned are simplified representations of vertical rows of aedicules quite similar to those seen on the façades of false-storey superstructures. Thus, on the central panel are seen elongated aedicules with a prominent median gable; corner panels bear square corner aedicules with ribbed bulb finials (as is the superstructure itself) while the recessed intermediary panels clearly correspond to miniature galleries. Even when the work is far more sophisticated – see for instance the Liṅgarāja Temple at Bhubaneshwar – it is undoubted that such a superstructure with strong vertical lines retains obvious tokens of its relationship with the two other types, a relationship based on the piling up of horizontal levels typical of a corbelling assembly.

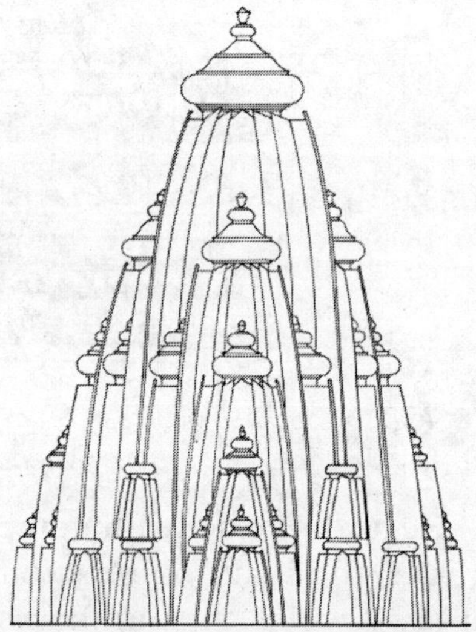

Fig. 29. Superstructure of Kaṇḍarīya Mahādeva Temple at Khajuraho (Dumarçay 1983).

This phenomenon is also obvious in the Kaṇḍarīya Mahādeva Temple at Khajuraho in spite of several secondary superstructures which, engaged in the main tower, suggest through a play of massive architectural structures the prominent position of the lord of the temple in the midst of his Attendants and gives its full meaning to the frequent comparison between temple and body of the god; each of the engaged superstructures suggest the presence of a non-existing chapel, of which the non-existing sanctum gives shelter to an attendant deity. Such a layout is seen elsewhere – see the Lakṣmaṇa Temple at Khajuraho and, to a lesser extent, in Orissa with Brahmeśvara (Fig.25) and Rājaraṇi Temples at Bhubaneshwar – but the Kaṇḍarīya Mahādeva Temple composition is obviously the most perfect example (see below p.72$).

Iconographic designs of temples with curvilinear superstructure are limited, as those of temples with a stepped superstructure and for the same reasons. However, the narrowness of the recessed parts allows saving some space on the quasi-vertical façades for images which would complete those placed in the false-dormer windows and similar elements. It happens also that the ground floor façades are covered with images as if to compensate for the iconographic void of the upper parts of the edifice.

Superstructures: Façades and Technique

Temples provided with any of the three types of superstructure can be interpreted as multi-storied edifices of which the stories would be false and more or less simplified. Simultaneously, all such temples are characterized by the thought of roofing the sanctum with vertical prolongations of its walls, each type of superstructure featuring a specific approach to the problem. Thus, properly speaking, false-storeys suggest successive corbelling levels separated by truly vertical parts, while a stepped composition seems to correspond to a continuous and gentle corbelling slope and a curvilinear one to the regular encasing of a corbelling shaft with quasi-vertical and straight inner walls.

However, things can be less clear in practice: a false-storey composition sometimes corresponds to a corbelling shaft with a continuous and regular slope, while curvilinear towers can comprise inner storeys which break their inner profile.[2] As a matter of fact, the use of a unique and same façade option in various construction contexts has led to the creation of three differentiated types; however, once defined and theorized in a norm, each of these three options has been used not only to cover the specific volume for which it had been created but also the two others.

An unsolved problem is of why the temple has been seen as a storeyed edifice (with true or false-storeys) and which has been so restrictive that there is always a more or less obvious mark of the storeys and whichever is the roofing option. Stella Kramrisch has proposed a solution which turns the storey composition into an exaltation of the temple in the guise of the "higher temple" located at the top; however, that is conceivable only when the top of the edifice is made up with an attic-roof-finial composition, that is to say, an image of the temple. It cannot be applied when the attic and roof are omitted, which is often the case.

From a Simple Building to a Complex One

A pavilion attached to the front of the entrance is a normal addition to the building housing the sanctum. This pavilion can be attached straight to that main body or to its porch-like forepart or both can be linked by a covered corridor (*antarāla*) which may comprise side latticed windows or even side entrances

2. It is difficult to have a look to the inside of a superstructure, unless it is ruined or dismantled for restoration. As regards Indian monuments, the cross section drawings as found in books are most often conventional and approximate. Thus, the very same ross section of the Kaṇḍarīya Mahādeva Temple at Khajuraho is found in several works and shows numerous horizontal divisions which are as incomprehensible as they are incredible.

(see for instance at Thanjavur, Gangaikondacholapuram, Darasuram, etc.). Such compositions are very common in India as well as South-East Asia. In India a second pavilion is frequently added in front of this composition and on the same line.

Pavilions

'Pavilions' (Skt. *maṇḍapa*) are described in technical literature as hypostyle edifices. More often they do not comprise upper-storey(s). They are either bordered by a portico and thus open outward or are closed by surrounding walls. They are defined as being provided with a three level elevation (basis, level of pillars and entablature [combined with a flat roof]). In practice, a flat roof is the most common type of roofing but false or real roofs with two or four slopes as well as lowered stepped superstructures are also found. The hypostyle structure makes easy the building of very big pavilions just by multiplying the rows of pillars. In South India, main shrines often boast a "thousand pillars pavilion" which often has been built during or after the Vijayanagar period.

Pavilions are typical all-purpose buildings and they can shelter a wide range of activities.[3] As soon as a temple is of some importance, several of them are found in its enclosure. Numerous ceremonies are performed in temporary pavilions which are of simplified types (they are often designated as *prapā* that is to say "light building"). Their pillars (mostly bamboo

---

3. *Mayamata* devotes a full chapter to pavilions and gives there in a list of their uses which does not claim to be exhaustive (see *Mayamata* 25.3-5): "pavilion as habitation, sacrificial pavilion, pavilion for consecrations and ceremonies of that sort, wedding pavilion, pavilion for alliances (*maitra[-maṇḍapa]*), pavilion for *upanayana* ceremony, audience pavilion [for the god at the time of festival or for the king], pavilion for military reviews, pavilion for negotiations, pavilion for hair-cutting, pavilion for meals and entertainment".

ones) rest upon the bare ground without a base and their flat-roof is made of straw or palms; they may be of 12 or 16 pillar compositions (such as those often used for oblations) or far bigger, where are drawn large diagrams and where numerous vases are placed, used for performing "great baths" (up to a thousand vases and even more). Similar huge temporary pavilions are built to protect from the sun the crowd of devotees which assemble at the time of temple festivals.

A Complement to the Sanctum

The permanent pavilion which is built in front of the sanctum door (*mukhamaṇḍapa*: lit. "pavilion built in front (of sanctum/of the god?)" has a wider inside room than the sanctum itself (Fig.30). It has several purposes. As regards liturgy it is the

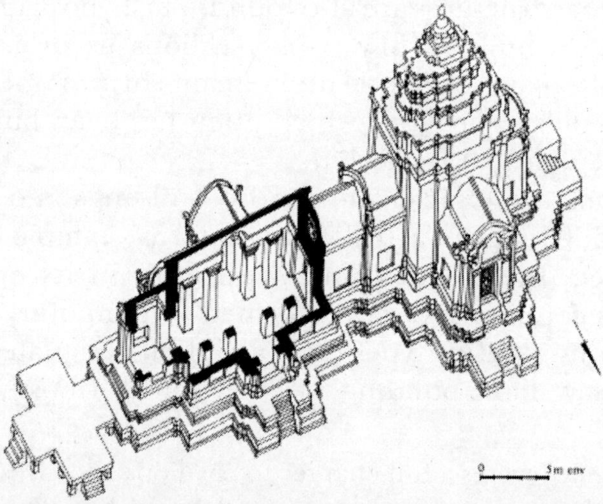

Fig.30. Axonometric view of the temple with pavilion at Nang Sida (Laos, 12th c.) (Dumarçay 1998). Built on the axis of the sanctum, the pavilion is linked to it by a corridor. As often in the Khmer area, it comprises a central bay provided with a corbelled vault and separated by two rows of pillars from the side-aisles which are roofed by half-vaults. There is a porch in front of the three outward doors of the pavilion as well as on the sides and the back of the sanctum.

place where are performed rites or episodes of daily cult which cannot be done in the sanctum itself: thus, the fire ritual which needs one or several fire-pits (*kuṇḍa*) in which the fire is lit and oblations received; another example is the "dance" to be performed in front of the god; in the same way it is in this pavilion that are ritually prepared and then arranged on a diagram the vases to be used for performing the daily "baths" offered to the god in the sanctum.

Lastly, that pavilion built just by the sanctum and provided with a door which can be closed and which makes it a "safe" building, is generally the place where are kept worship instruments and often, even god's ornaments (when they are not kept in a specific "treasury room") and portable images for processions. On the other side, opposite the sanctum, this pavilion is open to lay devotees (or at least to some of them). It is the best place to *see* the god through the sanctum door and to receive from the priest the "prasadam", i.e., a small part of an offering which has been in contact with the god and allows devotees to participate in his divine character.

Forms and Variations

The pavilion attached to the main body of the temple generally follows the same decorative option and its three elevation levels are equal in height to the corresponding ones of the temple itself. This may result in articulated façades provided with niches for images, etc. However, and unlike the sanctum, this pavilion is very often decorated inside, especially on its ceiling and its pillars which can have a very rich iconography. Lastly, it may comprise an only entrance (on the axis of that of the sanctum) or be provided with side doors (and porches) (Fig.30).

When there are two pavilions in a row in front of the sanctum entrance, it often happens that the first one is closed by walls while the second is a fully open hypostyle structure. This case is common but multiplies in the Vijayanagar period.

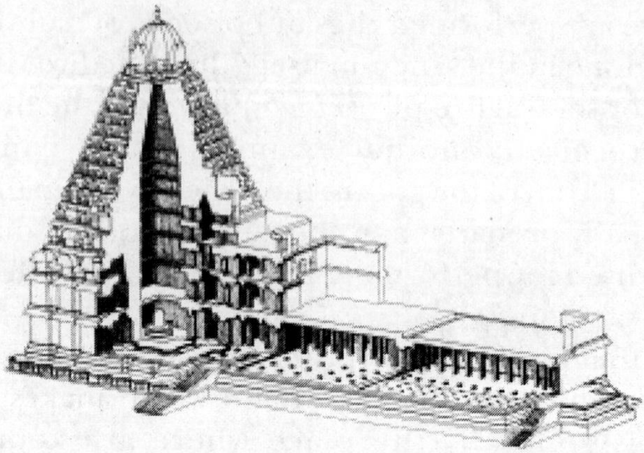

Fig.31. Axonometric view of Śiva Rājarājeśvara Temple at Thanjavur (state temple, beg. 11th c.) (PICHARD 1995). The twin pavilions are separated from the sanctum by a large vestibule; at the start they were planned with several storeys but have been modified, probably around the 17th-18th centuries.

In the 12th century several twin pavilion temples were built in Tamil Nadu, where the second pavilion is fully hypostyle and shaped like a chariot. The study of the well-preserved one at Darasuram (Fig.32) has allowed Françoise L'Hernault (1987) to show that it was to be seen as the chariot of Śiva and Gert Mevissen to specify that it was Śiva Tripurāntaka who was thus going to fight. This chariot-pavilion is closed by a wall to the north and open to the east and south; the chariot is going south as is shown by the position of the wheels and horses as well as that of Brahmā who is the chariot driver (at least at Darasuram). This composition results in creating a north-south axis at a right angle to the main west-east axis of the sanctum, temple and sanctuary: the new axis' importance is emphasized by the southern position of the stairways leading to the chariot pavilion and from it to the closed pavilion and then to the sanctum. Thus, the open eastern façade of the chariot pavilion allows the eyes of the god and his power to extend from the sanctum to all over the world. What is interesting is that at Darasuram the whole temple composition – the main body encasing the sanctum as well as the closed pavilion and chariot pavilion – is obviously the result of one single project and that the double-axis arrangement was thus arranged from the beginning. It is probably the same for the other contemporaneous Śiva temples following the same option in Tamil Nadu. The case is thus totally different from that of temples where a second axis was created as the result of a change of persuasion.

In a sense, this Tripurāntaka chariot is similar to the well known one of the Sun god at Konarak (Dagens 2009c). However, it is different from the "chariots" which are found later in the enclosure of some temples, mainly Vaishnavite ones: these last are stone copies of the huge wooden chariots used to take the god in procession at the time of temple festivals. There, the copy is sometimes very realistic: wheels turn freely round axles, a feature well in the spirit of the amazing feats often carried out by sculptors in the Vijayanagar period when these chariots were probably built. One such Vaishnavite chariot may be seen at Vijayanagar itself in the Vitthala Temple enclosure; another one,

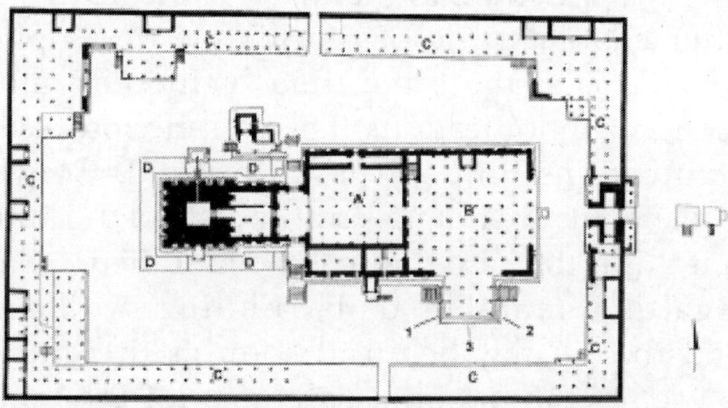

*Fig. 32. Darasuram: First enclosure of Śiva Airāvateśvara Temple (Dumarçay 2001). **A**: closed first pavilion; **B**: chariot-pavilion; **C**: cloister-like gallery (see p.59$); **D**: reflection basin (p. 100-101$). The chariot pavilion is open to the east and south but the position of horses and wheels (**1** and **2**) as well as that of Brahmā, the chariot driver (**3**), shows that the chariot is supposed to go to the south. The access to pavilions is gained by the southern stairway of the chariot pavilion or from the side-stairways at the junction of the sanctum and the closed first pavilion.*

found in the Kṛṣṇa Temple at Guruvayur (Kerala), is probably a little later. However, there the option is different: these stone Vaishnavite chariots join in the "petrifaction of the festival" as does, most probably, the "chariot-porch" of the Skanda chapel at Thanjavur (see below Fig.56, p.106$).

Conclusion

The creation around the sanctum of a more or less complex edifice marks the transition first from the temple *programme* to an *architectural project* true to the environment (in every sense of the word) and then to the *material rendering* of that project. The composition developed around the sanctum is concentric of course but it is also strongly orientated: that results in a lengthwise extension of the temple along its main axis, that of the sanctum and of the god. The temple is thus inscribed in an oblong plan where a wide covered area, that of the pavilion(s), lies in front of the sanctum and of the god. Generally, this oblong arrangement is passed on to the whole sanctuary.

Another characteristic of the temple development is its ambiguity as it is at the same time "achieved" and open to enlargements or modifications. The central body itself ignores such modifications unless it is unfinished. Conversely, its secondary elements are not necessarily parts of the initial project and even if this is the case they can be modified, enlarged, etc.

As regards a temple's daily running, we have already mentioned that it may begin as soon as the god has been installed, even if the opening ceremony of the temple as an edifice normally has to await the completion of its main body and the establishment of its finial. More than that, its "official" opening ceremony is sometimes delayed due to various reasons which can be astrological – the choice of an auspicious date – or economic: the temple authorities, patrons and others may choose to wait for enough means to organize an opening ceremony in accordance with their ambition and the glory of the god.

Chapter IV

Sanctuary and Temple Precincts

As told before, the "sanctuary" is primarily a cadastral entity, as it corresponds to the bounded estate attributed to the god and on which the temple is built. It pertains to the third category of already defined developments and its extent of the inside arrangement may change once the temple has been established. Being god's estate, it is part of a far wider but at the same time a slightly fuzzy notion, that of the "space of the temple" of which it is simultaneously the central part and the only one which is clearly delimited and definable.[1] As a matter of fact, the presence of the god and that of his temple are felt outside the limits of the sanctuary. Sometimes it can be just an expansion beyond the walls which is required for performing some ceremonies – especially the important festivals – and which occasionally corresponds to a socially delimited area such as a city or a village. But more generally, the main principle ruling the potential extent of the space of the temple is the 'radiance' of the divine power. More or less quantifiable and more or less marked, that radiance can combine with that of the very human power which has patronized the temple construction and/or which patronizes its running. Keeping for the second part of the book the question of interpretation and "staging" of these various forms of space,

1. Regarding the various aspects of the "space of the temple", see the papers edited and collected under the title "Espace du temple" by Jean-Claude Galey (2 vols., 1985-1986).

we shall now try to define them using the data of theoretical treatises and then to give two concrete examples, one derived from South India and the other from Cambodia, both marked by a strong historical element, but in different ways.

Definitions

A Sacred and Delimited Space

We can define a sanctuary as being a "sacred" area of which the temple is the centre in one way or another. Better than "sacred", the word to be used would usually be "consecrated", as that would clearly underline the necessary ritual preparation of the site. Thus, all the presentations regarding the choice of a site to build a temple insist upon the quest of an already sanctified ground. This divine space contrasts with the one which surrounds it and which is by essence "outside". Outside the divine, and thus human or mundane, perhaps even diabolical, it is also as we shall see later outside the world of which the sanctuary is an image. The limit between these two spaces is normally marked by a wall supplemented by a moat in Cambodia.

- Variations of Enclosure

The definition just given calls for several comments, the first of which relates to that which we may call "variable geometry" of a sanctuary. To start with, the central position of the temple is often very precise, but this is not a necessity and various reasons can lead to displace that "centre". Thus, history can modify its identification amongst the various elements making the sanctuary and thereby its precise position in the compound. A religious ensemble may be different from what was planned when it was founded: a deity who was at the start a secondary one may become the main god of the place without its original off-centre position being modified, a fine example of this being found in sanctuaries dedicated to Śiva at the start and where Skanda, his son, later supplanted him (p.27$).

In the same way, the sanctuary's borderline is not necessarily fixed and unchanging. Historical events regarding the status of the temple in the religious scenario as well as its political role are liable to vary its extent: the effect of this is the building of a new surrounding enclosure wall. In most of the cases it results in an enlargement of the sanctuary due to the 'success" of the temple and to the growth of its fame; that is very common in South India. On the contrary, the sanctuary of the Bayon Temple at Angkor has been reduced by the building of new surrounding wall very close to the temple – only a few meters from its base frontage – and which even cuts across the Eastern access terrace, this having been done most probably less than a century after the death of its founder.

Lastly, it is to be noticed that temples without enclosure walls do exist, especially in Nepal, in respect of most of the temples built in the cities of the Kathmandu Valley and of which the few existing walls are more or less reduced to nothing (Juramie 2001). Two explanations have been proposed – the enclosure wall of the temple being either the same as for the city or made up by the edifices built around the temple yard: these are possible but, as has been noted by Anne-Claire Juramie, there does not seem to be any general principle in this matter. We may conclude that, as regards Nepal, the enclosure wall is not an important feature of the temple lay-out.

Elsewhere, the situation is not always clear. In several places are seen wide compounds where, in a unique enclosure more or less obvious and apparently in no particular order are found several temples without being clear as to which is the main one. This phenomenon is clearly visible at the Papanasanam sanctuary not far from Alampur in Andhra Pradesh: here it results from the fact that Papanasanam was in the past (9th-10th c.) a very popular holy place (*tīrtha*) (Dagens 1984a Vol. II, pl.XI). Later, we will deal in detail with a different case, that of Tiruvannamalai, where the several "temples" surrounding a sacred mountain are to be considered simply as chapels, being annexes of that mountain itself (below, p.63$).

- *"Density" of the Sacred*

Apart from the 'abnormal' cases just mentioned, the sacred and delimited space which is the sanctuary is structured, arranged and organized into a hierarchy in a concentric and orientated manner which often results, we have seen, in a lengthening of the whole composition on its main axis and in a backward pushing of the temple on this axis. One of the elements of that arrangement is what may be called the "density" of the sacred which varies from one place to another. Quite naturally, it is higher as we get nearer the centre, that is to say the temple, the god, and the main axis which is the one with the god's eyes. We shall deal in our second part with the social importance of this phenomenon, related to the fact that in the Indian world the approach of the sacred is inseparable from the social rank of those who can participate in it or want to do so (chapter VI). We shall see also – in another connection – that the earliest manifestations of the phenomenon in the arrangement of a religious area probably occurred in a Buddhist context (see p.110-111$). For now, it can be noticed that there is most probably some connection with the "five circles worship' (*pañcāvaraṇapūjā,* see above on the subject of aedicules) which is characterized by the concentric and hierarchic organization of the pantheon around the main god. Here it is already perceptible in the distribution of a multiple and varied divine society around the main god according to different criteria, the hierarchy combining with other elements such as the orientation, which follows particular rules for each member of the pantheon. More than that, each of the attendant deities of the main god is himself the head of a hierarchy: the materialization of his attendants can lead to the creation of a secondary sanctuary delimited by its own enclosure wall inside the sanctuary of the main god (see above à propos the Goddess). Thus, according to a process similar to what may be seen at Papanasanam (see above) the well structured organization of some big sanctuaries is hidden by the numerous secondary foundations attracted by the fame of the main temple (see for instance the numerous secondary shrines in the Liṅgarāja compound at Bhubaneswhar or in the Jagannātha at Puri), or by the great number of service buildings needed for the large crowds gathered in a holy place (see for instance Viṣṇu Veṅkateśvara sanctuary at Tirupati in Andhra Pradesh).

A Beyond-the-Walls Space which is a "Necessary" One

Some ceremonies, most of which are related with festivals, require that the god goes out of his estate, i.e. out of the sanctuary. This may be, for instance, for reaching a place which, provided with precise characteristics, cannot be found inside the sacred and delimited space of the sanctuary. It is often the case with the water place (*tīrtha*) where the god is taken in procession for the performance of a bath, which marks the apex of Śiva's grand festival. The same may be said about the wild place where is to be performed the "hunt", another important ceremony of the grand festival (Barazer-Billoret 1999, p.156). In both these cases the place and the way to reach it are extensions of the sanctuary: they have no material limits and most often are temporary, as their "sacred" nature is linked to the ceremony organised there.

Festive promenades of the god out of his temple may go through the social space as when the god is taken in procession – often on a chariot – through the city or around it, along the "chariot road" surrounding the sanctuary. On this occasion the god is presenting himself to his faithful and at the same time takes possession of the social space and thus of the universe, or more exactly, this solemn festival allows the renewal of the taking of possession which goes back to the installation ceremony of the temple. Things are sometimes complex: at Varanasi for instance a "five leagues" roundabout (hence its name "*pañcakrośa*") places Śiva's mythology in the space that corresponds to the tour made around the holy city by Śiva at the end of the wandering he had been condemned to in order to atone for the murder of Brahmā, his father. In Panauti (Nepal) the meeting of processions coming from the two temples of a god and his spouse respectively renders the reiteration of their union (Barré *et al.* 1981). When dealing later on with Tiruvannamalai Śiva temple, we will see that its grand festival goes out from the social space to go around the mount at the top of which has been lit the Fire Liṅga and which has thus became a part of the immediate surroundings of the temple of which it is one of its founding elements.

Lastly, there is an interesting variation based upon a centripetal idea of the temple space (see also below p.94$). It concerns Śriśailam temple located in Andhra Pradesh in a forested and mountainous massif overlooking the south bank of the Krishnā River. This temple gets an enclosure wall ornamented with narrative reliefs, but according to tradition it possesses four faraway "doors" which are placed in the main directions at quite a distance from Śriśailam. They correspond to four small cities and each of them includes a holy place which may be considered as a starting point for a pilgrimage to Śriśailam. Thus, these four "doors" mark a sort of virtual expansion of the god's estate, in brief of his sanctuary, of which they would be the entrance pavilions of its outermost enclosure (see also [insert] p.102-103$).

A Wide Space Theoretically Unlimited

Beyond the "necessary space" we have just dealt with, the space of the temple can extend faraway but in a far less perceptible manner. We are dealing now with the area where the god is able to make his authority, his influence and his power felt; that area exceeds the more or less ritualistic limits we have just stated and one may say that it starts just beyond these limits. The community which refers to a god is often discontinuous and the numerous faithful living faraway are susceptible to become "pilgrims from abroad".

This wide space is not precisely delimited and in order to define it and to try to determine its approximate extent, one has to combine and/or to add one to the other the data provided by different kinds of markers. Amongst these are data which are very practical, even statistical, as for instance the geographical distribution of charitable institutions (pilgrims lodges, hospitals, etc.) which are managed by the temple authorities (Dagens 2003, about ancient Cambodia) or of the lands which have been offered to the temple or of the places from where come the pilgrims at the time of the temple grand festival (Guilmoto *et al.*, about Tiruvannamalai). Other elements are not quantifiable, such as the personal devotion of a sovereign, of a mighty landlord, or of a community, which commences from a long forgotten event. In this field most clear cases are those of state temples with which we will deal later (see p.88ff.$). Presently, let us only say that their space is more or less the one of the kingdom. However, the political basis of such temples often limits their functional longevity, and incidentally of the space they can generate. There are several scenarios, amongst the most interesting of which are those of the Jagannātha temple at Puri or of Angkor Wat in Cambodia: in both cases they have remained alive up to now in spite of a disruption of the initial political context and even – in the second case – of religious persuasion. It also may happen that the precise origin of the influence is changed: it now emanates less from the god – even if he is still worshipped – than from the temple itself, which has become a source of pride more than of devotion (see for instance Thanjavur or Khajuraho temples).

Theoretical Data and Practical Realities

Regarding what we call "sanctuary", it is sometimes described in technical treatises by the Sanskrit word (*bhavana*), which the same works apply very often to the 'palace', that is to say the building complex in the compound containing the king's living quarters, which underlines the parallel often drawn between god and king. However, what is apparently not found in these treatises is a word that is able to render the multiplicity of notions that we have seen, which are included in the expression 'temple space'. In spite of this deficiency, treatises take care of these topics in different occasions and contexts. Regarding temple construction, they deal with the space where the temple-to-be will be built and in the narrow and limited area which that temple is to generate once built, and which corresponds to the sanctuary. When the treatises deal with rites and ceremonies which are not confined to the sanctum and its direct annexes, they allude to the space where these are performed and which may be either the "necessary space" already mentioned or the limited space of the sanctuary: as a matter of fact it is in the latter that most rites are performed, while its sacred character may lead to restricting its access, which is not necessarily by right for everybody.

The Space where a Temple-to-be will be Built

The data dealing with the space where the planned temple is to be built are mainly found in the chapters dealing with the site choice and urbanism (Dagens 2009).

- Factors to be taken into account for choosing a site

The main factors taken into account when choosing a site to build a temple comprise its "holiness", its "purity" and – in a more general way – its "normality". At the beginning of their theoretical presentations, treatises often give a sort of religious geography of India in the guise of a list of holy places, some being specific to the period to which the treatise pertains, while others are more universal such as Kurukṣetra where was fought the big battle of *Mahābhārata* and which the first verse of the *Bhagavad-Gītā* deems as being the "Field of the norm" (*dharmakṣetra*). Whichever the case, the main idea is to "propose" sites of which the acknowledged holiness makes a temple installation very fruitful. On the whole, the lists are pan-Indian, even if some holy places listed there are mostly of regional importance. They are supplemented by enumerations of places deemed as very appropriate *per se,* such as forests, confluences, etc., which are certainly more immediately useful than that of well known but generally faraway holy places.

Purity and normality are often dealt with simultaneously, for both imply careful tests of the proposed site: some of these examinations may be considered as providing technical data about the permeable or impermeable nature of the ground or about it being compact or expansive : a purely visual examination concerns the look of the site (orientation of its slope, presence of some kinds of trees, shape, etc.) but to study the inner nature of the ground a pit would have to be dug (in the centre of the site, if possible). The examination also concerns the living beings which frequent the site and, in a more general way, that which we may call its "neighbourhood": thus, one must ascertain that it is not touched upon by the shadow of a socially impure building (abode of an outcast, of a procurer, etc.). However, it is noticeable that such rules vary widely from one text to the other in spite of some permanent features.

- *Inside or Outside the City*

The location of temples in a city is ruled by some precise principles. However, as far as we know, it is never stated that a temple is to be the central point around which a town is to be arranged, contrary to the royal palace which is given such a role in presentations regarding a capital city. It is interesting, and even surprising, that temple-cities which exist in South India – for instance Madurai, Srirangam, Tiruvannamalai – do not seem to have given rise to theorising texts. As a matter of fact, while treatises deal with temples provided with several concentric enclosures (see below), they do not suggest that there may be a shift from such a sanctuary arrangement to a city, as is very perceptible in the cases we have just mentioned above. An explanation could be found in the fact that most probably this kind of city is no more than an incidental outgrowth of the temple which it surrounds, an outgrowth resulting from the 'success' of that temple. However, this is a mere hypothesis which is difficult to apply for South-East Asia where very good examples are found wherein the city, and the temple which marks its geometrical centre, are both parts from one and the same project and are thus perfectly complementary; for instance Angkor Thom city around Bayon state temple or P'imai city around Vimāya Buddha Temple, or else the large composition of Prah Khan of Kompong Svay.

To come back to the insertion of temples in the urban fabric as presented in Indian treatises, these works broach it most often when dealing with orientation and with the allotment of a particular part of the city to a particular deity. To that, we may add that the relatively central position of temples has been used in sectarian quarrels but nothing indicates that the *de facto* hierarchy between the temples deduced by protagonists is more than just an *a posteriori* speculation based upon an already existing situation. Ram Raz, one of the first scholars to have studied technical treatises dealing with temples (see below p. 119ff.$) makes mention in his work published in 1834 of a sectarian book according which the superiority of Vaishnavism over Śaivism was clearly justified by the fact that some architectural treatises located the Viṣṇu temple near the centre of the city and that of Śiva on its periphery. Nevertheless, it is obvious that such a repartition is more linked with the nature of these gods than with the superiority of one over the other: Viṣṇu is a deity far more "urban" than Śiva, whom mythology often associates with wanderings in a wild environment.

Lastly, it is told about some violent deities that their temples have to be outside human settlements and even far away from them. This is the case for Viṣṇu Narasiṃha "Man-lion", Mātṛkās (the "Mothers" who are also deemed as child-eaters) or Śiva Bhairava Kṣetrapāla (a terrible and murderous form appropriately designated as 'guard of the field"). There is probably a double reason for their isolated location: first, a wish to place them in the position of guardians 'dominating' the whole territory they have to protect (for instance at Tiruvannamalai one of the goddess temples located to the north of the city) and also to place separately those characters dangerous even for their devotees.

- Definition and Delimitation

The place where the temple is to be built has to be prepared by ritual and technical operations, often carried on together with those regarding examination of the site and dealt with above. One of the first of these is ploughing, which together with the sowing following it enables testing the 'fertility' of the site, thus foretelling the fertility of the temple to-be. Moreover this operation is reiterated in a symbolic way at the start of any important ceremony through a rite during which seeds sowed in specific vessels are to sprout in a very short time (generally one day only) in order that the ceremony is fruitful.

The site orientation is more technical even as it serves many purposes. Performed with a gnomon it results in a full transformation of the selected ground which is made into an orientated space extensible to the Universe; as a matter of fact what is prepared is the installation in this space of a Lord (*īśvara*) often deemed as the Lord of the Universe (*lokeśvara*). That orientation is normally carried out at the centre of the temple to-be (that is to say at the geometrical centre of its sanctum where the god will be). That can possibly raise technical problems during construction works, for the position of that centre will have to be recorded as the building rises and the orientation elements will have to be transferred from the centre to the periphery. The important point is that this centre also has to be the centre (even if not necessarily 'geometrical', strictly speaking) of the whole compound which, whether simple or complex, will develop around the temple. Thus, there is a shift from the very common idea of a "building site" to that of a reduction of the Universe, which reduction is defined by its orientation and by its centre which will seat the god.

At this stage, the notions of limit and periphery remain a little vague but they are introduced through a diagram (*maṇḍala*). This last is established on the already orientated site which, theoretically, it covers fully (Fig.33). Its immediate role is to make easy the fixing on the ground of a chthonian and a dangerous character who is not precisely defined and which is named "Spirit of the site" (*vāstupuruṣa*): he lives in the ground of the site and his convulsive movements may endanger the buildings to-be. To avoid this evil, deities are summoned in order to keep him still and each of them is given a precise place on the diagram; outside the diagram, on its periphery, are installed eight terrible or harmful deities who have been just expelled from the site and who are in charge of its close protection.

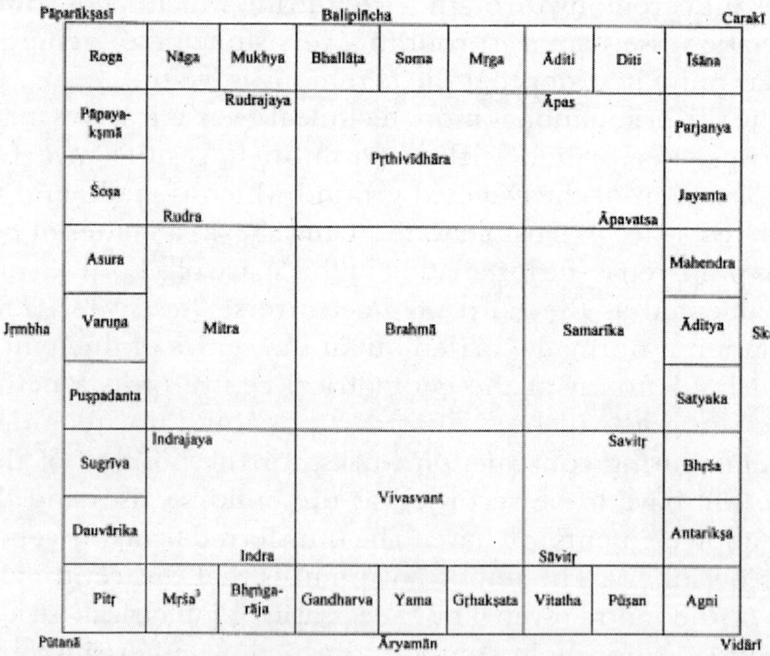

Fig.33. Diagram of the site (according to Dīptāgama*).*

From a very practical point of view this diagram is to be used as a reference grid for the material arrangement of the sanctuary and the precise locations of its various elements, the first of which being the temple itself; the position of these elements is marked by the name of the deity/deities ascribed to the corresponding square/squares of the diagram, without however having any connection other than an incidental one between that deity and the temple or the chapel installed on his square.

A similar diagram is to be drawn at the place of each of the elements of the site, temple and others: for each of them it will play the same role as before, namely, fixing the *vāstupuruṣa* of the precise place and locating various components.

The notion of 'limit' introduced through the diagram implies that of "measure" which is important for the root meaning "to measure" also means "to build" according to Indian tradition (Staal 1992). Thus, reaching the stage of "measuring" is to go from the choice of the site for a temple to the construction of that temple.

The Sanctuary, a Space Born from the Temple

- A Limited, Measurable, and Measured Space

The sanctuary ends with the outside face of its enclosure wall, in the event of this being its only enclosure, or the outermost one if there are several in a concentric arrangement. According to treatises, this limit is a wall, which is the normal way in India. However, in Angkorean Cambodia this wall is itself generally surrounded by a moat which replaces (or sometimes supplements) the reservoir, which in the Indian world usually provides the water supply for the temple as well as the neighbouring human settlement.

Temple Moat

The moat which surrounds most temples in Cambodia is a feature unheard of in Indian practice as well as in the architectural treatises dealing with temples (which, however, accept moats as an indispensable defensive element of forts). This Cambodian innovation results from the meeting of the regional tradition of "round cities" with an Indian ritual necessity – that of providing the temple with a permanent water-reserve and with an Indian cosmological conception – that of a concentric arrangement of the Universe with alternating mountain ranges and oceans.

"Round cities", well known in Mon region of present-day Thailand, actually comprise a large space occupied by villages and rice-fields; being more or less rounded (often elliptical) they are limited by a wide moat which may be a broken line of oblong reservoirs placed end to end (see for instance Dagens 2005 p.299). Such a moat has no defensive function and is just an arrangement for storing water to be supplied for village consumption as well rice-field irrigation (with such villages and rice-fields being inside and outside the "city").

The Khmers have borrowed from their Mon neighbours that very functional form but they have fitted it into their own tradition by giving an orthogonal and orientated plan to what was roughly ring shaped. While reinventing the water supply for use in Indian temples, they have given a material translation of the well known cosmological arrangement whereby Mount Meru is at the centre of the Universe with a central continent at its foot favoured by the gods - the Jambudvīpa (that is to say India) - which itself is surrounded by the Ocean. In Khmer composition, the Meru is the temple-tower or the full pyramidal ensemble of state temples, enclosures and annexes which surround it to make the Jambudvīpa, while all around the moat is the Ocean.

Further on, the Cambodians who mastered the art of piling up symbolic images have, as early as the 9th century A.D., bordered the causeways crossing the moats with railings in the form of mythical serpents. As has been shown in the past by Paul Mus in a magnificent paper, according to *Khmer* tradition serpents represent rainbows, rainbows which according to *Indian* tradition are bridges linking the land of mankind to the divine one.

Inside its enclosure, the sanctuary is theoretically arranged according to a complex interplay of measurable and measured relations whose starting point is always the "centre", i.e., the temple building itself which is the only essential part of the sanctuary. The dimensions of all other elements – annexes, open spaces, enclosure walls and entrance pavilions as well as images, offering altars, etc. – are governed by a one ratio-system of which the reference unit is taken from the main temple, with the temple itself being proportionate to the cult object installed in its sanctum.

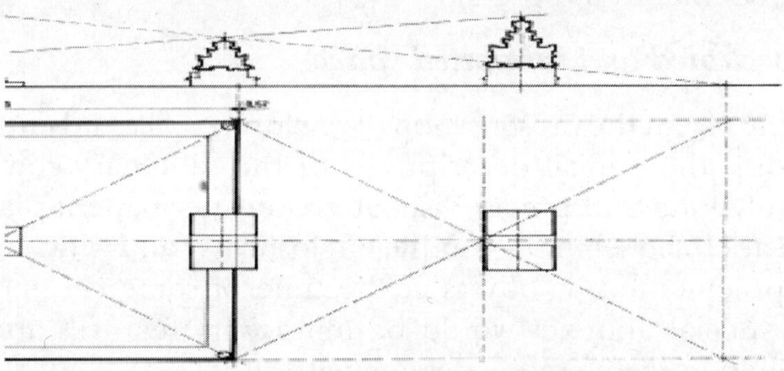

Fig.34. Proportional composition of Śiva Temple at Thanjavur (PICHARD 1995).

According to treatises the measurements of the one or several courtyards surrounding the temple are proportionate to the width of the main temple, which width is then designated as *daṇḍa*, a very appropriate Sanskrit word since it is used by the same treatises to designate a "module", another relative unit based on the width of pillars in India as it is in the West. Actually the ratios, when they can be verified, appear to be very complex and sometimes may link horizontal and vertical measurements. A fine example is found at Thanjavur as shown on Figure 24: the whole organisation of the sanctuary – size of enclosures, placing of the Bull and size of entrance pavilions – is integrated into a ratio system referring to the height of the temple (Pichard

1995). Twenty years later a similar arrangement was used for Gangaikondacolapuram temple (*ibidem*).

Information about measurements is given together with directions for their use. Such directions are at the same time both precise and open, which leaves a wide leeway for their use. Thus it is said that figures given for the length of an enclosure wall may be applied on its inner or outer face or else on its median axis; in the same way, all figures as provided may be slightly modified in order to comply with a complex set of calculations ending by a division, of which the remainder is to be a number deemed as auspicious for the success of the building work (Schildt, in the press).

- *An occupied and inhabited space*

Apart from the presentation of enclosure walls and entrance pavilions, theoretical descriptions of the sanctuary comprise relatively long and precise lists of various permanent features which are to be set in the temple enclosure(s) and which would be supplemented by others at the time of some ceremonies; these special annexes would be temporary features and are described in the chapters dealing with rites.

Permanent features are first attendant deities' chapels and service annexes: they may be separate buildings or parts of cloister like galleries built against the enclosure wall(s). It is regarding the chapels for Attendants that the information provided is most precise and also the most constant from one text to another, as well as that regarding position, orientation, type of building, etc.). Service annexes are mainly pavilions used for rites: the sacrificial pavilion (for fire ritual and oblations), dance pavilion, audience pavilion (where are kept mobile images used for processions), pavilion for the wedding of the god and goddess, etc. Besides, there is a treasury where are kept god's ornaments, sheds for ritual instruments, a granary, a kitchen for preparation of food offerings together with its storerooms, a hall for religious discourses, a school, etc. (Dagens 1984b §

5.9-10). The lists also comprise wells, reservoirs and the like, and possibly a stable for the temple elephant, gardens and orchards for providing flowers, fruits, coconuts, banana fruit and leaves, etc., for daily offerings to the god.

Beside the buildings and facilities, are some other quasi-indispensable features. These are the offering altars used every day (especially at the time of a procession deemed as "daily festival", *nityotsava*) and placed upon the main axis of the temple between the door of sanctum and the entrance-pavilion (and sometimes outside it). On the same axis is the flag-pole: it is very often dealt with in the treatises when they present the grand festival which begins and ends by the rising and lowering of the god's flag; generally the pole is said to be erected before the festival and sometimes we are told it is to be destroyed at the end of that same festival. Actually, it however appears that it is a permanent feature and more than that, a landmark of the sanctuary, especially as regards the social hierarchical organisation of the god's estate (below p.84$).

Setting in place of these features and buildings as well as their proportions and orientation (etc.), are precisely ruled (even if the rules may vary from one treatise to another). As already stated, their localisation is often given with reference to a diagram. Their dimensions are proportionate to those of the temple and their general arrangement follows concentric and orientated settings centred on that temple. Orientation is marked by allocation of precise directions to each of the attendants chapels (they normally face the temple, at least when they are just by it). Similar rules relate to some other annexes, like the well always located in the north-east quarter or the kitchen placed in the south-east one.

From Theology to Architecture through Concentric Setting of the Sanctuary

- *Archaeological Evidence*

The concentric arrangement which, implicitly at least, is the base of the setting of the sanctuary may be materialised by an architectural division of the space lying between the temple and its outermost enclosure wall. It can be simply the result of the arranging of concentric rows of similar chapels (see for instance in Indonesia at Candi Sewu where the chapels of the two first rows are facing outward and not towards the central temple). However, in South India and in Cambodia, the arrangement is far more articulated, even if it results in various forms and follows various modes. Thus, the division may be marked either by the setting of intermediary enclosures, or by the arrangement of a stepped pyramid topped by the temple itself, or else by combining both these options. Concentric enclosure walls and their respective entrance pavilions may either be of increasing size as one goes outward or are all of similar dimensions. Lastly,

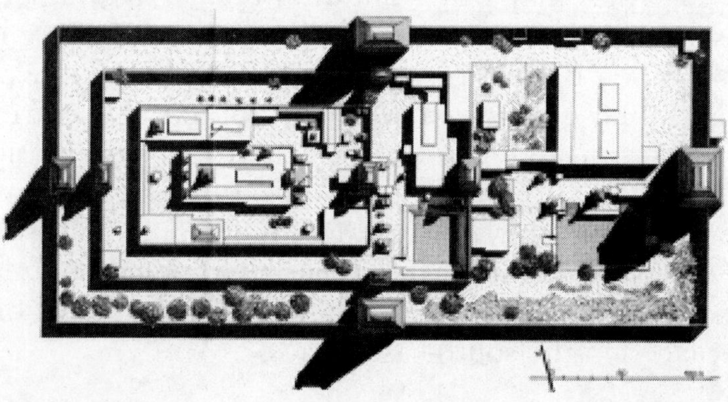

Fig.35. Tiruvannamalai: Śiva Aruṇācaleśvara Temple (roof plan according to Pierre P*ICHARD,* Tiruvannamalai *2). A: 1st and 2nd enclosures (they are nearly fully roofed); B, C and D: 3rd, 4th and 5th enclosures. The double central enclosure is provided with a single entrance pavilion (on the East) while all the others have four of them.*

such concentric arrangements often result from a dynamic process which may spread over several centuries.

South India ignores the pyramid arrangement and uses only the one where there are several enclosure walls and entrance pavilions with increasing sizes, as is theorized in the regional Sanskrit technical literature. This arrangement appears in the beginning of the 11th century at Thanjavur and soon becomes the rule for all temples as soon as they are of some size. Thus, it appears that it is mostly the fruit of the historically progressive enlargement of the sanctuary by the successive building of new walls, each surrounding the preceding one and each bigger in size and provided with bigger entrance pavilions. Such a dynamic phenomenon is never mentioned in theoretical presentations. It is however obvious, as seen at Tiruvannamalai. There the temple was surrounded at the start (beginning of the 11th c.) by a solitary enclosure and it is through successive stages in the 17th century that the present composition comprising five concentric enclosures was obtained (Fig.35 and below p.61ff.$). The same arrangement may also be seen at Srirangam, Madurai or Cidambaram, even if these monuments are less documented.

In Cambodia, two types of arrangements are used, the one with a stepped pyramid and another with enclosures which are concentric but provided with walls and entrance-pavilions, both of more or less identical size. Both seem to appear as early as the 9th century (perhaps a little earlier). The stepped pyramid option is a specific feature of the state temples (alias "mountain temples") and its most ancient perfect rendering is to be seen at Phnom Bakheng (end of 9th c.) (Fig.37, insert p.57$). Thereafter, the main stages are marked first by the Ta Kév temple (end of 10th c., with the first instance of a cloister-like gallery on the 2nd floor) (Fig.38) and by Angkor Wat (12th c., (Fig.46, 65$) where the type reaches its peak (for details see the insert).

The arrangement with several enclosures seems to appear in Cambodia with the Prah Ko temple (middle of 9th c.) where two concentric enclosures surround the six tower group, making the core of that monument dedicated to the ancestors of its founder. At the end of the 10th century, the composition where there are several enclosures with walls and entrance pavilions increasing in size when going outward, is seen at the Śiva Temple of Banteay Srei (inaugurated 967 AD). The phenomenon, short lived in Cambodia, however makes the Banteay Srei sanctuary the oldest known instance of such a composition in the whole Indian world, for it is around forty years older than the Thanjavur Temple (deemed as the first well established achievement of the type in India). As far as Cambodia is concerned, the arrangement with several concentric but similar enclosure walls is carried on till the big sanctuaries of the 12th-13th centuries (Beng Mealea, then Ta Prohm and other foundations of Jayavarman VI), which mark the end of great religious foundations in the Cambodian kingdom.

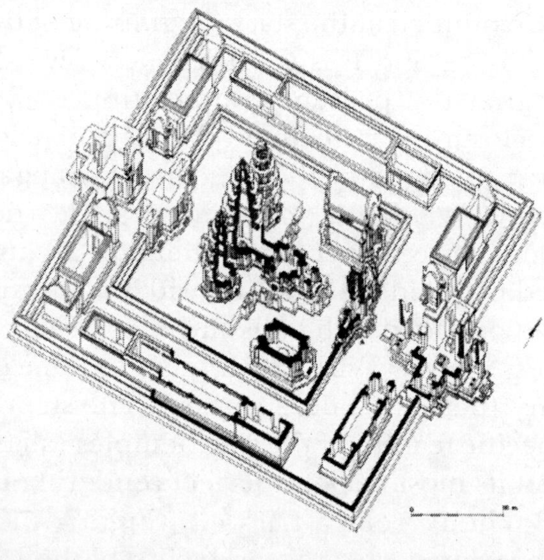

Fig.36. Śiva Temple at Banteay Srei (founded in 967): Enclosures I and II (DUMARÇAY 1988). In the 1st enclosure are found the main temple and its pavilion together with two secondary temples all rising on the same base; they are supplemented in front by two pseudo-libraries opening to the west. The 2nd enclosure contains long halls – most probably service buildings – and its entrance pavilions are far bigger than those of the first enclosure; its wall is bordered on the outside by a wide moat (not appearing in the drawing) which is itself bordered by the third enclosure wall.

As regards Banteay Srei, it is worth noting that it is also marked by an important renewal in the field of iconography where new images appear, of which the origin cannot be found elsewhere than in South India (*e.g.* image of Kāreikkālammeyār, a Tamil poetess who was a devotee of Śiva). We may assume that the idea of successive enclosures of increasing size was in the air at that time and that it was one of various new concepts which came to the knowledge of the founder of Banteay Srei Temple, a learned Brahmin, who then implemented them in his foundation.

Mountain-like Temples and Concentric Enclosures in Cambodia

After the Ak Yum temple and, better still, the Bakong temple which is the first well characterised "mountain temple", it is the state temple built at the end of the 9th c. at Angkor on Phnom Bakheng which marks a first stage in the evolution of the type with its stepped pyramid covered with many towers.

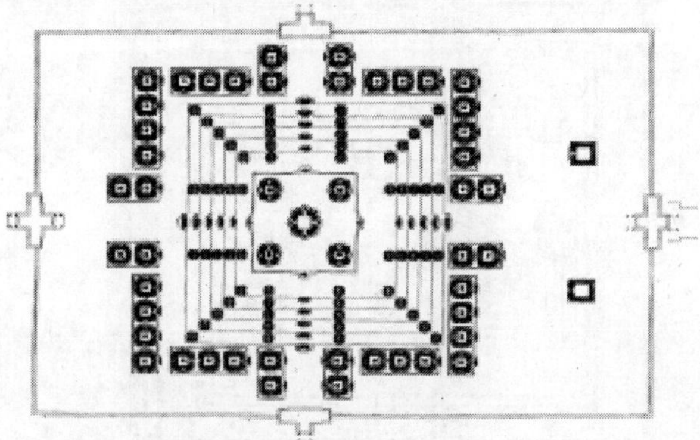

Fig.37. Śiva Temple, Phnom Bakheng (state temple, Angkor end of 9th c.) (DUMARÇAY 1972). The pyramid comprises fives steps on each of which are twelve towers, each containing a Liṅga.

Its central temple is surrounded by 108 chapels regularly arranged on the five steps and at the foot of the pyramid of which the height is increased through perspective effects. On the top level, the main temple and its four more important chapels are arranged in a quincunx. Later in the 10th century, will appear the combination of such a pyramid with several concentric enclosures (see Pre Rup temple, inaugurated in 961).

The next major stage concerns the construction of the mountain-temple of Ta Kèv (Fig. 38). Building work started around the time of the founding of Banteay Srei (that is to say around 967) and it lasted up to the beginning of the 11th century without ever reaching its end. The pyramid is a three stepped one, its first step being bordered by an enclosure wall. The great novelty of this monument (where perspective effects are very important) is that its second step is bordered by a cloister-like gallery surrounding a courtyard, in the centre of which rises the enormous three-level base of the third floor. On this is found again the quincunx towers seen at Phnom Bakheng and which has become a perfect rendering of the five-fold supreme form of Śiva. The gallery is a blind one on its outside face (where is seen a row of false-windows) and an open one with bar-windows on the yard: this suggests that it is isolating the yard it encloses. However the function of that gallery can be only symbolic or aesthetic, as there is no door to enter it.

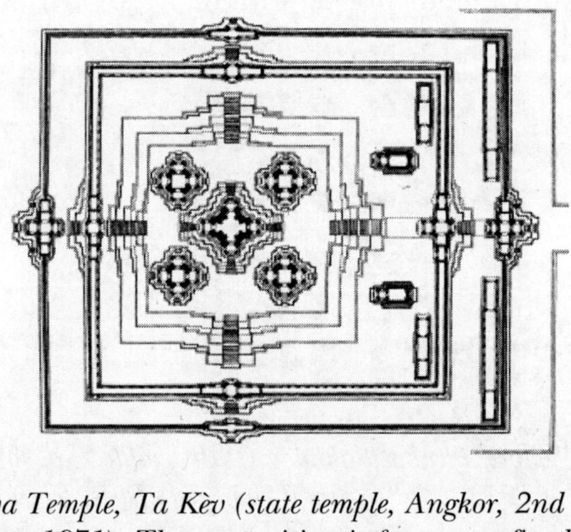

Fig.38. Śiva Temple, Ta Kèv (state temple, Angkor, 2nd half of 10th c.) (Dumarçay 1971). The composition is far more refined than that of Phnom Bakheng. An enormous three-level base replaces the three upper floors of the pyramid; the 1st floor is bordered by a wall and the 2nd one by a gallery which cannot be entered and which comprises open windows on its inner face and false-windows on its outer one.

> During the following centuries which are the last of the Angkorean period, the composition with a stepped galleried pyramid, first improved at the Baphuon, reaches its peak at Angkor Wat where the organisation of the central part in concentric zones which are by turns open and closed is very fine (see below p.65-66$); in the second floor there is a gallery similar to that of the 2nd floor of Ta Kèv but here it may be entered and thus allows access all around. As for the quincunx organisation of the 3rd floor, it has lost its theological meaning due to the now Vaishnavite context and it has been changed in that that the four secondary towers have become corner pavilions of a gallery going around the 3rd floor and open on its inner and outer faces. The last example of the type is Bayon state temple at Angkor which again takes some of the Angkor Wat novelties (see for instance the 2nd floor gallery) but in its own baroque way. Moreover, it omits the peripheral gallery of the 3rd floor where the quincunx pattern is replaced by a massive composition which is at the same time more complex and more unitary.

- Theorising the Concentric Pattern

As far as theoretical treatises are concerned, the setting with concentric enclosures of increasing heights is the only one that they consider. It is clearly the "normal" one: the best sanctuary is the one which gets the maximum number of concentric enclosures allowed by the concerned treatise. In that perspective, a temple provided with only one enclosure is to be seen as the lower term of a more or less continuous series which goes up to the best type. Confused instructions are given when dealing with temples which do not reach the highest number of enclosures and more especially those with one enclosure only. The general idea seems to be that the only enclosure is to be bigger than the innermost enclosure of a sanctuary which comprises several of them. Lastly, let us add that in most of these treatises, five is the highest possible number of enclosures. Some Vaishnavite texts reduce that number to three while others, more numerous but of the same persuasion, increase that number in order, most probably, to include in the norm Srirangam Temple: the largest and one of the most venerated temples dedicated to Viṣṇu, it comprises seven enclosures (or eight, according to the reckoning mode) (Rao 1967).

Thus, according to theoretical presentations, the concentric enclosures pattern is a coordinated project which is to be carried out at one time, whatever the planned number of the enclosures. The dynamic process of a long term progressive composition is never taken into account, even if it seems to be the rule in India, where the adding of one or several enclosures is done around an already existing ensemble and never, it seems, by insertion of an intermediary enclosure between two existing ones. The sole and very slight hint about such a dynamic process would be a very vague prescription often mentioned when dealing with renovation or repairs, according to which the result of such work is to be a temple identical to the original one, or bigger than it.

Things are different in Cambodia where Angkor Wat is a fine example of a four enclosure composition – three on the stepped pyramid and the fourth one twinned with a moat to make the border of the sanctuary – projected at the start and built at one time. The Bayon was first following the same pattern, the so-called Angkor Thom wall and moat enclosure marking them as its border; however, later its central pyramid was surrounded by an intermediary enclosure wall making a new border smaller than the initial one. Elsewhere various options have been followed. Thus, some temples without stepped pyramids (see for instance Ta Prohm or Ta Som at Angkor) have been provided with a large new outermost enclosure which widely enlarged the original sanctuary, itself surrounded by a wall-moat binomial. It happens also in some cases that an intermediary enclosure wall has been added between the original first and second enclosure walls, without being clear if it was some ad hoc arrangement or, like for the Bayon, the result of the will (or the necessity) to diminish the size of the sanctuary.

In India, as elsewhere, the composition with concentric enclosure patterns comprises two specific architectural features which are found also in sanctuaries provided with only one enclosure but which here play a peculiar role. We shall deal with them now before going back to the concentric pattern and its aim. These features are first the entrance pavilions – monumental gateways crossing the border wall as well as the intermediary enclosure walls when they exist. The other feature is the galleries or similar continuous elements which possibly are built against enclosure walls or sometimes replace them.

- *Entrance Pavilions*

Two types of temple entrance pavilions are found in India. The first one is a fairly simple building provided with a flat roof and devoid of an upper-floor or superstructure. Designated by the word *pratolī*, it seems unknown south of the Krishnā River – especially in Tamil country – and it does not appear in concentric enclosure patterns. Finc cxamples of it are found at Nivṛttisaṅgameśvara temple (Saṅgameśvara, Andhra Pradesh) located just on the Krishnā bank and where two of the four entrance pavilions are of this type, the two others being of the second one (see below Fig.50, p.78$).

That second type (Fig.39) is provided with a (false-) storey supcrstructure which is similar to the one already described for temples. Treatises prescribe that such entrance pavilions are to be " temple-like" (*prāsādavat*). Technically they are designated as *gopuras*, which is ambiguous, as the same term is also used to designate the border wall entrance pavilion when dealing with concentric enclosure patterns.[2] Used in concentric or single enclosure patterns, this type is generally found solely in South India and Cambodia. In India, its superstructure is constituted

2. *Gopura* is also used to designate monumental gateways of civilian architecture (towns and palaces, see J. Filliozat 1959); the same may be said about *pratolī* which however is only sparingly used when dealing with sanctuaries. Both terms are used simultaneously in the *Rāmāyaṇa* description of Laṅkā (*gopurāṭṭapratolīṣu caryāsu vividhāsu ca/* VI.62.6ab).

of real storeys made accessible by an internal stairway and their height can be very significant (for instance around 60 metres for those of the Madurai temple outermost enclosure). To the contrary, in Cambodia where such *gopuras* have been "re-invented" (see below) they are characterised by a crossing passage arranged as a sanctum and by a superstructure made up of false-storeys and of a modest size (below p.114-115$ and Fig.59).

Fig.39. Entrance pavilion (17th c.) of the outermost enclosure of Śiva Temple at Tiruvarur (Tamil Nadu) (Ram Raz 1834). The entrance pavilion comprises eight floors (including the ground floor); the upper storeys may be reached by an interior stairway. Plan is oblong which results in a wagon-roof comprising five finials lined up on its ridge piece.

- Galleries and Similar Structures

Frequently, a gallery or some similar feature is built against an enclosure wall or even replaces it; the second case is usual in

Cambodia where the back façade of such galleries, used as enclosure walls, may comprise bar-windows or be ornamented by false windows. These galleries can be organised as a row of cells or chapels, or as a circulation bordered by an open portico, or else by a wall with windows. Such galleries often open toward the centre of the sanctuary and thus look cloister-like (for the opposite pattern see below). When dealing with Angkor Wat we shall see that they play an important part in the symbolical organisation of the sanctuary where they strongly emphasize the "close" or "open" character of the various concentric areas.

The row of chapels built against a single enclosure wall and thus directly facing the central temple probably refers to a Buddhist pattern, where monk cells or Buddha chapels border a courtyard, in the centre of which stands a stūpa (below p.110-111$). This pattern is found quite early outside Buddhist circles and all over India as is shown in 8th c. Tamil Nadu by the Kailāsanātha Śiva Temple at Kancipuram or in 9th c. Kashmir by the Śiva and Viṣṇu temples at Avantipur. Later on, it is found in Karnataka Hoyṣala temples (Somnathpur), etc. As for the cloister-like gallery built all around the main temple, it may be seen in the Cola period state temples of South India (Thanjavur, Gangaikondacolapuram, Darasuram, etc.) where it shelters Liṅgas and statues, being thus a follow up of the Kailāsanātha row of chapels at Kancipuram. A similar pattern is to be seen in Cambodian state temples first at Ta Kèv (end of 10th c.) then at Angkor Wat (12th c.) and lastly at the Bayon (12-13th c.). Such a similarity between Tamil Nadu and Cambodia regarding cloister-like galleries and state temples suggests that this feature may be present in the definition of state temples in both these regions (see below p.90$). If such a pattern is quite common, the galleries which lean on the *outside* face of an enclosure wall are far rarer: the best examples are most probably the Cambodian ones where the back walls of such galleries are adorned with a long frieze of bas-reliefs (see below, about Angkor Wat or Bayon).

- *What for a concentric pattern?*

One may wonder about the purpose of a concentric pattern and of its arrangement. It is obvious that such compositions manifest the implicitly hierarchical organisation of the inner space of a sanctuary, creating limits between various levels of sacredness, which are as much levels of prohibition, being all the more restrictive when one enters deeper into that which is sacred. One may say that the basic aim is to reinforce the protection of the god against potential pollution. Such a hypothesis may explain why the organisation into concentric areas may be the result of a single project. It may also justify the creation of such a sanctuary and then its progressive growth by successive additions of enclosures reinforcing the protection of the god against outside pollution and, at the same time,

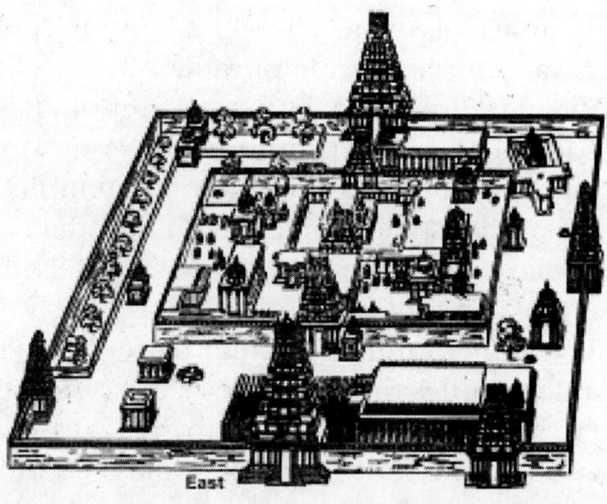

Fig.40. Śiva sanctuary at Tiruvarur (Tamil Nadu 10th- 17th c); bird's eye view (RAM RAZ 1834). The sanctuary comprises three enclosures but the central one contains a double Śiva temple. Entrance pavilions of the 3rd enclosure are irregularly located: three main ones are at the centre of the East, North and West faces respectively, while two others which are smaller have been added in the east-north-east and south-south-east areas. In the eastern part of the same 3rd enclosure is seen the thousand pillar pavilion. The Goddess temple is in the north-east corner, facing west with a slight variation.

increasing the place where temple annexes may multiply. However, such a view does not clearly explain why walls and entrance pavilions increase in size as one goes outwards from the centre.

In order to justify such a regular increase, a purely geometrical or better architectural explanation may be offered. It will be to consider this increase as an attempt to maintain – at least on a visual plan if not on a mathematical one – a constant ratio between the length of the side of enclosures and the height of their wall as well as the size of corresponding entrance pavilions. Simultaneously there could be an image – here also geometrical – of a ray of light which becomes wider as it moves away from its source. Such a ray would be the one which flashes out of the eyes of the god. Such an image is common, especially as regards Śiva: it is with a ray born from his third eye that he strikes Kāma the god of love who was attempting to disturb his ascetic stance. On a more pacific mode there is the ray that flashed out from Buddha's forehead which illuminates the worlds, as is told endlessly in famous Mahayanist texts. In both cases we again find the leading axis of the temple, that which surges out of the sanctum, in a centrifugal motion.

On the way, we may notice that through a reverse effect of perspective, the composition results in the bringing closer of the landmarks of that rectilinear motion to the outside world. The increasing size of the South Indian entrance pavilions results in an apparent decrease in their distance from the centre, unlike what occurs in Cambodia, where the homogeneous size of successive entrance pavilions lead to an apparent decrease in their size, proportional to the distance. We shall see later that the leading axis of the temple may be seen differently, and perhaps in a more satisfactory mode, if we consider it from the view point of the devotee progressively approaching the god (p.103$).[3]

3. For another interpretation see Pierre Pichard in L'Hernault et al. 1990 p. 94-96.

Beyond the Border of the Sanctuary

Little is found in technical literature dealing with temples about the space which extends outside the sanctuary while being ruled by the temple. Treatises sometimes comprise a chapter dealing with town planning, where the position of temples in a city is dealt with. There are found general rules regarding prohibitions: thus, outcasts and other polluting groups are not allowed to use the street leading to the main entrance, as it most probably leads to the temple *and* is bordered by Brahmins' houses. Therefore, the consideration of that outside space falls in the province of social studies, as is clearly shown by the rules regarding the temple approach as that of the god who lives in such temples.

However, putting aside the few cases we have just mentioned, treatises give very few hints on this matter. They especially ignore the large space which may be defined as "the zone upon which the temple spreads its influence", that which is the future of the temple, as its extent determines the temple's success. However, such "ignorance" is easily understandable, as the success of the temple is "normal" as long as the norms given by the treatise have been followed, keeping in mind that long lists of atonements allowing for some deviations from the norms make such deviations free from serious consequences. To that perhaps is to be added that what constitutes the influence of the temple outside its outermost border wall pertains – at least for authors of treatises if not for us – to the category of unquantifiable phenomena: in any case, their theoretical quantification could have been only prior to any realization and could result only in establishing a pattern of restrictive rules which are inconceivable when dealing with divine power.

Tiruvannamalai: Temple and the City

A Bipolar Holy Place

Tiruvannamalai, an important city of Tamil Nadu and a holy place dedicated to Śiva Aruṇācaleśvara, is marked by the juxtaposition of a large sanctuary and a 'sacred' mountain. Built against the mountain, the sanctuary is located in the heart of a city to which it has given birth but which, very early, has become a large economic centre due to its strategic position on an important trading road. The archaeological and epigraphic history of the site may be followed since the end of the 9th century A.D., but it is also known through older Tamil literary texts pertaining to the 7th or 9th centuries. All these sources show a regular growth of the sanctuary and other monuments from the 10th century to beginning of the 17th.

Well known through an important monograph written by several scholars (*Tiruvannamalai* 1 to 5), this holy place allows us to examine the space of the temple, of which we have just seen some of the theoretical features, through a very representative and very usual built reality.

The mythical background of the place is well established. It is on the mountain that Śiva appeared to Viṣṇu and Brahmā in the guise of a fire column, which event is commemorated each year at the time of the grand festival performed in the month of Karttikai (November-December). It is also at Tiruvannamalai that Śiva and Pārvatī had merged themselves into one being, the Lord-half-woman (Ardhanarīśvara) and it is here too that occurred their "holy lovers' tiff", famous in Tamil country. Sometimes it is also said that it is at Tiruvannamalai that Durgā, sent by the host of gods, took the form of Mahiṣāsuramardinī and killed the Buffalo-demon. Lastly, according to the sacred geography of the Tamil country, Tiruvannamalai is the seat of the "Liṅga of Fire", one of the five Liṅgas made from the gross elements (see above, p.7$).

The combination of a sanctuary and a mountain in the same holy place is in no way exceptional in the Indian world. However, amongst the specificities of Tiruvannamalai is the fact that its topographical layout gives to the mountain an independence of a sort from the sanctuary and, simultaneously, allows organising of several ceremonies on the mountain at the time of big festivals, linked to those which are performed in the sanctuary. Thus, on one side the mountain is an extension of the sanctuary and, on the other, a substitute for it, in such a way that the man-made sanctuary may be seen as a double of the 'temple', which is the mountain and its surroundings. This appears clearly at the time of the Karttikai Grand festival when two big fires are lighted at the same time to commemorate the appearance of Śiva as a column of fire, one on top of the mountain and the other in front of the temple.

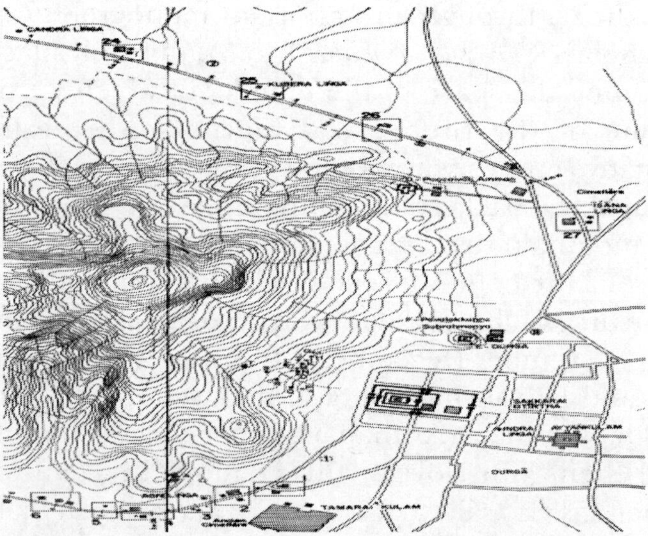

Fig.41. Tiruvannamalai: General map (Tiruvannamalai 2). The city is to the South-East of the mountain; it is built around the temple of which the orientation is slightly out of line. All around the temple's outermost enclosure there is the "chariot street" used for processions. The road which goes around the mountain is lined by temples and repose-platforms used during processions.

Temple, Sanctuary, and the City

In its first stage, prior to 1030 AD (the base having probably been built at the beginning of the 10th c.), Tiruvannamalai temple was a single body building comprising a forepart as vestibule and surrounded by a single enclosure wall. Between the 11th and 17th centuries modifications and additions led to the present five enclosure pattern, each enclosure corresponding to a stage in the growth of the sanctuary (see *Tiruvannamalai* 2 and Fig. 35 above). Establishing of the second enclosure wall resulted mainly in an extension to the east of the original layout, while the addition of other enclosures corresponded each time with a concentric extension of the sanctuary (see Fig.42). Entrance pavilions that face north, south and west emphasize this concentric growth but they appear only with the building of the fourth enclosure. As for the fifth and last enclosure, it was obviously planned at the same time as the fourth one, even if it was built only one century later.

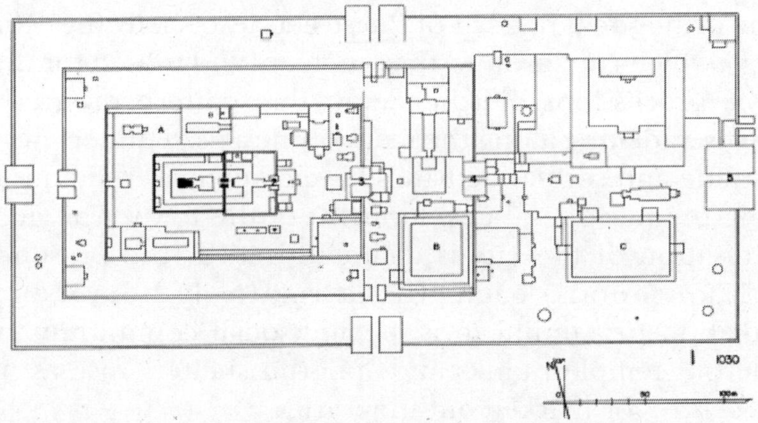

*Fig.42. Tiruvannamalai: Śiva Temple (Tiruvannamalai 2). Parts prior to 1030 are drawn with bold lines (temple and 1st enclosure), the 2nd enclosure (just an eastward extension of the 1st one) dating from the 11th c. The Goddess temple and its compound (**A**) are in the 3rd enclosure while the two big reservoirs (**B** and **C**) are in the 4th and 5th enclosures respectively.*

Since the 10th century the main temple has been subjected to additions, amongst which are two pavilions lined up on the axis of the sanctum door. However, the temple remained a modest building compared to the huge gateways, to say nothing of the big pavilions of the 5th enclosure. Currently, the enclosures are cluttered up with numerous annexes (apart from the western, southern and northern parts of the 4th and 5th enclosures). One may note the huge hypostyle features in the 2nd enclosure and in the eastern part of the 5th one (it is here that the "thousand pillar pavilion" exists) or the two big reservoirs in the south-eastern quarters of the 4th and 5th enclosures). In the 3rd enclosure are located important annexes used for rites: sacrificial pavilion (north-east), kitchen (south-east), pavilion for the wedding of the god and goddess (south-west). Quite a number of small shrines are found in the enclosures and as usual the Goddess has a full-fledged sanctuary set in the north-western corner of the 3rd enclosure.

Outside the fifth enclosure has developed the city to which the temple has given birth, as is well revealed in its central part by the orthogonal pattern of the streets, especially the "chariot street", which runs around the sanctuary and is used for the big festival processions. Further away, that pattern progressively changes, radiating along the main traffic axis: it underlines thus that trade and secular activities have taken over religious ones during the peripheral development of the town. The general organisation of the city is characterised by the presence of neighbourhoods, each with a relatively homogeneous population pertaining to a specific social community, while numerous temples, tanks and "pilgrim shelters" are as much local centres or marked out itineraries.

The town looks like an extension of the sanctuary outside its border wall. The "chariot street" is a characteristic element of what we have designated as the "necessary" space, used for performing several important ceremonies beyond the sanctuary walls, and numerous temples complement the already important pantheons accommodated in the main temple and its surrounding chapels. In a more subtle way the neighbourhoods express a concentric social pattern where the 'pure' castes live near the centre while the 'impure' ones are on the periphery, thus emphasizing the idea of a varying "density" of the sacred as perceptible around the sanctuary as it is around thc temple itself.

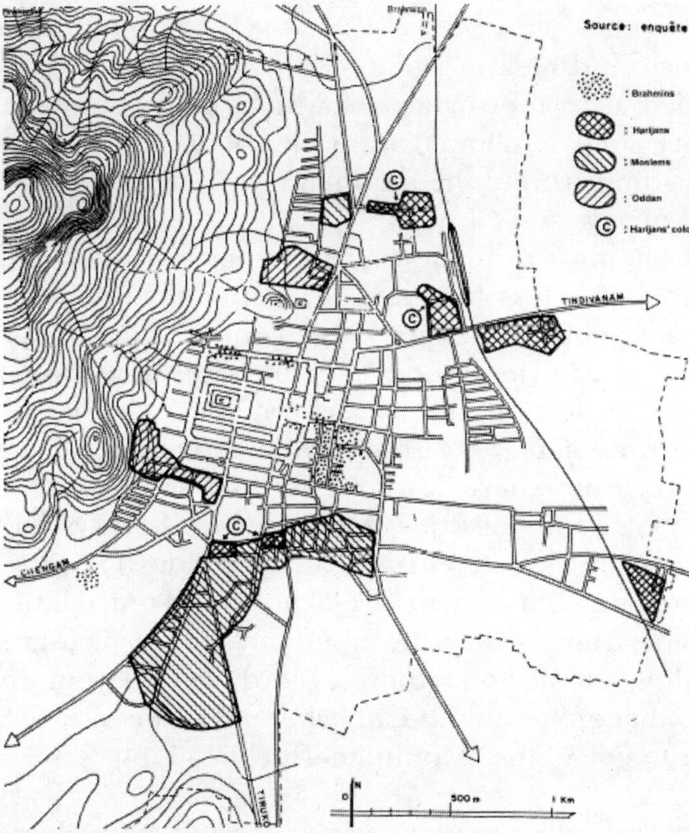

Fig.43. Tiruvannamalai: Social hierarchy in the city (Tiruvannamalai 5). On this map are only located the Brahmin neighbourhoods (dotted parts, north and east of the temple and south-west periphery) and those of lower classes (outcasts [harijan, oddan] and Muslims, oblique lines, periphery). The small group of Brahmin houses located on the south-western periphery is just near the hermitage of a holy man.

Thus, on the whole the town looks like a mixed space which is half religious and half lay. On the religious side it appears as a kind of intermediary space where the sacred is present but only in a diffuse way, as the god is not living *in it* but goes *through it* when he travels from one centre of the site to the other.

The Mountain

Massive and clearly isolated, the mountain (Fig.41) is surrounded at its foot by a road which, used twice a year by huge processions, is followed at any time of the year by individual devotees going around the mountain with the hope of getting countless merits.

While being the pivotal axis of that circular road, the mountain is far less frequented. Being the pedestal and hypaethral temple of the Fire Liṅga lighted at the time of the Karttikai festival in December, it is at the same time the support and house of the God and as such one may say that it is his body. Its divine nature is also shown by the part it plays as the water-source from where flow rivulets which supply water to the tanks and reservoirs of the sanctuary or of the city. All these rivulets are as much Ganges (*alias* Gaṅgā goddess) flowing from the head of Śiva according to a well known and much illustrated myth. Visible from faraway, the mountain is also a gigantic signal announcing that the god is there, according to a layout which is similar to that of Vat Phu in Laos where the sanctuary of Śiva is built on the side of the "Mountain which is a Liṅga" (see above p.7$).

The surrounding road, a permanent and main element of the site, is at the same time a divine way and the materialisation of the border of the sanctuary centred around the mountain. It makes up a 14 km itinerary, along which, at more or less regular intervals, are found twenty seven stations with tanks, repose-places, etc. and where processions stop off. Often founded by specifics communities, the resting places allow members of such communities to "see" the god when he goes around the mount. To that are added numerous temples located on the road itself or nearby. Some of them are connected to processions and to related myths. Amongst others, eight are located roughly at cardinal and intermediary points: each containing a Liṅga named according to the concerned direction, they locate the bearings of the mountain sanctuary. All of them face the mountain and are devoid of enclosure walls: thus they are no more than chapels attached to the mountain and underlining its role of "temple", as already dealt with.

By way of Conclusion

As far as the temple and sanctuary are concerned, Tiruvannamalai's space is marked by a strong historical element where politics play a discontinuous part. Even if important political interventions have been mainly sporadic such as those at the end of the 13th c. (at the time of the last of Hoyc alas kings, Ballala III [1291-1312]) and further in the 16th century where important works were carried out, especially in the 5th enclosure by Kṛṣṇadevarāyā, King of Vijayanagar (see also p.88$). However, if these royal interventions have marked important stages in the growth of the sanctuary, it is obvious that the continuous character of that growth is mainly the result of the efforts of various groups of the local community which, while being various and organised according to a strong hierarchy, are united around a god who, for all the members of that community, is the Lord, Master of the world.

Angkor Wat: Temple, City, and State

Angkor Wat – the "monastery (*wat/vat*)" which is a "city (*angkor*)" – is a kind of antithesis of Tiruvannamalai. The contrast is naturally marked in the architecture, even if by a paradox the Cambodian sanctuary with its pyramid and the large space of its

4th enclosure unites the elements of the Indian holy place in an only composition: temple, mountain, and city (that last appearing in the name given to the temple since the 16th century). But the dissimilarity is also visible in the architectural history of the two monuments. In contradistinction to the continuous growth and aggiornamento of the Indian temple, Angkor Wat has practically never changed since its construction in the 12th century. One may mention just some works appropriate to the monument carried out by Jayavarman VII who ruled Cambodia some decades after its founder. Later on, in the 15th or 16th century there was the closing of the main sanctum and then in the 16th century the sculpting of some bas-reliefs left unfinished up to then and some timely arrangements (especially on the top floor) linked with the temporary reinstallation of the Cambodian king at Angkor; around the same time, a Buddhist stūpa was built to the east of the temple. What remains to be added are the preservation and restoration works carried on since the beginning of 20th century, to acquire all the elements of the very modest technical history of a religious monument which since its founding in the 12th century has never ceased to function.

On this last point also, there is complete divergence, even if Tiruvannamalai has known a similar continuous functioning since its foundation. As a matter of fact, Angkor Wat was founded by King Sūryavarman II as a state temple dedicated to Viṣṇu and that religious allegiance was confirmed by Jayavarman VII at the end of the 12th century. It is probably in the 16th century – or perhaps some decades earlier – that the monument was converted to its present persuasion, the *Theravādin* Buddhism (*alias* "Small Vehicle"), but without any architectural change, except the occupation mode. The original sanctum was then closed and the centre of the worship shifted to the cruciform galleries of the 1st floor while two Buddhist monasteries where installed in the fourth enclosure to the north and south of the temple; these monasteries are shown on a map of Angkor Wat drawn in the 17th century by a Japanese pilgrim and they were still existing in 1970 on the eve of the war.

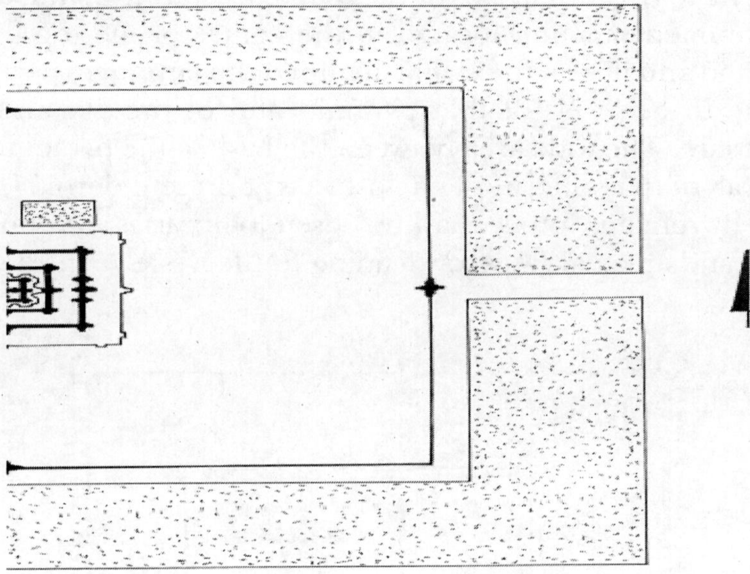

Fig.44. Angkor Wat: General map (DUMARÇAY 1983). The main entrance is to the west where the elongated entrance pavilion is an image of the main temple; to the west of the main temple are the two mirror-tanks where the pyramid is reflected.

Sanctuary Setting

Orientated toward the west, the sanctuary is bordered by an oblong enclosure wall (ca. 1000 x 800 m.) twinned by a 200 meters wide moat with stone-faced banks. A single body entrance pavilion is found on the north, east and south sides of that wall while there is a complex arrangement to the west. There a central triple body building is extended to the south and to the north by an outward facing gallery at the ends of which are two chariot-gates; we shall come back again to that arrangement which aims at giving a first view of the main temple (below p.79-80$). As for the moat, it is crossed by a causeway to the west and to the east, the eastern causeway being unfinished; the northern and southern entrance-pavilions directly lead out to the moat bank.

The four cardinal axis of the sanctuary start from the doors of the main sanctum located in the centre of the top of the pyramid and it is on them that are lined the entrances pavilions of the three levels of that pyramid and of the 4th and last enclosure. The wide area between the base of the pyramid and the wall of that outermost enclosure is at present devoid of any ancient remains, other than two pseudo-libraries, two mirror-tanks and an axial causeway leading to the western entrance.

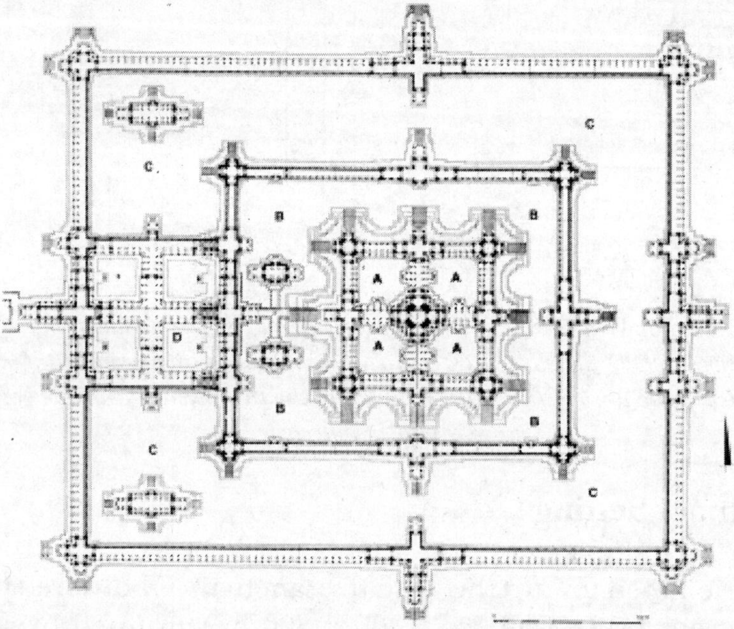

Fig.45. Angkor Wat: Layout of the central part (DUMARÇAY 1983). A: 3rd level; B: 2nd level; C: 1st level; D: cruciform galleries on the 1st level.

The central pyramid stands on a large platform (ca. 340 x 250 m.) linked to the western entrance of the sanctuary by the raised causeway going between two mirror-tanks and then two pseudo-library type annexes. The pyramid comprises three levels, the first and the second being of an oblong plan while the third one is square. The first level (*alias* "3rd enclosure") is bordered by a gallery opening outward with a double colonnade ("bas-reliefs gallery"); this gallery is interrupted by cardinal entrance pavilions and at the corners by square pavilions with groined vaults. The entrance pavilions of the western and eastern sides are treble bodied while the two others are single-bodied; the western entrance pavilion is linked with that of the second level (alias "2nd enclosure") by an arrangement of cruciform covered

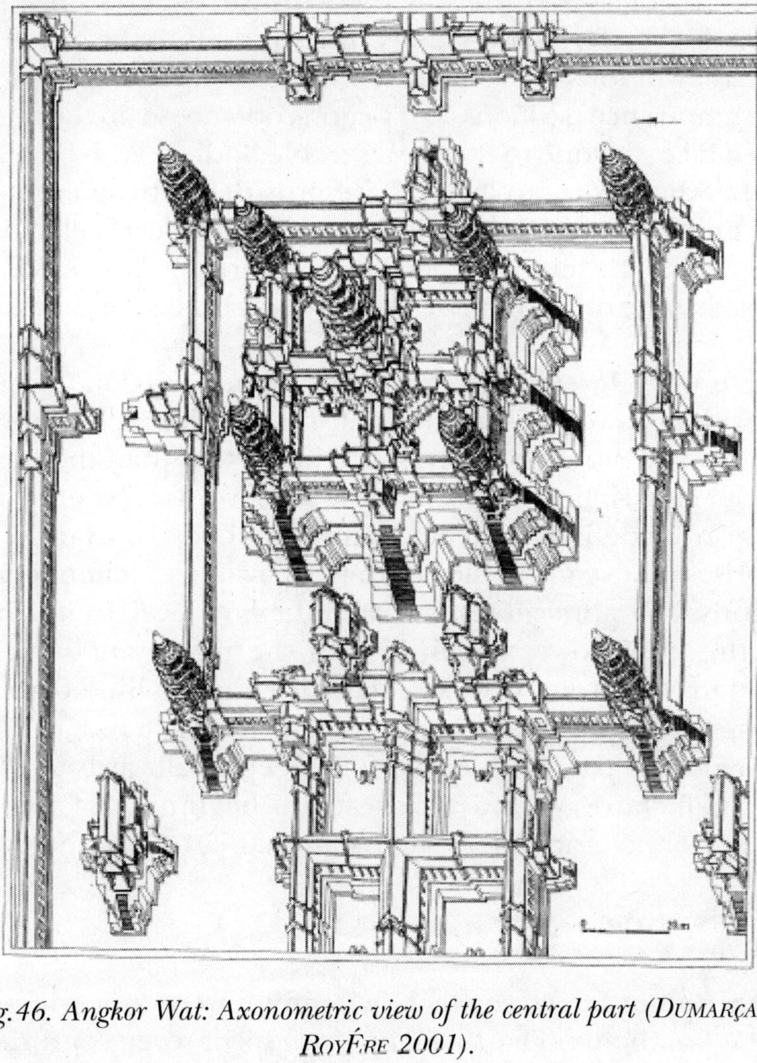

Fig.46. Angkor Wat: Axonometric view of the central part (Dumarçay & Royère 2001).

passages. The inner courtyard of the first level is bordered by the blind façades of the 1st and 2nd levels galleries, the façades of which are decorated with false-windows (below and p.99$). In the south-west and north-west corners of that courtyard are located pseudo-library type annexes provided with a very high base, so high that these buildings may be seen from outside above the roof of the first level gallery.

The second level (alias "2nd enclosure") stands on a high base and is bordered by a gallery with windows to the inside and with false windows to the outside where the façade is blind (see above). Entrance pavilions with wagon-roofs are set in the middle of each face, the one to the west is treble bodied, and the others single bodied; corner pavilions are provided with a false-storey tower and stairways lead to them from the first level. The inside courtyard, in the middle of which stands the third level, is paved with flagstones and comprises two pseudo-library annexes in its western part.

The third level (alias "1st enclosure") stands on a double base with a powerful moulded set; it is a square plan but the western main access stairway, more important than the others, introduces a slight dissymmetry. This level is bordered by a gallery provided with (true) windows on its two facades; it comprises four single bodied entrance pavilions and four corner pavilions with storeyed towers as on the 2nd level. In its centre rises the huge tower which houses the main sanctum. It is provided with four doors, each of which is linked to the corresponding entrance pavilion by a hypostyle passage. These four hypostyle passages delimit four deep small yards to which lead small stairways and which at the beginning of the 20th century were considered as small water-tanks by archaeologists.

Space Setting

We do not know exactly how temples were functioning in ancient Cambodia. The giving up since six or seven centuries of the Brahmanical and Mahayanic faiths for *Theravādin* Buddhism, the practices of which are very different, has cut the lines of handing down traditions. If the Indian technical literature makes us well aware of the theoretical basis of ritual practice, we do not know how such practice was implemented in the social and cultural context of ancient Cambodia. Thus, the organisation of the architectural mass of a monument such as Angkor Wat allows reconstructing of some elements of its hierarchic structure. It appears that the last is set at the same time on a horizontal plan – here it is simultaneously concentric and orientated – as well as in a vertical one – and it is articulated on the various levels and their peripheral galleries which indicate the open or closed status of each of the concentric zones of the whole building.

At the start, one notices the very strong architectural unity of the third level. It is obvious that having arrived in front of it, the general impression is of being at the foot of an inaccessible place: the square plan, the isolated position in the centre of second level courtyard of which the oblong plan allows some decentring, as well as the huge height of the base and the steepness of the stairways, even if it is slightly attenuated for the western one. At the top of the third level the impression is different. The unity remains, but it is expressed in a different way by numerous circulations through which the eyes roam (especially through the peripheral gallery): the temple remains imposing but the four corner pavilion towers multiply it and soften the impression.

Such singularity of the third level is, on the whole, better understood if one thinks of what has already been told about the pattern of cloister-like and other types of galleries surrounding the central part of temples in South India as early as the 7th c. or in Cambodia from the building of Ta Kèv temple in the 10th c (above p.59-60$). As a matter of fact, we have seen that at Angkor Wat the third level surrounding gallery does not close that level while at the second level the courtyard and the base of the third level which occupies its centre are fully isolated from the outside world by a double barrier formed by the second level gallery which is blind to the outside and the first level courtyard which looks like a kind of no-man's land bordered by blind walls on both its sides. Let us add that it is only through the arrangement of cruciform passages that one can reach, from the inner of the temple, that fully open world which is the first level gallery.

To summarize, Angkor Wat by and at large is organized in three large zones, each of them being well differentiated. At the bottom of the pyramid it is the fourth enclosure wide area to which may be added the gallery of the first level, its bas-reliefs being open to the view of all those who are allowed to enter that fourth enclosure. This public space ends with the cruciform passages which are yet on the first level. Stairways at the end of these passages allow only authorized people to climb to the fully blind second level.

However, some elements appearing above the roof of the galleries shoot up from this blind area and thus constitute a third zone, which again may be seen by all. First amongst them is the tower of the central temple – the God's body – surrounded by corner pavilion towers, just as the god is surrounded by his Attendants. That first batch appears between the two pseudo-libraries - rising on their huge base in the blind first level courtyard - where probably were performed rites which, unknown to us, pertained to the "visible" sphere.

Changes in the Space Organisation once the Temple shifted to Buddhism

It has already been stated that Angkor Wat shifted from Brahmanical faith to Buddhism without practical changes in its architecture. The doors of the sanctum were then closed and the main ritual activity was transferred from the second and third levels to the cruciform passages at the back of bas-reliefs galleries on the first level, but still in the open part of the sanctuary. This new arrangement was well in accordance with Buddhist practices marked by community celebration of the deity (see above chap. II). The higher zone of the temple is still there and stays visible above the galleries. However, the closing of the main temple has converted it to a sort of stūpa (or *prang*); in short the god has changed and is Buddha, and no more Viṇṇu, but his body is still visible to all eyes.

Conclusion

Through the two cases we have just presented the sanctuary may be seen in two very different contexts as a cadastral unit with a variable geometry. At Tiruvannamalai, historical variation has resulted in the increase of the surface area of god's estate, but the variable geometry of the holy place mainly rests in its bipolar arrangement: the centre of activity shifts from one pole to the other according to the time-table of festivals. At Angkor Wat, history has resulted in a shift of ritual activity from the third level to the first one, i.e., from the closed area of the sanctuary to its open one, according to its original arrangement. However there was no change in the god's estate surface area.

Moreover, it appears that at Tiruvannamalai the idea of inaccessibility being more and more marked as one goes deeper inside the sanctuary is very perceptible in the present day-to-day ritual practices. A similar idea may be perceived at Angkor Wat with the plain break marked by the first level inner courtyard bordered by two blind walls ornamented with false windows; this pattern was developed from a characteristic arrangement of state temples in South India as in Cambodia, important enough to be included in the architectural programme of such temples. Now, if we look again at Tiruvannamalai we may see that the wall bordering the double central courtyard is crossed by only one entrance pavilion which emphasizes the closed character of the central area; the same may be said of the fact that most of this central enclosure has been covered by hypostyle structures built over centuries. That has resulted in the making of a "private" area in the middle of the sanctuary which is less imposing than the Angkor Wat arrangement but nevertheless similar to it. One may wonder whether or not this posterior arrangement resulted in the rise of the Tiruvannamalai temple's fame and also whether or not it is a mark of the will of its staff to put it on the same level as a "royal" temple.

PART II

USAGE OF THE TEMPLE

Chapter V

Temple, Mirror of the God

As the temple building goes up, its divine character and its nature of a living being are progressively and simultaneously taking shape. They are complementary and during the complex ceremonies which mark the putting into service of the temple – installation, opening ceremony, etc – they will combine in order to make this temple the god himself. However, while being thus made up through rites, the divinity of the temple, its living nature, and its identification with the god are also displayed in a far more practical way. As already alluded to, various processes are used which concern the architecture or iconography of the temple itself or the arrangement of the sanctuary surrounding it. Their results are more or less visible which can be justified by their dual objectives. The first one (and the most tangible) is to show off the god to the exterior world and to make his presence materially perceptible even to those who – by will, necessity or any other reason – cannot approach him and would, however, be able to see it directly and materially, which ability is an instrument of devotion. Their second aim is more subtle as it is to transpose to the open the reality of the god's self, his theology, his mythology, etc., which as a matter of fact is just a way to affirm his consubstantiality with the universe which goes together with that of the temple.[1]

The Ritual Construction of the Temple

The ritual process in temple construction starts with the selection of the site. In that field, as in that of the construction proper, many rules are common to all architecture – human or divine. However, it appears that the selection criteria relating to a site meant for establishing a temple are more specifically linked to an association with an already recognized holy place or with a place that is naturally open to sanctity.

Once the site has been selected, one of the first necessary operations is its ploughing, about which we already know that it is a way to verify the fertility of the site and thus the future success of the building work. More than that, bringing the site under cultivation together with the sowing which follows it, suggest an analogy of the temple-to-be with the living world even if it is only with plants, the living beings said to be "immobile" (*sthāvara*) as opposed to the "walking, mobile" ones (*jaṇgama*), i.e. animals and humans as well as the gods figured like them. This vegetal character shows everywhere in the temple through foliage scrolls, branches, other wall decorations and, more than that, through the countless doucines of moulded sets, doucines which in the Indian world borrow their profile and their name from the lotus, the most perfect and the holiest of all plants.

The temple orientation process is another important stage, for it renders the plot of land where the temple is to be built comparable to the universe and thus makes it ready to receive the god who, whoever he is, is Lord of the Universe. It is also at the time of orientation that the main axes of the temple are

---

1. We borrow the expression "transposition to the open [French "transposition dans l'espace"]" to Édith Parlier-Renault (2006) who uses it to define the wall iconography in her study of iconographic programs.

fixed, the first of them being that of the god's eyes, the basic directrix of the sanctuary. Such organisation starts with the making of a diagram on an already orientated ground, which is also the collective taking of possession of that ground by the pantheon in order to ensure stability and protection, while the placing outside of the very same diagram of malevolent beings clearly establishes the difference between the sanctuary which is of divine nature and the external world which is not so (see above Fig.33, p.53$).

Preparations become more precise when a foundation deposit is installed under the future temple, an operation which initiates the beginning of practical construction works. This installation is to be seen as an insemination of the site through the placing in a pit of an "embryo" (*garbha*), the name given to that deposit which includes seeds, recalling thus the sowing made after the site selection. This ceremony also is a first definition of the future lord of the temple as the components of the deposit and the mantras used during the ceremony are related to his identity.

Then, there is apparently a break in the ritual activity as building work goes on. However, dismantling of monuments in the 20th century for restoration or other reasons in India (see especially Andhra Pradesh) as well as in South East Asia (especially at Angkor) have revealed that many secondary sacred deposits were found at various levels inside temple walls, under thresholds, at the bottom of upper false-storeys or steps of superstructures, etc.[2] Treatises make more or less clear mention of deposits related to doors but we have not found any indication

2. Like the central foundation deposit, such secondary deposits have at all periods lured looters, due to their comprising gold or gems and the like, and has thus been the cause of damages to superstructures sometimes at a very early date. In India or in Cambodia, this is clearly shown by stone layers lifted and displaced in order to reach the small cavities housing these deposits

about those which are set in the roofing superstructure. However, their regular disposition and their significant number in each monument clearly emphasize that the temple is progressively divinized as its construction goes on. This is particularly noticeable with regard to the Cambodian towers provided with big human faces where such deposits were installed just behind these faces (Dumarçay 1973, p.45-46).

Whatever are these secondary deposits, the ritual process starts again with full splendour at the time of preparatory ceremonies for putting the temple into service, ceremonies which concern the building as well as the cult object housed in it. Without going into the particulars of these ceremonies, let us mention that concerning the temple itself, the first one aims at making it "watertight" by placing the finial, the installation of which goes together with that of a new sacred deposit symmetrical to the one in the foundation, that being followed by a consecration watering of the whole building. As regards the cult object, it is its practical and ritual installation which is performed if not previously done, before the construction of temple walls (see above p.19$).

Once all these ceremonies have been performed, it can be said that the temple and cult object have attained life as well as divine status. As regards the cult object, the attainment of life is evident, for it has become a god who by nature is a living being and some phases of the installation ceremonies emphasize this point. This is the "installation of the breath of life" mentioned in some Yoga related manuals or, even better, the "opening of the eyes" which is often deemed as the most important part of the installation ceremonies while it is no more than its normal consequence; it is just the presentation of the material world (in the guise of some auspicious items or beings: ghee pot, cow, Brahmin, etc.) to bring the god to life.

As regards the installation of the temple itself, things are more diffuse but as obvious. As I have shown elsewhere, a very common attitude in India, whichever the religious persuasion concerned, is to consider the temple as a body and more specifically as that of the god it houses (Dagens 1996). Such an attitude is sensible at the semantic level as well at the speculative one. A heterogeneous series of metaphors using an anatomic vocabulary provides the basis of a set of equivalences which, even if muddled, may suggest a first analogy between temple and body. Such metaphors most probably are the source of speculations which have developed in order to confirm the analogy and to go further, first by making the temple as the body of the god of which the sanctum image would be the soul, and then by taking the temple as the god himself as it is the case for the image. These speculations are found expressed in the same way in works pertaining to various persuasions. Most often they go together with a new set of far more rigorous and logical equivalences between a temple façade and a body, as is shown by this modern drawing illustrating a work from Orissa (Fig.47).

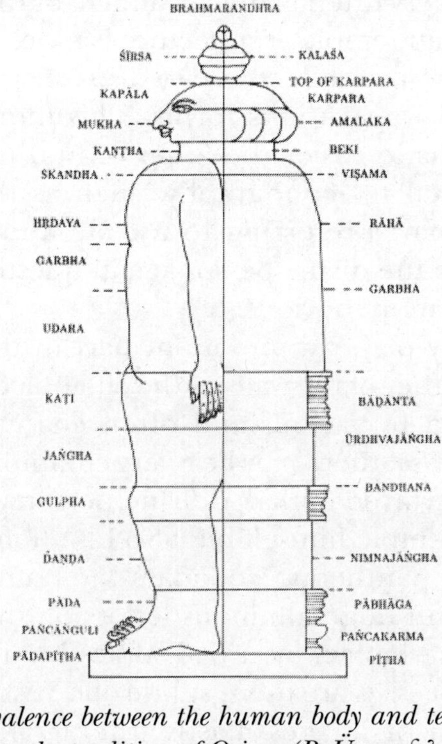

Fig.47. Equivalence between the human body and temple elevation according to the tradition of Orissa (BAÜMER & DAS 1994).

Their materialisation in the architectural dressing of the temple has led to transform the latter into a monumental representation of the god, even if more or less obvious, and to confirm that the temple is the "Visible form of divine power" ("Apparaître de la Puissance divine") as says Gérard Colas (1987).

From Temple to God

Prolegomena

The general principles ruling the architecture of a temple mainly mirror time and place. On the whole they show little sectarian bias. This being the case, architecture is used in different ways to display the identity of the god, lord of the temple, or the persuasion to which it pertains through some precise forms, arrangements, effects, etc. On this aspect, architects have very often taken advantage of the fact that most of the time Indian temple architecture is more "sculpted" than "built". Thus, these architects are to dress structures which are little diversified with various forms. This implementation of sculpture has made easier the architectural use of processes generally applied to iconography, such as the insertion of characteristic marks referring to a code appropriate to the persuasion or to the divine personage in question and making their definition more obvious.

Iconography plays an important part in the definition of the temple, whether of the walls or the cult object, this last being often concealed by various and often changed ornaments. Whichever the case, there may be a very common and very open display of the involved faiths or divine personages, not only of the god of the temple himself but also his attendant deities, or even the whole pantheon. Nowadays the name of the god is often displayed in huge luminous letters on the façade of the main entrance pavilion or inscribed endlessly on enclosure walls. Some other processes are more subtle and rest for instance on the distribution of images. Lastly, the arrangement of the sanctuary may be used to specify the definition of the temple. On this point, we have already mentioned the importance of orientation but all the processes related to architecture or iconography which we have seen applied to the main temple may also be applied to all its annexes and thus lead to a multilevel definition. Thus, for instance, the sub-shrine housing an attendant deity is defined according to that deity and according to its relationship of subordination to the main god, which subordination is often marked by the orientation of the sub-shrine, normally facing the main temple. Sometimes the definition is two sided as is shown, for instance, by the increase in the power of the goddess from the 12th or 13th centuries, which increase is marked by an enlargement of her chapel – it becomes a real temple, even if secondary - and by the change of its orientation – it is now parallel to that of the main god's temple and no more facing it (p.20-21$).

The more or less obvious signifying elements of the temple definition assume great importance when the definition is modified, or even at least partly changed. Such an event gives a good opportunity to know the precise value of these elements and also the value which they had for those who were responsible of the modification.

Architecture as an Instrument of Definition

Even in the absence of any iconographic element, it is possible to use the architecture of the temple to precisely identify the god it houses. Precision may result from the layout of the temple plan, and more than that from the arrangement of its facades. On this point, it is possible to take advantage of the placing of some supposedly purely decorative elements, of the use of the perspective, of the rendering of the god's aspect through the general form of the temple or through the treatment of some parts of its superstructure.

- The Plan as a Signifying Element

As regards the temple plan, the choice of certain options is linked with particular deities, even if that does not always exclude other gods. Here we shall consider two distinctive types of plan (already dealt with in the first part), the apsidal and the width-wise oblong ones.

The apsidal plan originally seems to be a Buddhist feature, connected with the ritual necessity of assembling a monastic community to honour the Buddha under his symbolic form of a stūpa. This explains why big elongated apsidal halls appear at the beginning of the Christian era in Western India and why they have survived, later losing their apse but keeping their elongated form in some Buddhist countries (see below). This being the case, the apsidal plan was adopted very early on by Brahmanical movements and apparently without any ritual necessity. Examples may be seen at Sonkh for a temple presumably dedicated to the Nāga cult at the beginning of the Christian era at Sonkh (Haertel 1993) or later in the 3rd–4th centuries at Nagarjunakonda: here, several temples of this type are found, some being dedicated to Buddha and others to Śiva or Viṣṇu (Sarkar & Mitra 1966). The metaphorical designation of this plan – "elephant's back" – is used as early as the 6th c. and less than one century later apsidal temples were built for gods linked with the elephant, Gaṇeśa in the first place, but also others. Thus, it is very common to find apsidal temples dedicated to Śiva, see for instance at Tiruttani (above Fig.6, p.29$) or Tiruvottiyur (Tamil Nadu, 11th c.). As a last remark, this plan has not travelled outside the Indian subcontinent and it is unknown in South-East Asia (where however the list of plan types used is a short one).

The case of the width-wise oblong temple is more complex and probably more interesting. Used at the beginning for Durgā Mahiṣāsuramardinī – most probably due to a formal necessity (width-wise elongated image) – it became a feature more or less characteristic of temples dedicated to the Goddess, probably due to the fact that her archetype as a major deity was the form of Durgā. Therefore, it appears that several Goddess' temples which look like having a width-wise oblong plan are actually square planned, a width-wise elongated plan being just simulated by a special treatment of their roofs (see above, p.32$). The call to such a process clearly shows that the width-wise elongated plan was considered as a significant *mark* of the presence of the Goddess, in such a way that simulating this plan by the use of a wagon-roof or of double slope roof was enough to announce her presence from afar. However, once again the specialisation is in no way exclusive, and the same width-wise elongated plan is also applied to temples of other deities. Some of them get width-wise elongated images (e.g. the reclining Viṣṇu) in accordance with the original plan, but for others this kind of explanation does not exist, for instance in the case of Sūrya (see above p.18$).

Lastly, there is the length-wise elongated oblong plan which may correspond to double function sanctums (above p.14$). It was most probably the case at the start of the apsidal plan and of its functional heirs in Theravādin countries: thus, the Buddhist monasteries of Sri Lanka, Thailand, Laos, or Cambodia ordinarily comprise a temple of which the sanctum is a wide elongated hall which is at the same time the house of the Buddha in the guise of a huge seated statue and the place for a pious assembly. We have already seen that the pseudo-libraries of Cambodia are also an example (even if less evident) of double function rectangular sanctums, being at the same time the house of a god and the place for oblation rites. The elongated plan was certainly a feature important enough to be simulated by the use of a double slope roof with a well marked ridge, when the real plan was a square one.

- *The Suggested Pantheon*

A god, whatever his identity, is at the head of the whole pantheon at the level of his temple, and members of this pantheon who are closely related to him are generally housed in chapels surrounding his temple. The necessity to display such pre-eminence upon the pantheon most probably is amongst the origins of a very common option which, as already mentioned, consists of decorating a temple with images of temples. These, for instance, are the rows of more or less complex aedicules set on the horizontal levels of superstructures (false-storied ones or others), the "*pièces d'accent*" proper to Cambodian temples, or else the secondary superstructures surrounding the main one as may be seen at the Khajuraho Kandariya Mahadeva temple (see Fig.29, p.43$). This Khajuraho arrangement, where everything is just suggested, is to be set in parallel with the similar extraordinary composition of the Bayon temple at Angkor where face towers of the subshrines canton the main face tower, like the sanctums of chapels canton the main one which houses the Buddha.

The highly decorative aspect of such compositions is unquestionable, but it is also obvious that each of their elements is to be seen as the virtual chapel of a divine Attendant to the main god, as is indisputably the case for the deities housed in the Bayon chapels. In fact, such an arrangement repeats at the temple level a kind of sanctuary with a concentric pattern or else – and it comes to the same thing – it makes up a diagram (*maṅḍala*) as used in rites and of which the main god always occupies the central square. In the present architectural transposition of the diagram, this central square may be figured by the topping aedicule which often crowns the superstructure and especially the false-storeyed ones (above p.36-37$ and Fig.19). The idea of Stella Kramrisch who was considering this "higher temple" as a projection of the main sanctum and of the god it houses assumes its full sense here, especially because this "higher temple" is at the end of the long way followed by the eyes of a devotee from the time he enters the sanctuary enclosure (see p.103$).

Such compositions with images of temples may either remain fully non-iconic or comprise more or less precise deities' figures.

This is of little importance as the main point is the display of a collective presence of the pantheon, well attested by the simple existence of aedicules. The precise individual identity of its members may rely on the position of the aedicules when there is no divine image and it remains a matter which devotees voluntarily leave to rites specialists. These arrangements which thus appear anonymous are in some way parallel to the "five circles worship" (*pañcāvaraṇapūjā*) and similar observances. For such rites, a full pantheon is to be visualised on a diagram, this pantheon being materialized by rows of uniform pots surrounding a main one which is "the" god, subject of the cult (p.38$, insert). Some members of the portrayed pantheons are very abstract (see for instance the mantras), which is most probably true of the pantheon housed on the façades of a temple. A fine example of the acknowledged presence of abstract entities appears on the façade of the second enclosure entrance pavilion of Darasuram temple: five images located in niches are identified by inscriptions as being those of the *śaktis* ("Powers") between which are distributed the *tattvas* ("essences") according to Śaivite theology (L'Hernault 1987, p.120).

The Figured God

In the case of the apsidal plan or the (real or feigned) width-wise oblong one, the identification of the deity through this temple characteristic is no more than a questionable suggestion, because the identification mark is ambiguous as much as it does not necessarily convey the precise meaning which it may possess. The case is however different when the temple or an important part of its elevation are arranged to be a clearly recognizable representation of the god. Without being numerous, examples of this process are interesting as they use either one or the other of the two main modes of Indian iconography, symbolic and iconic.

The best example of architectural transposition of a symbolic divine figure is certainly the Śiva Temple at

Gangaikondacolapuram (Tamil Nadu), an 11th century state temple of which the whole elevation – measuring around 60 metres – displays a gigantic regular Liṅga with its three sections – square, octagonal, and circular – exactly like the symbolic Śiva image housed in the sanctum of the very same temple (Pichard *et al.* 1994, p. 89-91).

To obtain such a result, the architect has transposed, while re-inventing it, a type of building well known in technical literature, namely a temple of which the lower part (base, ground floor body, entablature and possibly false storey(s)) is of square plan while its "attic" is octagonal and its roof and finial circular. At Gangaikondacolapuram temple, the superstructure comprises seven false storeys and the change from a square to

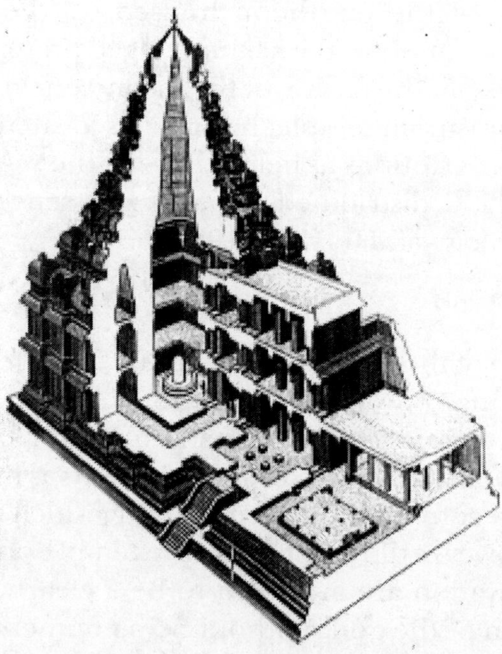

*Fig.48. Axonometric view of Gangaikondacolapuram temple (*Pichard *et al. 1994). The change from a square to octagonal plan and from that to a circular one is clearly visible in the arrangement of the intrados of the inner shaft. Like at Thanjavur (Fig.31, p.45$), the sanctum is topped by two rooms with wooden floors, which are most probably gantries used to make the watering rites easier.*

octagonal plan occurs at the level of the third one. It is a true technical achievement as the plan of the corner aedicules which is normally at 90° angle had to be warped in order to accord with the 135° angles of the octagon. As for the change from octagon to circle, it occurs at the level of the last false storey. The inner section of the corbelling shaft follows the same changing pattern and thus it changes from square to octagon and then from octagon to circle (see Fig.48).[3] To summarize, this temple is thus made a monumental symbolic image of Śiva, a faithful reproduction (but with a big change of scale) of the one housed in the sanctum (and which itself is of quite a huge size). The temple is the image of the god and thus it is the god himself, in accordance with speculations already dealt with.

Similar arrangements resulting in making the temple a symbolic image of the god can be simpler from a structural point of view, while remaining just as significant. Thus in Indonesia and Burma, the roofing of a Buddhist temple is often used as a significant mark. The most ancient examples are most probably to be found in Indonesia from the end of the 8th century, especially in the big compound of Candi Sewu. There, all roofs – those of the main body, the foreparts and the aedicules of the main temple as well as those of the 240 chapels surrounding it – are given the form of a stūpa, that is to say the symbolic form of Buddha, who is thus made omnipresent. The general

---

3. Without entering here into the details of a complex demonstration, it may be said that apparently the transforming of the temple into a Liṅga as fully materialized at Gangaikondacolapuram, had already been virtually achieved at the state temple built at Thanjavur twenty years earlier by the father and predecessor of the Gangaikondacolapuram founder. At Thanjavur, it is variations in the number of aediculae on each storey which suggest variations in the section of the superstructure, which variations would correspond to the change first from square to octagon and then from octagon to circle (see below Fig. 20 and 31, borrowed from Pichard 1995).

composition which is not without analogy to the many stūpas of Borobudur is also found at Candi Kalasan, another temple of the same period. By a curious manifestation of sectarian mimetism, it appears that when some decades after the building of Candi Sewu temple a dynastic change led the region to shift from Buddhism to Hinduism, the Śiva temple built at Prambanan by the new rulers got a roofing similar to that of Candi Sewu but for some slight changes of form, which made the roofs look more like Liṅgas, well in accordance with the new religious context. It is difficult to imagine that the relationship with the stūpa-like roofs is not deliberate. Whatever the case, it looks like a fine assertion of the power of the new dynasty through the appropriation of the marks used by the previous one.

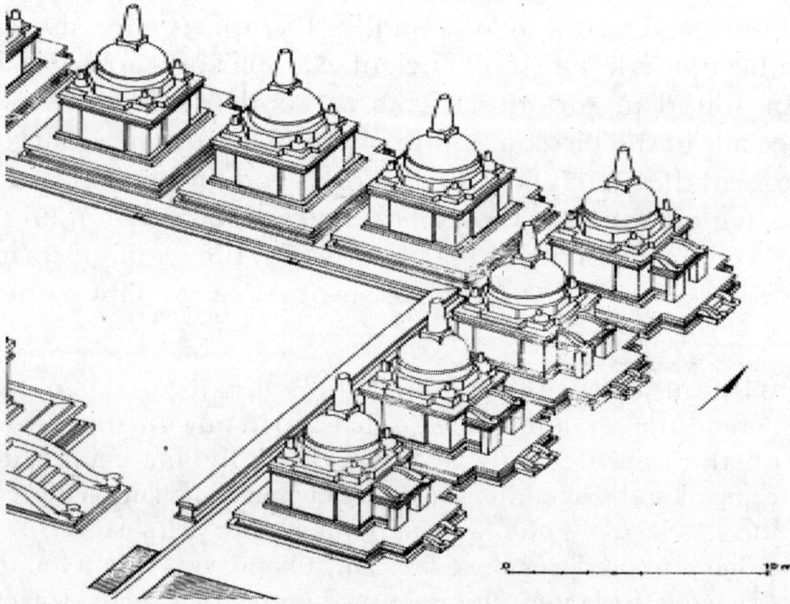

Fig.49. Candi Sewu (Indonesia, 8th c.) (axonometric view by DUMARÇAY 1993). Main temple and corner of the first row of chapels (see p.55$); all roofs are in the form of stūpas.

This use of the stūpa as an element of roofing of Buddhist temples is found again in Burma during the 12th century (Pichard 1992-2001). The genesis of these Burmese temples is different as is the religious context – we are now in a Theravādin country. However, the result is the same, that is to say the display of the identity of the temple as Buddha.

As for the practical transformation of a temple into an iconic representation of a god, it seems to be met only in ancient Cambodia with the well-known "face-towers" of Jayavarman VII monuments. Unless we are mistaken, the only known parallels are Nepalese and they do not concern temples but stūpas (a Buddha face being painted on each side of the square *harmikā*). The Cambodian face towers are well known and we have already dealt with them elsewhere; let us only recall that they pose many problems such as the identity of the god(s) who is/are figured, all the more complex since such towers are found in several positions (Dagens 2005, p. 220 ff.). In only one unquestionable case, such a tower is found roofing the main sanctum of a sanctuary (see Prah Stung temple at Prah Khan of Kompong Svay) but it was probably the same for Bayon at Angkor. Elsewhere, these towers are above the chapels (Bayon, Banteay Chmar) as well as the cart entrance-pavilions of sanctuaries (Bayon-Angkor Thom, Banteay Kdei, Ta Prohm, Ta Som). The most likely hypothesis perhaps would be that these gods are those whom Indian tradition calls "keepers of territory" (*kṣetrapāla*) and who are "gods of the soil" according to Cambodian tradition. We shall see later that such interpretation allows giving a specific and interesting meaning to the presence of a huge number of such towers at the Bayon (see below p.91$).

- *Perspective Effects and Religious Persuasion*

Perspective effects are currently used in the Indian world to visually increase the dimensions of a building; they play a big part in the aesthetic treatment of façades and are an important feature in the temple staging (below p.103$). This technical process has been sometimes used to display the religious persuasion to which a monument pertains. There is no doubt about this as regards Indonesia, but as Jacques Dumarçay suggested to me it may also happen in Angkorean Cambodia. The interest of the Indonesian case lies in the very sectarian bias with which these effects are used or avoided. Of common use for the first Brahmanical temples built on Dieng plateau, they are conspicuously absent from the Buddhist monuments dating from the middle of the 8th century (e.g. Candi Sewu) while their use is again systematic in Brahmanical temples built some decades later in the 9th c. (e.g. Candi Prambanan). The sectarian bias is very clear at Borobudur, of which the construction was started around 770 A.D. by the Sañjaya dynasty, which had in mind a Brahmanical monument. While that construction was going on, the monument-to-be was taken over by the Buddhist Śailendra rulers who made from it the stūpa which it now is (Dumarçay 1998). Transforming the already built parts of the monument, the Śailendra Buddhist architects modified the elements which were subject to perspective effects in order to suppress these last (*ibid.*). This suppression being without any technical justification, it clearly shows that the use of perspective effects rests on ideological grounds. The suppression, with the advent of Buddhism, could just be the affirmation of a difference like the restoration of their use (for instance at Prambanan) was a return to tradition after the Śailendra Buddhist dynasty had been ousted.

- Architecture and Persuasion

Up to now, we have presented several "positive" examples where the architecture is used to display, in a more or less visible way, the religious persuasion to which the temple pertains, and the identity of the god it houses. Even if, properly speaking, it does not concern a temple, the last of those examples, that of Borobudur, shows how the architecture may be used to signify a disruption in official faith, following a brutal shift from Brahmanism to Buddhism. Now it remains for us to show that there exist some counter-examples.

The first one concerns temples of which the architecture is arranged in a deliberately deceptive way in order to let us believe that they are not temples. It originates in Goa, where at the end of the 18th century, Indian temples which look like Portuguese catholic churches were built. We have dealt with them elsewhere and we have only to remind here that the construction of such monuments was provoked by colonial civilian authorities in order to maintain peace in the territory by allowing its Indian inhabitants to follow their religious practices without incurring the anathema of the all-powerful Church, for which the only aim of Portuguese presence in India was the religious conversion of the Indian people (Dagens 2000). For our present topic, this aspect presents several interests. First, the architectural combining of Hinduism and Christianity could have been grotesque but on the whole it remained harmonious and did not seem to have posed unacceptable problems to Indian devotees. In any case, the Christian dressing of the temple did not go beyond architecture and even beyond the architectural part visible from outside. It would probably have been difficult to Christianize images of Indian gods even on the surface, which probably explains why the façades of these temples are devoid of any iconographic feature. Similarly, we may mention some churches built in the second half of 20th century in Tamil Nadu, which are apparently like Hindu temples. Thus, these monuments do not aim at concealing a Christian presence but want to express, formally at least, an ecumenical open-mindedness. Like in the case of Goanese temples, the deceptive dressing is only applied to outward façades.

Another counter-example is provided by temples of which the religious attachment has changed and the adaptation to the new faith has been made through a reorganisation of the ritual space without any significant change in architecture. Several such temples are found in continental South-East Asia where the end of Angkorean period is marked by a shift from Brahmanical and Mahayanist faiths to a Theravādin one, which has often used cult places previously linked to relinquished faiths. We have already dealt with the exceptional case of Angkor Wat, but Vat Phu shows another far more common example. Here, the narrow sanctum of the Angkorean temple was deemed unsuitable for the community meetings in front of one or several Buddha images according to the Theravādin practice. To make up for it, the sanctum of the ancient Śiva temple at Vat Phu was deserted and Buddha images were installed in the wider pavilion which is in front of the sanctum door. Lastly, we may mention, for the sake of curiosity, a small temple in Ban Chaniang (Surin Province, Thailand) built under Jayavarman VII (end of 12th - beg. of 13th c.). The whole of the sanctuary including the temple itself, and its pseudo-library, has disappeared under a Theravādin temple; the enclosure wall of the Angkorean temple being used as a retaining wall for the base of the new Buddhist temple, which base has been built by filling up the whole interior space enclosed by that wall (Dagens 1991)!

Iconography and Definition of the Temple

The divine identity of the cult object installed in the sanctum is the main factor that defines a temple; however, it is not necessarily perceptible by merely looking at it. The object – a symbolic representation or image – is not necessarily a true to life representation of the god and it may even be in opposition with his iconographic definition as given in normative treatises. In any case, this object is (most often) barely visible, which means that it establishes the definition of the temple without directly helping to spread it.

- Images on the Temple and its Annexes

The situation is different when one deals with images which are *upon* the temple, that is to say outside its sanctum, and the function of which *inter alia* is to emphasize the divine nature of the temple and to show how the presence of its main god and his surrounding pantheon is made manifest through the temple itself. More or less linked with ornamentation, the wall iconography plays a part in the beautification of the temple and the images which form it are marked by an obvious concern for aesthetics.

Their quantitative importance may vary and depends upon very contingent factors such as the decorative option chosen for the temple or the regional fashions followed in its implementation, to say nothing of its size and the means of its patron/patrons.

As it has just been implied, it is through the decorative programme of the temple that its iconographic programme is inscribed in its architecture. That may be done in various ways. To mention only the most frequent case, the images (or narrative ensembles) can be placed in niches or simply put against the walls or else sculpted straight on the walls; but they can also occupy pediments on gable walls of double slope roofs (either on the main body or on foreparts) or on decorative lintels. They are also seen on dados of pillars, on miniature pediments of false dormer-windows or inserted into foliage compositions, scrolls and others, running on pilasters as well as on side panels of doorframes, etc. As for the long (pseudo-) historical or mythological tales, they may occupy elongated narrative friezes; either continuous or segmented into panels placed side by side, possibly arranged in several tiers one on top of the other, they run around the building either thinly and inserted in moulded sets or occupying the wall on the full of its height or on a part of it.

Images, whatever their kind, are not necessarily gathered on the ground floor façades of the temple. They are also found on upper parts of the building and especially at the attic level as well as on false storeys, where they underline and specify the meaning of aedicules and other accessory elements. In these higher positions, they are often amongst the "non-visible" parts of the temple and are thus presented only to the eyes of the god. (p.96$).

All buildings surrounding the temple may also bear images: chapels and sub-shrines, but also pavilions (their pilasters often get a narrative ornamentation) as well as galleries where painted or sculpted friezes may especially be found, to say nothing of enclosure walls and entrance pavilions (see below). As a matter of fact, iconography goes on with all the architectural "developments" we have dealt with in our first part, whether they pertain to the initial program or mark out the temple's history.

- *Iconography and Iconographical Programme*

The choice of images and their arrangement on the temple walls first lie on the "iconographical project", which goes together with the architectural one, and for which theoretical treatises provide some examples. However, such theoretical models centre on the main images and do not take into account the extreme richness of iconography which may actually be noticed on the temples themselves. Thus, whatever its scale, the project makes provisions for iconic representations which are straightaway intelligible, that is they are images of the god and his retinue under various forms and in various situations which mythology ascribes to all of them. What is meant is to "transpose the myth in the space", according to an already quoted expression of Edith Parlier-Renault (2006). That the temple is used for such a transposition is one more reason to make it the body of the god. We may even use on this point a fine expression created by Buddhism and say that the temple becomes the "glorious body" of the god. Let us add that the increase in the number of images enlarges the transposition, and hence that "glorious body".

The project rules the choice of images as well as their arrangement on the temple walls; it is obvious that their implementation on the monument meets various constraints which do not necessarily take into account the practical visibility of those images, as has already been mentioned. Some requirements are hierarchical: the importance of a god is marked by the place of his image on the main axial directions, the first rank naturally being given to the axis corresponding to the sanctum door and to which is often ascribed a form of the main god. Some other requirements are more "personal" like those linked to the orientation appropriate to the deity: Brahmā and Durgā generally are to be on the northern face of Śiva temples while Skanda, who has some connection with Indra, is found on the eastern side of the attic. The god's form is also to be taken into account. Thus Śiva in his teaching form of Dakṣiṅāmurti (lit. "Southern manifestation") is in a sense "naturally" placed on the southern face of the temple, while as Liṅgodbhavamūrti he is on the western one. The function of the god also may play its part: it is enough to mention the obvious cases of the eight Lords of directions (*lokapāla*) or, even more, of the door keepers (*dvārapāla*); for each of these the requirements concern the orientation of the door as well as the doorkeeper's position on the right or left of the door, as there exists for each god four pairs of doorkeepers, one for each cardinal direction.

The general composition follows a spatial pattern most of the time, not very different from that of a diagram (*maṇḍala*), of which the centre would naturally be the sanctum and the god it houses, while concentric zones take the form of surrounding arrangements which may be repeated or extended on successive elevation levels of the building. Therefore, one of the basic principles is that the reading order is to follow a right hand turnaround (*pradakṣiṇa*) and that it is marked out by images, the most important of these being on the cardinal axis (or the so called ones when orientation is not regular). There are however exceptions; such is the case for lengthy friezes where they are connected with narration requirements (*e.g.* battle scenes centred on the clash between enemy troops) or with the narration continuity (see for instance the boustrophedon tiers noticed by M. Carnis on Viṣṇu's temple at Tadpatri). Other exceptions mark the choice of a reverse reading following a *left hand* turnaround (*prasavya*), which we may etymologically call "sinister", as it often goes with a relatively negative signification of the figured story or of the monument, without that being systematic. Thus, Angkor Wat bas-relief friezes are to be read according to this left hand turnaround without clear reasons, especially since the hypothesis of the funerary character of that state temple has been ruled out.

Some arrangements are very significant regarding the definition of the god, Lord of the temple. One of the best examples of the kind is the central part (temple and pavilion) of Vimaya Buddha sanctuary at P'imai (Thailand, end of 11th c.). The outside iconography of the building (doors of the foreparts of the temple and of its pavilion) is purely Brahmanical (with one exception, see below); more than that, a Dancing Śiva's image tops the main door of the pavilion which is on the axis of the sanctum and the eyes of the Buddha it houses. The only Buddhist elements of the outside iconography are small images of a secondary Buddhist deity found on the bottom of door pilasters where they mark the start of a rising scroll (Dagens 2003, p.177-178 and Fig. *ad loc.*). On the other hand, all inside doors are decorated with Buddhist subjects (lintels of four doors of the sanctum as well as of its inner forepart linking it with the pavilion). This ensemble in fact makes a quite common diagram; the Buddha installed in the sanctum is surrounded by two rows of images sculpted above the doors; the first and inner one is Buddhist while the outer second one is Brahmanical and aptly corresponds to the world of appearances. Thus it results in a temple, that is to say the body of a god whose identity is explicit only to devotees being in the "non visible" field, concealed to the eyes of onlookers who are "exterior" and thus outsiders to Buddhism. The divine body is perceptible only to those who have made the effort to cross the limit of the world of appearances and thus doing can reach that Buddha who is "out of illusion" (*vimaya*, lit. "devoid of illusion") and who will lead them to liberation. This complex iconographical pattern displays a foundation of Buddhist theology and is very interesting as the set of themes used is clearly part of an esoteric trend which again justifies the extolling of the "non-visible".

Lastly, we have to recall that wall iconography is sometimes "rewritten" in order to adapt to a new faith. If such a process is not indispensable as is shown by the example of Angkor Wat, it may however also be violent and complete as at the Bayon of Angkor where it had fully concealed the previous faith which could then be identified only through some elements left untouched for they were non-visible or supposed to be so (Dagens 1969).

Organising the Sanctuary

Due to what it comprises – chapels, ritual annexes, etc. – a sanctuary reflects the image of a god through the worship which he is to receive and also through his retinue being made visible. Its limits and their crossings – walls, doors and moats – are different mirrors which announce in various ways the presence of the god through that of his house or supplement his definition by showing the temple in the universe of which it is the centre.

- *The Sanctuary as a Projection of the Temple*

The words "sanctuary" and "temple" refer to one or the other. We have already seen how various architectural processes, sometimes supplemented by iconography, come to suggest the presence of the god's retinue in the temple itself, that of a pantheon of which the main members are normally housed in chapels or similar structures installed in the sanctuary. However, it has been already noticed that other components of the sanctuary are also used to rectify the orientation as given by the sanctum, mainly its access (entrance pavilions or just doors).

Thus at Narttamalai, the only entrance pavilion (leading nowhere) has been placed at the east of the Vijalayacolīśvara Temple, which opens to the west due to topographical and/or historical reasons (p.20-21$).

In the same way, the most visible mark of a change in the allegiance of a temple is the modification in the access to the sanctuary. We have seen that in Andhra Pradesh where, due to the popularity gained in the 12th-13th c. by Vīrabhadra – a violent form of Śiva – the orientation of Śiva's sanctuaries has been shifted from East to North when they have become Vīrabhadra's ones, north being his normal orientation (Dagens 1984a). As it was generally not possible to modify the orientation of the building which houses the sanctum, it is the whole sanctuary which has been modified by the opening of a new entrance on

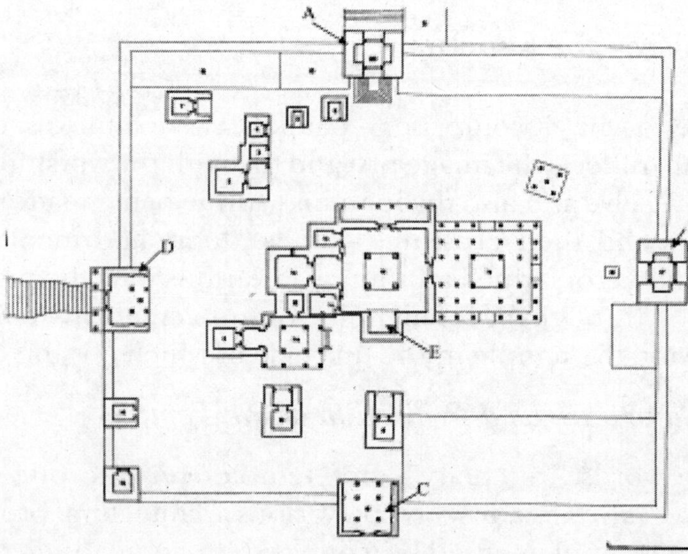

Fig.50. Śiva Nivṛttisaṅgameśvara Temple (9th-16th c. Andhra Pradesh) (DAGENS 1984a). The main entrance pavilion (A) is located to the north on the axis of Vīrabhadra chapel (E); it is a storeyed gopura as is the eastern one (B) while southern (C) and western (D) entrances have flat-roofed pratolīs (see p.59-60$). Western entrance-pavilion opens on the Krishnā bank (which explains the row of steps).

its north side. In Sasenur temple where a Vīrabhadra statue had been added in the sanctum to the side of the Liṅga, a door was thus pierced in the northern wall of the enclosure. At Nivṛttisaṅgameśvara a chapel has been added to the side of the temple in order to house Vīrabhadra's statue (Fig.50) and it opens to the north inside the pavilion, which is in front of Śiva's sanctum. That pavilion itself has been modified in order to get a new door with a huge porch on its northern face in front of Vīrabhadra's chapel. Lastly, a new entrance-pavilion has been built across the northern enclosure wall in order to be on the axis of Vīrabhadra's eyes. All these show that the lordship of the sanctuary has been shifted from Śiva to his violent form.

There are other examples of such modifications leading to reorganized sanctuaries, in order to express a new religious allegiance. One of them concerns the famous Cidambaram Temple which seems to have been very early refocused on the *sabhā* sheltering the Dancing Śiva image and which had supplanted the original sanctum housing a Liṅga.

- *Bordering God's Estate*

It is not uncommon to see images of the god's mounts arranged on the coping of the enclosure wall. They may be placed only at the corners or regularly spaced all along the wall. Such use of the god's mount's image as a visible token of god's identity is not rare. Four such mount images are often placed at the corners of the temple's attic level, while it is a standard practice to install a statue of the same mount in front of the door of the sanctum as well as to draw its image on the flag raised in front of the temple at the time of festivals.

In ancient Cambodia this fashion to place the god's mount on the enclosure walls seems to be unknown (Garua's images applied on the Prah Khan enclosure wall have another function, see below p.98$). Therefore, in the 12th-13th centuries Buddhist temples built by Jayavarman VII, there are enclosure walls of which the coping bears a kind of crest decorated by images of the meditating Buddha, which may be numbered by the thousands due to the length of some of those walls – they may reach several kilometres! The importance of these images in the identification of the temples' allegiance is shown by their systematic destruction – in spite of their high numbers – when in the middle of the 13th century the Khmer kingdom shifted from Buddhism to a sectarian form of Śaivism. This destruction, which came together with a full rewriting of the iconography of the temples, shows how significant was deemed this "decorative" crest of the walls.

In some rare cases, an outermost enclosure wall is covered on its outside face with narrative reliefs. At Śrīśailam (Andhra Pradesh) they represent the local mythology of Śiva, Lord of the temple, which is a appropriate way to prepare for entering into the god's estate, an entrance which follows a lengthy pilgrimage through "wild" hilly country, as is appropriate for a holy place dedicated to Śiva. More than that, the presentation of Śiva's mythology here is punctuated by regularly spaced images of the eight Bhairavas – fearsome forms of Śiva – which face the eight directions and protect the sanctuary and its Lord from all evil beings usually met in such a wild context.

Lastly, let us say that the moat, which in Cambodia generally is twinned with the outermost wall, while not being an precise identification token however marks the sanctuary as an image of the Universe (see p.102$).

- *The Pictured Temple*

It has been said that in South India and in Ancient Cambodia, entrance pavilions located on the outermost or intermediary enclosure walls are given a 'temple form' as is prescribed in normative treatises. This is specially rendered by their storied superstructure. However, in India, the similarity of form with the temple gets a very special meaning, as it very often happens that such high-rise buildings obstruct the view of the temple itself from outside. As a result, the temple "seen" from faraway is just its *image* as provided by its huge entrance pavilions.

The case of Cambodia is very interesting for, as we shall see, the prescription of technical treatises have led to the transformation of such entrance pavilions into chapels. Besides, Khmer architects seems to have been aware of the suggestion that such buildings were to be an image of the temple to which they were giving access; see for instance the example of Angkor Wat's western entrance pavilion or of Bayon's Angkor Thom gateways; the same arrangement was also probably that of the Baphuon (where a similar outermost entrance pavilion was seemingly added in the 12th century).

At Angkor Wat the phenomenon concerns the main access to the compound, namely the western entrance pavilion of the outermost wall, which pavilion is developed on a length of ca. 230 metres, a little bigger than the width of the first floor of the temple pyramid (Fig.44, p.64$). The central part of this large entrance pavilion comprises three doors, each crowned by a tower and which gives to this part the profile and width of the third floor of the pyramid. Two porticos extending to the right and left of this central part present a convincing image of the gallery with bas-reliefs, which borders the first floor of the same pyramid. The causeway crossing the moat outside the enclosure is an compulsory viewpoint and the spectator proceeding on it has in front of him *an image* of the temple, which itself he will see having once crossed the entrance pavilion. This image of the temple is all the more remarkable since the entrance pavilions of the three inner "enclosures" (the three floors of the pyramid) are devoid of towers and thus do not obstruct the view of the central structure of the third floor.

Half a century later, the arrangement of the Bayon is simpler. The outermost enclosure wall of this state temple is the same as that of the walled capital. Its monumental gateways are provided with a single passage but are crowned by three towers with faces; the ternary group refers to Angkor Wat while the faces express that the doors are the entrance pavilions of the Bayon temple (even if, formally, the picturing of the temple through the entrance pavilion is less accurate than at Angkor Wat). Let us add that that the city and temple wall comprises *five* entrance pavilions of which the fifth – similar to the four others - is not facing the temple but the royal palace!

The significance of these compositions, of which have just been given the most outstanding examples, is to transmit the image of the god outside the sanctuary through that of the temple; in other words, they contribute to guiding the eyes searching from faraway for a view of the god – in everyday language a 'darshan' (*darśana* in Sanskrit) – which is a favour sought by devotees when approaching their Lord. As such, these compositions play an important part in the staging of the temple.

- *Entrance Pavilions and Temple Enrichment*

The iconography of storeyed entrance pavilions is, of course, related to that of the temple itself. In South India, where they reach sizeable heights, the iconography is of a great richness which is rarely found on the temple itself, even when it gets an important superstructure. The few rather exhaustive surveys that exist (see Harle 1963, or better Delaruelle 1999) show that beyond the richness of its set of themes, the iconography is marked by a careful placing of images. This concerns the directions they are facing as well as their distribution among inward and outward faces of enclosures. There also exist complex relations between deities (Delaruelle 1999). It results in an enrichment beyond the iconographical arrangement of the temple itself, enrichment which goes together with frequent updating. Adding new enclosures to a temple compound is a common historical phenomenon and the iconography of entrance pavilions established on each new enclosure follows the evolution of doctrine and faiths and thus of the nature of the god himself and of his real identity. For instance, at Darasuram, the placing of images of the five abstract *śaktis* on the added entrance pavilion of the 2nd enclosure (see above) is probably related with a broadening of the textual basis of the monument and of the definition of the god it is reflecting.

Conclusion

The god installed in a temple is by means of that temple installed in the space. The whole building contributes to this through all the technical tools of architecture or iconography. More visible, the second image of the god is also richer and more expressive than the cult object housed in the sanctum. In some rare cases it may happen that it bears a good likeness to the god as pictured in the sanctum. This is then a clever reminder of the similarity of the two images and of the fact that the god in the sanctum plainly corresponds to all that is shown by the image installed in the space. What is offered to our eyes through such an image is – to paraphrase the title of the eleventh chapter of *Bhagavad-Gītā* – "the vision of innumerable body" as Emile Senart was rendering an expression – *viśvarūpa-darśanam* – which may also be rendered by "the vision of the manifestation of the Whole" or "the vision of the universal form". As a matter of fact, that chapter deals wholly with a dialogue aiming at describing such manifestation of the Whole and introducing the next one, where the devotion (*bhakti*) which is at the origin of the invention of the temple is defined. Here, concerning the temple, we have mostly dealt with the divine components of the Whole by dealing with the pantheon coving the body of the god through architectural and iconographical decorations. In our following chapters, it will be seen that many other actors are performing on the temple stage – human beings, animals, plants – which echoes the injunction of Kṛṣṇa to Arjuna, to whom he has already enumerated his numerous forms and the several divine manifestations who appear when He shows himself as the Whole: "See here in my body [...] the whole universe, with all the beings – living or inanimate – and whichever thing you wish to look at"

(*Bhag.G.*11.7). On this point, we must recall that every god is the main one as far as his temple is considered which explains why Hanuman may be deemed – like Kṛṣṇa himself – as a "manifestation of the Whole" (*viśvarūpa*) in an new temple built some time ago in Tamil Nadu (p.122$). This cosmic vision of god which the temple offers to our eyes is installed in the centre of the sanctuary, which confirms if necessary that the sanctuary is at the same time a projection of the temple and an image of the universe.

Chapter VI

Temple, the Mirror of Man

Introduction

The temple reflects an ambiguous view of the Indian social body. Without being by nature a meeting place, it is well known that it may attract huge crowds. Their view, especially during grand festivals, easily suggests a kind of universal consensus which could make one forget that the temple also is at the centre of an exclusion system, or more exactly of a social segregation, which possibly may even affect the gods.

Shifting from social issues to political ones, things are not always very clear, for the "King" gets a special role. First, he is more or less deemed as the paradigm of patrons, those who are technically called *yajamāna* ('sacrificing one'), which explains why he is often talked about when dealing with temples and ceremonies. However, treatises concerned more specifically with such topics, commonly use many synonyms to designate the King: this may not necessarily be taken literally for it is well known that the same words also are common designations of people pertaining to the second class (usually called "Kṣatriyas'). Moreover, the best manner to emphasize the qualities of patrons is to give them the title of the most glorious one! In a practical way, such emphatic tendencies appear in the glowing honours – they may be said "kingly" – which the officiating priest renders to the patron during the installation ceremony of a temple or even of just an image.

As for the real holders of royal power, the temple provides them with several opportunities to manifest their necessary qualities of a "good king" but, for them, the temple is also a remarkable instrument of power, especially when it is a state temple or some similar monument which, in one way or the other, is the architectural manifestation of such royal power. That purpose may be expressed by the temple arrangement or iconography, or more commonly by its huge size and by the care taken to build and ornate it, which puts buildings of that category amongst the most beautiful monuments engendered by Indian genius.

Temple and Human Hierarchies

The Right to Enter Temples: Social Hierarchy and Religious Law[1]

Nowadays, a panel can be seen at the door of many temples which reads " Non-Hindus not allowed" or something similar. As a matter of fact, this prohibition with an obvious religious

1. For greater convenience, let us recall that Indian traditional society is organized according to two different hierarchical systems which superpose or combine one with the other. The first and more ancient one is in a sense theoretical: it organizes the social body into four "classes" (*varṇa*) corresponding to Brahmins, *Ksatriya, Vaiśya* and *Sūdra*, respectively and to which are to be added the "others" – excluded or not integrated, they are at best out of the hierarchy (case of religious ascetics) and more commonly at its bottom. The second system is dealing with castes (jāti), properly speaking; built upon a socio-professional basis, its hierarchy is ruled by a pure-impure dialectics related in part to the original craft linked to caste (as well as to the membership of the one or the other amongst the four classes defined above). The bottom of the hierarchy is occupied by the numerous castes and sub-castes deemed as "untouchable" and here are also found the "others" of the first system.

character replaces an older one which was different and which was useless to display, as it was part of what was obviously left unsaid. Following several more limited measures (Pillai 1953), the Indian constitution has *de facto* rendered it obsolete by abolishing the caste system of which it was just one of the manifestations in the religious area (Derrett 1968, p.468 ff.). This prohibition related the access to a temple with two opposite notions pertaining to the foundations of the caste system and grading the castes according to purity, or conversely, to their polluting character. With the divine nature being defined by its purity, as clearly shown by the numerous purifying rites during ceremonies, to bring it into contact or even to make it approachable by members of groups deemed as polluting, was reprehensible. To this was added the idea of strongly relating approachability to the eyes which pollute, as much as the touch. Thus, the curtain which usually accompanies the door of the sanctum, is in part aimed at protecting the god against polluting eyes (see p.19$). The idea of pollution itself most probably originated from the concept that purity is a necessary condition for the success of rites. This being the case, the prohibition regarding entrance to temples is principally the result of social segregation being applied to the religious field. Such collective segregation comes in addition to some other cases (duly listed in technical treatises) of individual segregation related to temporary personal impurity, such as those of a woman during her periods or due to the death of a close relative.

Treatises of ritual do not fail to mention social prohibition but they have often developed a sophisticated casuistry about it. They broach this topic from two sides: on the one hand from the god's side and thus that of the officiating priest - the question is how to overcome a possible pollution – and on the other from the side of the devotees who try to understand their own position regarding the prohibition. In both cases, the treatises inscribe the prohibition within the topography of the temple precincts, of which the divine character (hence the purity) is all the more pronounced as one gets closer to the temple and to the god who lives in its sanctum.

As regards the officiating priest in charge of the worship in the sanctum, he has to identify a pollution inflicted upon the god or the temple through touch, sight, or just an approach by a polluting individual and then to evaluate the seriousness of the lapse in order to fix the precise atonement rite to overcome it. According to what has been just said, it is obvious that the more the polluting element is near the sanctum, the more the pollution will be noticeable, and the more the necessary atonement will be complex and, let us add, costly which explains the importance given to the assessment. A ritual treatise gives a good example of the scale of atonements necessary when an "untouchable" enters Shiva's sanctuary. The first degree corresponds to the crossing of each enclosure of the temple, starting with the fourth one (which, according to that treatise, makes us presume that the fifth and last one is supposed to be open to everybody which is not always the case, see below). The degrees that follow concern the pollution occurring in the pavilion facing the door of the sanctum and at points nearer and nearer that door (*Rauravāgama,* chapt. Kp. 56). Another chapter of the same treatise deals only with the pollution occurring inside the sanctum itself (touch of the Liṅga or its pedestal by an "untouchable" or a woman during her periods) (*ibidem,* chapt. Kp.44).

As regards devotees, they need to know up to which point their respective social status allows them to approach the temple and the god in its sanctum, it being understood that to pollute a god or his temple is an offence which is to be avoided or atoned for. A small Śaivite treatise ascribed to a famous theologian from the 11th century (but most probably by a later author), presents things in quite a clear manner. According to a well-known method, it uses the authority of quotations supposedly borrowed from canonical treatises in which however they are not found. This treatise (published in Filliozat 1975) gives a hierarchical list of about thirty social categories of Śaivite devotees. The resulting table is very comprehensive, at least as concerns its beginning and end. The two categories at the top respectively comprise Śiva in the first one and the priest in charge of the temple in the second, while at the bottom are found the most polluting "untouchable" groups. To members of each category is fixed the limit in the temple surroundings up to which they can approach the god as well as the acts of devotion or of service to the god that they are allowed to perform, the first of which being to get a 'view' (*darśana*) of the god. The descending hierarchy of devotees corresponds with an approach towards the sanctum that becomes more and more remote, as well as an increasingly difficult view of the god, and progressively lowlier acts of devotion. Thus, the officiating priest enters the sanctum where he performs the worship while Vedic Brahmins stop under the porch of the sanctum from where they contemplate and extol the god. On the other end of the scale, the lowest ranked "untouchables" are not allowed to cross the peripheral street of the village and they show their devotion by sweeping the ground there. The rules are not to be infringed, even if it is only to see the god; the evil results would be countless for the polluter, but also could rebound on the village, the King and the kingdom.

The framing of such rules in the space follows a very linear view. All the markers fall into line with the door of sanctum, that is, with the eyes of the god who dispenses his grace and with those of the devotees who seek to look at him. First, there is the porch of the sanctum mentioned earlier, then the various positions inside the pavilion in front of it, then the flagpole and the entrance pavilion. Beyond are the points where the temple axis crosses the "chariot street" (*rathavīthi*), then the "peripheral street" (*bāhyavīthi*) - the first named street being followed by god's chariot when he goes around the sanctuary inside the city (p.63$) while the second is the limit beyond which extends the "untouchables' quarter" (Tam. *cēri*). Some of inhabitants of this quarter are forbidden to go out of it for approaching the temple. Thus, the relevant area is the whole village. It extends not only beyond the sanctuary enclosure, but also outside the festive area marked by the chariot-street and encompassing the "untouchable" quarter, until it reaches the limit of the social space of the community united around the temple, even if only some of its members can enter it.

Social Hierarchy, Temple Hierarchy and Gods Hierarchy

The rules, of which an example has just been given, concern the temples of "great gods" related to the Brahmanical tradition (sometimes said to be the 'great tradition') and which are simultaneously at the centre of an important community where the entire hierarchy based upon pure and polluting dialectics are present. However, things can be more complex, and even if the temples we have just alluded to are usually the most visible and, at various levels, the most prestigious of the village or of the city, they are not necessarily the most numerous. As a matter of fact, any group may build a temple for its own use. The main difference with the preceding case is that on one hand the entrance or the approach to such a temple is forbidden to groups more polluting than its patrons and, on the other, some groups may abstain from entering it in order to avoid the touch of these patrons. Such refusal does not mean that they deny a divine presence in that temple nor the power which it has, but just that the social status of its patrons is transmitted to the temple and in a sense to the god which it houses.

From this phenomenon results a hierarchical organization of temples which may be deemed as 'social' as it is based on the same requirements as the society attending the same temples. What is important is that the strong division into social sectors which marks most Indian cities or villages (excepting some big metropolises) goes along with a similar division of temples. The phenomenon perhaps is more perceptible in small towns and villages where the "untouchable quarter" is often well delimited in the topography of the settlement; most of the people from other areas as a rule avoid entering it as also for the temples which can be found there. Some of these temples are dedicated to village deities (*grāma devatā*) and ceremonies like bloody rites, meat offerings, as well as fowl or goat sacrifices, etc. are performed there, all of which are deemed to be polluting. However, it appears that some deities related to the Brahmanical tradition retain at least a part of their higher status, in spite of the "polluting" rank of the patrons of their temple and of its officiating priest. A good example of such complex relations is the Goddess temple built by "untouchables" in their quarter in a village in the Pondicherry area. Due to bonds of kinship uniting that goddess with the Brahmanical pantheon, the temple inauguration ceremony was performed by a Brahmin but things stopped there and the priest in charge of worship belongs to the patrons' group or to a similar one (Viramma & Racine 1994, p. 151 ff.).

The Festival or the Temple as a Unifying Centre?

The temple is a meeting point for festivities. Its life which is also that of the god is marked by ceremonies which increase and multiply as soon as it gets some importance. For instance, in the case of Tiruvannamalai, there are "more than a hundred days which look as very festive as the gods are taken into procession outside [the sanctuary]" (L'Hernault & Reiniche 1999, p. 43). Such ceremonies are collectively called 'festivals' (*utsava*) and are major occasions to demonstrate the inscription of the god and his mythology in time and space. As regards time, the inscription appears in the succession of festivals in accordance with various calendar rhythms: a week, fortnight, month, or even a season, year and, sometimes, more. Thus, one of the festivals of the great temple of Ziva at Kumbhakonam (Tamil Nadu) is performed every twelfth year to commemorate the meeting of all the main sacred rivers of India at Brahma's instigation. To all these regular ceremonies is added the 'daily festival' (*nityotsava*), which is a normal part of daily rites but which, as in the other festivals, comprises a procession taking the god outside the sanctum.

The common feature of all festivals described in ritual treatises comprises one or more processions which includes the god, and are deemed as "promenades" (*yātra, yāna*) or more often 'turn the right side towards' (*pradakṣiṇa*) corresponding to their normal itinerary. During the daily festival, such a procession is performed around the temple but inside the sanctuary, while in most other cases it goes outside and around the sanctuary, all along the chariot street in a village or city, but sometimes further on beyond the settlement limits. We have said previously that at Tiruvannamalai that some processions go outside the town to reach a road running around the sacred mountain. Leaving the sanctuary, that is to say his own estate, the god goes through the social space in order to show oneself and also to take it over again; then, sometimes, he may go beyond. During such trips, he is never alone; mounted either on a chariot or on a palanquin, he is accompanied by some of his divine attendants – each of whom often have their own convenience – and he is surrounded by devotees when he goes through their space or more precisely through their own respective spaces.

The implications of such external processions are numerous, but they are most perceptible in their multiplicity at the time of the annual festival which marks the peak of yearly calendar cycle of the temple life and which treatises deem as a "grand festival" (*mahotsava*) or "Brahmic festival" (*brahmotsava*) and to which they devote long presentations (Barazer-Billoret 1999). Important temples have several festivals during the year, designated by one or the other of those names. However, one of them is obviously "*the*" festival of the temple: it is the one which each year draws the biggest crowds, thus showing the measure of the strong symbiotic union which then occurs between the god and the social body revolving around the temple. Thus, at Tiruvannamalai four "Brahmic festivals" are performed yearly, but the one to which the name of the city is attached and for which pilgrims crowd from far is twinned with the festival of the Karttikai month which immediately follows it, and of which the centre is the mountain, that is to say the second pole of the holy place.

Every Brahmic festival normally follows a regular time-table and lasts nine days: the god goes out of the temple twice a day donning several forms and riding various types of vehicles, all of which however are borne or drawn by devotees: palanquins and litters of various sorts, animal or monstrous mounts made up of wood (or metal, at times), chariots and even rafts (when the promenade is performed in a reservoir).

The chariot (*ratha*), a heavy structure often of a large size, is a genuine temple, sculpted in wood and provided with many wheels. It often runs on one day of the festival, which day if not necessarily the most important one, but is the most attended, the one which draws great crowds and which certainly can deemed to be the most spectacular. The weight of the chariot demands its movement to be a collective work, requiring numerous people to harness themselves to ropes which can be very long. People who are not engaged in drawing the chariot crowd around it and accompany it all along its trip on the chariot street, all this looking like a great flood of the faithful dragging the chariot. The scenes are similar in respect of the huge palanquins which again need numerous bearers, and which are surrounded and accompanied in their progress by a similar admiring crowd.

That episode of the grand festival has been mentioned as early as the 14th century by Odoric of Pordenone who, like later travellers, was impressed by the sight of devotees throwing themselves under the wheels of the chariot. It was popularized in the West in the 19th century through engravings showing crowds surrounding processions of the chariots of the Viṣṇu Jagannātha temple at Puri (Orissa), well known since long for this manner of suicides. Later, the name of that god was distorted as Juggernaut (English authors), Jaggernaut (Balzac) or

Jagarnata (Renan) and became the metaphor for religion being an irresistible and mankind crushing force.

If the huge number of spectators and actors engaged in common tasks displays the role of a unifier played by the temple, a careful examination shows that behind this apparently very collective religious function, several details betray the fact that the community while looking united, is in fact deeply divided and distributed The people who draw the chariot are lined up hierarchically in relation to the chariot, the mobile house of the god. The King will be just next to the chariot, with the Brahmins in front of him, then the King's councillors, and finally the crowd of devotees who, while apparently heading the procession, are in fact the farthest away from the chariot and the god it houses (*Dīptāgama*, chapt. 101).

Other remarks concern members of civil society who are technically in charge of these processions (Reiniche 1989, p. 117 ff.). Before the festival, repairs and preparation of the chariots and palanquins pertain, as may be expected, to specialized craftsmen. Such tribute to their technical talent allows them, for the duration of the festival at least, to receive marks of respect which are ordinarily denied to them due to their social status. The palanquin bearers and those in charge of driving the chariot (setting it in motion, making it take a bend, etc.) are also subject to socially related recruitment, but without a tangible relation between their craft – which is that of their caste – and their role in the festival. At Tiruvannamalai, they are builders, well-diggers (etc.), i.e. they pertain to groups about which nothing suggests that they might bear palanquins or guide the god's chariot; that they have the exclusive and hereditary right for such activity and their fulfilling it allows them to receive a token of respect which they ordinarily could not expect.

Another typical example concerns the Kartikkai festival, during which members of a fisherman caste have the exclusive right to light the fire on the top of Tiruvannamalai mountain. On this occasion, these fishermen first go to the temple to take the fire and take it in a procession to the top of the mount. There, at night and following a signal from the temple, they light a big vat full of ghee and thus turn the mountain into a fire Liṅga, which is a monumental doublet of the one that is at the same time lit up in the temple courtyard and which itself temporarily will play the part of the main representation of Śiva, replacing the Liṅga installed in the sanctum.

In the cases we have just mentioned, the festival is also an occasion to show the hierarchical division of society and to temporarily allow some groups to circumvent the rejection implied by their polluting social status. In the same way, the manner in which processions of the gods are performed allow some groups to assert their unity and their distinctive identity. Thus, when a procession goes through various neighbourhoods of the city, it often stops at different places where homogeneous groups living there can welcome the god, "see" him and glorify him – let us say – in a private manner. We already know that at Tiruvannamalai, during the Karttikai festival, such meetings with the god are organized in a very elaborate way during the long circumambulation around the mountain, prior to its ascent. At each break granted to the bearers of palanquins, the god and his retinue stop on altars of repose, these permanent structures being established and maintained by a caste from whom the bearers receive honours and offerings.

The Temple and the King

It is difficult to list all the links which may exist between the King and the temple. First, the King is the patron of excellence and the multiplicity of temples which he has helped to build, to enlarge or to make functional is by itself a manifestation of his power and a cause for glory; his epigraphic celebrations never miss a chance to emphasize this. However, as the state temples reveal, a temple also can be a real instrument of power, planned and built as such.

A Preference Relationship

There is more. The King, who through his consecration has attributes similar to divinity, often enjoys a special relationship with the god of a specific temple, a relationship that goes beyond the one resulting from patronage. This may appear through onomastics when the name of the god (and thus of the temple) is a derivative of that of the King's or through iconography when the King's features become those of the god's , a common phenomenon in India as well as South-East Asia. The royal titles, whereby the divine character of the King generally is asserted, are also used to establish a hierarchical relation between the King and the god, as is well shown for instance by the Puri temple in Orissa (Kulke 1979). There, in the 12th century, Codagaṅga, King of Orissa and builder of that temple dedicated to Viṣṇu Purucottama Jagannātha took the title of "vassal" (*rājaputra, rāutra*) of that god. Asserting thus his own subordination, he was also making the god the real sovereign, of whom he himself was only the terrestrial representative. The two-fold result of this was, first, to put the kingdom of Orissa directly under the god's protection and, secondly, to allow the King himself to leave to the god the full responsibility for all governmental actions, which thus became unquestionable, whatever sense may be given to that expression. In the 20th century, after Indian independence, and once the management of the Puri temple was taken over by the Orissa State government, the Puri Rāja who lost his terrestrial power does however intervene in the grand festival of the Puri temple. On the day of the chariot procession, his presence as first vassal of the god-sovereign is deemed to be indispensable for the success of the ceremony, which is to result in the prosperity of the State, successor to the Kingdom.

At roughly the same time as Codagaṅga's rule in Orissa, a similar phenomenon of the substitution of a King by a god through a temple occurred in Cambodia and is shown through the very structure of the nilometer-temples built at Angkor in the 11th and 12th centuries. These temples are arranged in such a way that it is the god to whom the temple is dedicated – Śiva, Viṣṇu or Buddha – who personally sets the irrigation calendar of the surroundings of the kingdom's capital city (Dagens 2009b)

Temple and the Rightful King

To establish a temple, install an image there, ensure through gifts its regular running and engage in similar actions, all that naturally is typical of a rightful King, eager for the well-being of his kingdom and of his subjects even if some dynasties, while being very active to favour temples and other religious establishments, seem prone to let local authorities involve themselves in the activity of building temples (Willis 1997). To multiply such pious duties on behalf of various religious groups of the kingdom is a way to parade one's own universal virtue and also one's power or just one's presence. It is a fact that Indian sovereigns and these of Indianized countries, with very few exceptions, have always been extremely open-minded regarding religious foundations, most of the time sharing them out among the various faiths of their kingdom.

The founding of a new temple is a fruitful act but a similar result may be obtained through the work carried out on temples previously built by predecessors of the patron. More than that, renovation works as well as the addition of new buildings or statues or similar enterprises are necessarily followed by a renewal of the inauguration ceremony – sometimes designated by the simplistic expression "consecration through vases" (*kumbhābhiṣeka*) – which renewal leads to the appropriation of the foundation by the new patron. Such a process is common, and sometimes, even practised on a large scale in India as well as in South-East Asia.

In India a good example of it is found when Kṛṣṇadevarāya (1510-1529), a leading monarch of the Vijayanagar dynasty, demonstrated his command upon Tamil Nadu by introducing important arrangements to several temples of that area, especially by providing them with huge towered entrance pavilions. Very often designated as *rāyagopura* with an obvious reference to his name, such pavilions often go together with the establishment of a new enclosure wall surrounding the existing sanctuary, thus enlarging the *temenos* and leading to a redefinition of the god's estate by the new landlord of the ground. Such is the case at Tiruvannamalai where Kṛṣṇadevarāya, among several other building works, adds a fifth enclosure. There he established many new buildings, amongst them a thousand-pillar pavilion, and more than that a *rāyagopura* on the eastern side which, with its height of over 65 metres, is the tallest building in the whole compound. The new benefactor thus becomes definitely tied to the holy place and, in accordance with the rules, his construction work was followed by a fresh inauguration, which makes him the new founder of the sanctuary. Moreover, the *rāyagopura* while being visible from afar, by the same token displays the god's presence and the might of the new temple's patron. What is interesting is that this type of entrance pavilion, especially in its monumental form, then multiplies in South India outside the Tamil area; Kṛṣṇadevarāya and his successors systematically used it to mark their territory. Trying to celebrate one of these Vijayanagar monarchs, an author glorifies him for having built "entrance pavilions, etc., for many temples", which shows well the importance given to such buildings (Dagens 1979).

Some centuries before Kṛṣṇadevarāya's rule in South India, King Jayavarman VII who was then ruling at Angkor, had followed a course of action which, even if less monumental, was as significant as that of his Indian counterpart. He systematically added new statues to temples built by his predecessors, amongst which were several state temples. This action – at times supplemented by the addition of some secondary buildings – was performed in all cases with a perfect consideration for the original faith of the temples. Thus, this Buddhist King who founded numerous Buddhist temples, added Brahmanical images to the Brahmanical foundations of his predecessors. The case is especially obvious at Angkor Wat, which is the only Cambodian state temple dedicated to Viṣṇu, and where Jayavarman VII installed numerous images of several forms of Viṣṇu. Such respect shows that the aim of that King was to take over the politico-religious legacy of his predecessors, most of whom had built the Angkorean power with the help of Brahmanical gods. His action was in no way a sectarian gesture aimed at annexing such ancient temples to the Buddhist faith, on which he was building his own rule. By contradistinction, some decades after his death his own Buddhist foundations were forcibly transformed into Śaivites holy places by changing or fully rewriting their original iconography.

State Temples

- Tentative Definition

That which we call a 'state temple' corresponds to a functional category of the Indian temple, which category while being obviously existent is, as far as we know, neither defined nor even considered in Indian normative literature. It also appears that temples which may be ascribed to this category follow various forms which are often not well defined. Besides, such monuments are in no way "royal chapels" aimed at the private use of the sovereign, for they are meant to be simultaneously an instrument and a manifestation of royal power. They are "royal foundations", even if in some cases their patrons belong to the King's retinue, as for instance some temples at Pattadakal which were founded by the queens (see below p.112$ regarding Virūpākṣa Temple). However, in the most obvious cases, their foundations are the responsibility of the King to whose person they are strongly linked. The building work starts at the beginning of the king's rule and is carried on either inside the capital city or nearby. The state temple often gets a name related to that of the king-patron and it is often abandoned or neglected after the disappearance of its founder. Its survival, if at all, is often the result of a takeover linked with its use as a symbol of dynastic continuity. In some cases, however, it is the result of a very contingent factor, little related to the original function of the state temple (see below regarding Tribhuvanam temple).

Generally dedicated to Śiva, a state temple may also be in honour of Viṣṇu (see for instance Puri in Orissa, Cangu Narayan at Kathmandu in Nepal, Angkor Wat in Cambodia) or Buddha (Bayon at Angkor, Candi Sewu in Java) but one may also wonder about Sūrya (see Konarak) or, else, a Goddess.

Countries and times where such state monuments are most easily identified are those where they generally exist as a homogeneous dynastic or pseudo-dynastic series, such as Cambodia in the Angkorean period where are found "mountain-like temples", or Tamil Nadu in the Pallava or Cola times, where big temples were built at Mahabalipuram (Shore Temple) and Kancipuram (Kailāsanātha Temple), and also at Thanjavur, Gangaikondacolapuram, Darasuram and Tribhuvanam. Fine examples are also found in Karnataka from the time of the Western Cālukyas (Virūpākṣa at Pattadakal) and later on perhaps at Vijayanagar – see the uncompleted Vitthala temple and perhaps the Acyuta temple – or else in Nepal where the series of false-storeyed temples often designated as *dega* is found (*e. g.* below Fig.58, p.113$).

Elsewhere, state temples probably are more isolated phenomena, but some famous examples are found in the Rāṣṭrakūṭa area at Ellora (Kailāsanātha rock temple, 8th c.) or in some capitals of Orissa – Bhubaneshwar (Liṅgarāja temple), Puri (Jagannātha temple), and perhaps Konarak (Sun-god temple) – or in Madhya Pradesh at Khajuraho, while in South-East Asia, they are in Java (Candi Sewu, Prambanan) or in Champa. To these, we may add some other possible examples, even if more modest, such as the Śiva temple at Bhojpur (Madhya Pradesh, 11th c.), and the ïiva Vijayacolīśvara temple at

Narttamalai (Tamil Nadu, 10th c.), which were both founded by kings belonging to local dynasties.

- State Temples and Architecture: General Features

There is no specific architectural form corresponding to these state temples, except in Cambodia, where have been created a "mountain-temple" type which is very meaningful as regards symbolism. Everywhere else, these royal temples follow regional or dynastic traditions – the curvilinear tower in Orissa, the multi-storeyed ones in Tamil Nadu and Karṇataka or at Ellora. Therefore, all these monuments are characterized by huge dimensions, usually without possible comparisons with other contemporaneous temples. The Kailāsanātha temple at Kancipuram (Tamil Nadu, beginning of 8th c.) was at the time of its building by far the tallest monument in the whole of India, but it was soon surpassed by the Virūkpākṣa state temple built at Pattadakal by a rival dynasty. This trend towards gigantic proportions is general and most of the definite or possible examples we have listed above show it well. We may add that in Cambodia the increase in size does not concern the building housing the sanctum itself, but the stepped pyramid above which it rises. In any case, the state temple always is the highest building in the compound, of which it is the centre. Even when the compound is organized in a concentric pattern where the dimensions increase towards the periphery, the temple is greatly higher that is annexes, including the entrance pavilions (see above Fig. 34, p.54$, Thanjavur composition, where the entrance pavilions are in proportion to the temple itself). One of the reasons which make us think that the Narttamalai temple pertains to the state temple category, even if it appears less than gigantic, is that the surviving base of its only entrance pavilion, which is in ruins, corresponds to a building of which the height could never equal that of the temple. Another important consequence of the great size of such temples is the important place occupied by its construction amongst the activities during its founder's rule. Pierre Pichard has thus been able to note that in each case the building of Thanjavur and Gangaikondacolapuram state temples made up half of the construction activity of their respective royal founders (Pichard *et al.* 1994).

Leaving aside the question of dimension, the architecture of state temples is often marked by an exceptional inventiveness regarding architectural forms – see for instance at Thanjavur, at Gangaikondacolapuram or at Bayon in Angkor – and more often regarding the perfection in execution. One real exception seems to be the Bayon, but it is well known that one of the most evident characteristics of the architecture during the rule of its founder, Jayavarman VII, was to combine an unrestrained inventiveness with a generally appalling execution. As for the perfection which is shown in the building work and proportions, as well as when dealing with ornamentation – arrangement and sculpting – it is a result of their perfection that most of state temples have been the aesthetic references of their time.

Lastly, if the first impression is that a state temple form was a purely regional phenomenon, a careful examination of its two well-defined series – that from Tamil Nadu and from Cambodia – makes one wonder about the possible existence of a common architectural element which would suggest a relationship that could be more than just functional. As has been told in the first part of this book, the common feature could be the cloister-like gallery or a similar element which is found in Tamil Nadu earlier than the 8th century (see Kailāsanātha Temple at Kancipuram) as well as in 10th century Cambodia (Ta Kèv Temple at Angkor) and which is continued in the later state temples of both those areas.

- State Temples and Iconography

Very rich when the chosen architectural option makes it possible, the iconography of the state temple is, like architecture, made use of even if perhaps in a less lavish way. Without going into details, here we shall only emphasize the diversity of processes used in the examples of the Thanjavur and Angkor Wat temples. At Thanjavur, the iconography of the lower register of first floor façades offers a panorama of Śiva's mythology, a panorama which is supplemented by paintings, especially those on the back wall of the gallery leaning towards the first enclosure wall and by the sculpture on the entrance pavilion, where it is enlarged to include other main deities of Hinduism. However, the most interesting point of the Thanjavur iconography as regards our present topic is that all the statues housed in the niches of the second register of first floor façades display Śiva in his warlike manifestation of "the Lord Conqueror of the three forts of Asuras" (Tripurāntakamūkrti). Thus, this basically royal conquering form faces the four directions and appears as a fine iconographic metaphor of the thirst for universal domination boasted by Rājarāja the 1st; more than that, the position of these images on the second and highest register makes them especially conspicuous.

At Angkor Wat, the bas-reliefs gallery surrounding the first floor of the pyramid is fully outward facing and gets a very significant set of themes. The narrative bas-reliefs are arranged in eight long panels, six of them extolling the victory of what is rightful, what is just, or what is good – all this shown through the two great Indian epics and other great mythological texts – while the last two panels (located on the southern face of the monument) figure, one, the big retinue accompanying King Sūryavarman II, the founder of this state temple, and, the other, the heavens and hells where good and evil lead respectively in their many forms. Here again there is an obvious metaphor, with the additional interest of the fact that the combination of these two non-mythological panels emphasizes that the King will be followed by his retinue in his afterlife, which is a way of reminding that the King's acts concern the future of the whole kingdom.

- State Temples and Symbolism

Our last point here deals with the symbolism of state temples. If we go further than some views which are actually rather simplistic, such as the trend towards gigantic proportions, it appears that symbolism is most often unexpressed as if it was pertaining to what is left unsaid. The only real exception concerns Cambodia. While Cambodian architects and theologians were re-inventing the Indian temple, they also tried in several ways to integrate their own view of what the Indians left unsaid in their own architectural interpretation of state temples, which interpretation relied on their own traditions separated from the Indian model (Dagens 2000b and 2009b). The pyramid, image of the mountain seen in the Indian way as Mount Meru, axis of the universe, is combined with the ocean-moat and its crossings already dealt with. Simultaneously, the pyramid may be a cosmic support for the pantheon, as has been shown in regard to Phnom Bakheng (Fig.37, p.57$; see Filliozat 1954). But sometimes a state temple is obviously an image of the kingdom as, for instance, suggested by the numerous gracious goddesses who cover the Angkor Wat walls and who most probably represent the many provinces of the Khmer kingdom. In the same way, at the Bayon a map and a history of the kingdom are drawn and written by a stupendous combination of face-towers most probably figuring deities of the grounds and of chapels housing the King's ancestors as well as gods pertaining to the various provinces (Dagens 2003, p.207-208). One may wonder if such obvious examples could not allow a reinterpretation of the row of Tripurāntaka's images sculpted at Thanjavur and already talked about. Such a row could be seen as part of an image of the Rājarāja kingdom's geography, if such an idea was not probably less Indian than Cambodian. In any case and as already mentioned, the Tripurāntaka row is at least a fine metaphor of that sovereign power (see also below p.103$).

- *Fate of State Temples*

The specificity of state temples is more evident when their raison d'être has disappeared, which in the most obvious cases is after the death of their founder. Regarding those built by the Cola dynasty from the 11th century to the beginning of the 13th (Thanjavur, Gangaikondacholapuram, Darasuram, Tribhuvanam), it appears that these temples nowadays have a very "archaeological" look, with the exception of the last one, which may be a counter-example. The others do not give the impression of being or having been main centres of religious life and nothing suggests that they have known that continuous growth which is so apparent at Śrīrangam, Madurai, Kumbhakonam or Tiruvannamalai. Arrangements posterior to the original project are few or do not exist and the whole composition, devoid of any congestion, extols the greatness of the central group. The most important renovations or additions pertain to the 17th-18th centuries, when the Thanjavur Kings endeavoured to enforce their power by relating it to their ancient predecessors of the Cola dynasty.

Nowadays, Thanjavur, Gangaikondacholapuram, and Darasuram temples have only limited religious activity and they are mostly visited by tourists who come to admire the monument and, in a very natural way, use this opportunity to express their devotion to the Lord of the temple. From time to time, some huge ceremonies are performed but that is mainly due to the historic and monumental reputation of the temples. At Darasuram, tourists sometimes look for a cursory *darśan* in front of the sanctum of the state temple itself; however, they make a much longer and devout stop at the subsidiary temple dedicated to the Goddess.

Regarding the Tribhuvanam state temple, it seems like an exception as it is marked by an impression of continuous activity enforced by the existence of various annexes – especially chapels - which have been added later to the initial composition. Presently, it is also the only state temple of that area of which the maintenance is not wholly under the national or regional archaeological offices. On this point, a good testimony is offered by the sub-shrine dedicated to Śarabha which around ten years ago was provided with an iron railing, of which the interlacings form an image of Śarabha himself. This kind of renovation is not in fashion in those designated as historic monuments (Barazer-Billoret 2009, Fig.8). Śarabha himself is a monstrous form of Śiva which the latter had given birth to in order to fight Viṣṇu-Narasiṁha. His image appeared in Śaivite temples during the 11th-12th centuries in the context of conflict between Śiva's and Viṣṇu's devotees. His image is to be seen in some 12th century temples (see for instance Darasuram or Tukkaci), but for unknown reasons the one installed at Tribhuvanam is the only which has been and which remains widely popular, to the point that this chapel is the most popular spot in the temple and appears to be the main cause for the comparatively higher attendance in this sanctuary.

Elsewhere, the abandonment of ancient political centres probably has brought about the neglect of the corresponding state temples. Thus, for instance in Karnataka, Vijayanagar has supplanted the ancient Cālukyas' capitals while being itself supplanted by Mysore (and recently Bangalore). In Orissa, to the contrary, Bhubaneshwar and Puri have kept their political place, up to the present in the first case, and at least up to the 19th century in the case of Puri. The two corresponding state temples have been taken over as dynastic temples by the successors to their founders. We shall not insist upon the last two state temples built at Angkor. The Bayon, which is now just an archaeological monument, had seen its sanctuary diminished by the building of a new and smaller enclosure wall in the decades following the death of its founder, while the earlier Angkor Wat soon became a national symbol and has never ceased to be a cult place since its foundation, even if it has changed from Brahmanical Vishnuism to Theravādin Buddhism.

Kings' Disappearance and Change for a Secular State

We know that after Indian Independence, the Constitution of India has changed the relationship between temple and society, at least from an official standpoint. One of the novelties is that India became a secular State, which implies that in a certain way the political authority no more intervenes in the religious field. While succeeding the kings as regards the holding of power, it cannot however play the part of patron in the building of temples. One of the consequences of this was that the number of trusts and similar foundations has multiplied (which results in many problems, especially in tax areas, see Derrett 1968). However, the question goes beyond that of financing for, due to the change towards a secular state, the strong relations which existed since the beginning between political power and religion has broken off. The implementation of the new situation has been very difficult, as was clearly apparent when in 1951 there was a conflict between the Indian President and the Prime Minister regarding the rebuilding of Somnath temple, the very one which had been plundered by Mahmud of Ghazni in 1026. Pandit Nehru, the then Prime Minister, insisted that neither the rebuilding nor the inauguration to follow were in any way in the Government domain and that the President of India was not to attend the inauguration *ex officio*, while President Rajendra Prasad who had been invited to preside over the ceremony, wanted to do it and did it (see Thapar 2004, p.197-201; and regarding Somnath below p.108$).

Many years later in the nineties, the takeover of power in a perfectly democratic way by political parties strongly marked by religious bias would lead some parts of India into a vicious cycle of violence centred upon another temple, that of Ayodhya (*ibidem*).

Conclusion

The next chapter will try to show that the temple is to be seen as a performance. Here we have shown it as what may be called a theatre of "human comedy", in the sense given to that expression by Balzac. Here, everybody has his own place and rank without practically being able to control one or the other, but compelled to cling to them for as long as they are known to be privileges. They are the marks that one exists in the eyes of the god in the representation of the universe made up by the sanctuary. Let us add that there is no abuse of the Balzacian metaphor, as we have recalled that the author of *Comédie humaine* is one of the leading people in the introduction of the god from Puri temple to European languages!

Changing to a political field, we have also changed to another theatre, that of the king's power and naturally of his *goodness*. We have seen that the new legislative norms of modern India, while drastically changing the social rules regarding temples, has also affirmed the official separation of political power and religion, and while so doing, has *de facto* broken the relationship which existed until then between the state and temple. The two examples we have just alluded to however show that such a separation cannot be easily implemented, even at the highest levels of the state. The reason for this is quite simple: the temple remains as an instrument of political power, but what it displays is no more the power itself but the ideology which that power promotes. When at the beginning of the 11th century King Rājarāja I was building the Thanjavur Śiva Rājarājeśvara temple to which he was giving his own name, he was showing to all his own power. Ten centuries later, the people rebuilding Somnath temple and, more than that, perhaps those in Ayodhya, wanted to show to the whole world the paramount power of an ideology – the *hindutva* - according to which India as a national entity may only be Hindu.

Chapter VII

Temple as a Performance

Introduction

Space and Time

If the architectural analysis of a temple must begin from its central part and then, little by little reach its periphery, the study of the usage of that temple is to be seen more as a centripetal process, for the temple is also a performing show. Its staging needs to call on all the resources of architecture in the field and it sets the progressive approach of the god across the several spaces generated by the temple, this last often being *mis en abyme.* The show is continuously renewed, for its performance adapts to the rhythms of time as well as to circumstances. In this way it takes into account the daily movement of shade and light, which literally gives life to the temple façades. As regards rites and ceremonies, the daily show rarely goes out of the sanctuary or even of the temple itself. On the contrary, at the time of festivals the stage extends beyond the bounded space of the sanctuary, fills up the social space which surrounds it, and may even stretch beyond. Simultaneously, the festival enhances the extended show and makes it run faster. Therefore, whatsoever their importance, festivals do not last more than a few days; however, skilled architects cum sculptors in charge of temple construction know how to "petrify" the festival in order to suggest that the celebration has become permanent due to a pause of time.

There is also the human time, that of history. First, it is that which through the patron's intentions fixes the initial frame where the show is to be performed. Later on, this same time provokes an increase in the size of the stage, also possibly a decrease; it may also modify its orientation or centre it again (in all senses of the expression); in short, it will set the duration for the performance. However, this historical time generally goes further than just the daily anecdotal life of the temple. A temple records the history with which it is entrusted and sometimes it so happens that the temple itself is the main hero of that history.

Spectators and Actors

A show needs spectators and actors. On a human plane and for the sake of presentation, we have clearly separated them in our initial definition assigning the actor's part to the officiating priest while that of the spectator (and possibly patron) was given to all others. Later on, while dealing with the approach to the god we were more balanced, thereby underlining that anybody, irrespective of his social rank, was capable of offering a service to the god, this ability also being a privilege. Thus, festivals were opportunities to open the performance to unusual participants.

At the divine level, the gods and their retinue are obviously privileged spectators. Regarding installation ceremonies, we have already noticed a rite which immediately follows the "opening of eyes" and consists of "showing" several auspicious beings and objects to the image become a god, and in order to introduce it/him to the world show which he will now lead. Moreover, it often happens that during some ceremonies a show is presented to the god; for this purpose, in many temples there is a building designated as the "dance pavilion" in front of the sanctum door. In its centre, there is a flat and smooth place, sometimes a circular one, where the temple dancer performs what is sometimes deemed as a "pure dance", under the gaze of the god engaged in his daily procession in the temple courtyard (see for instance *Rauravāgama,* translation). A similar rite with a wider scope occurs during the grand festival: then the god is presented a "dance festival" which truly is a festival within a festival and of which the performance may last several days (Barazer-Billoret 1999). The god may also be a spectator of a different kind when for his own eyes, as well as to the personal satisfaction of the people in charge (officiating priests, artists, or patrons), are performed some parts of the show which apparently are non-perceptible: such is the case of purely mental rites, or of non-visible but important architectural or iconographic features (see above).

Lastly the god is an actor. The staging of the temple is mainly that of his eyes which, flashing from the sanctum, go up to the world's limits. This staging is also of the mythology inscribed in the space, of which it marks the directions. On this point, it is noticeable that Indian tradition often gets a powerful strength of suggestion resting on the selection of images as well as on their arrangement on temple façades (Parlier-Renault 2006); however it is in South-East Asia – especially in Cambodia – that images sometimes extend to the size of the sanctuary. See for instance the presentations of the 'Churning of the Ocean' where the Bayon temple or the central tower of Prah Khan play the part of Mount Mandara, the axis of that churning. Sometimes, arrangement of an image may go beyond sanctuary limits as appears in the stupendous arrangement of the Angkor area by King Yaśovarman 1st (beginning of the 10th century). This arrangement extends up to the three hills marking the Angkor site. On the central one – the Phnom Bakheng – is built a state temple of which the pyramid is crowned by a quincunx of towers displaying the five-fold nature of Śiva, while each of the other two hills – Phnom Krom and Phnom Bok – is crowned by a triad of towers recalling that Śiva, who is housed in the central one, outclasses the two other main gods – Brahmā and Viṣṇu – who inhabit the two side towers. In India, this divine triad is displayed by a statue commonly installed on the western façade of temples. At Angkor, the same triad occupies twice the space of the capital city and, more than that, is accompanied by a cortege of about one hundred royal foundations arranged throughout the kingdom where, with most of them dedicated to Śaivite forms, they play the dual role of travellers' lodges and monasteries.

An Art of the Temple

A Necessary Beauty

Being, at the same time, an element and the central part of the show the temple is to be beautiful. That goes without saying, according to normative treatises, even if they do not give the why's of such beauty. In any case, it is a necessity for patrons, as is recalled by a quotation which we borrow from an inscription of the 5th century A.D. The text relates, often in a lyrical way, how some silk-weavers settled in Mandasor city in Central India and, there, made a building in honour of the Sun:

> "this incomparably noble temple [...]. Its [...] pointed tower is like a mountain, white as the mass of the pure rays of the risen moon, it shines, lovely to the eye; let a glorious crest-jewel set in the (turban of) the City [...]"

The inscription goes on to remind that around fifty years later the silk-weaver guild has repaired

> "this house of the sun [...], for the increase of their fame [...]. It is very high and white, as though touching the sky with its lovely pinnacles, a resting place for the first clear rays of the rising moon and sun. [...] this wholly noble city is adorned by best of temples [...]."[1]

All is said in these few lines, where the temple's necessary beauty is thrice justified, being simultaneously defined as a homage to the god, a beautification of the city, and a glory for the patrons.

---

1. Verses 29-30, 37-38, and 42cd according to the full translation given by Basham 1983 (p.94-105); for Sanskrit text, see Sircar 1965 (I, p. 299 and following).

In India, for a long time, art has been related to the temple and to power (which, as a matter of fact, is in no way surprising). The oldest known testimonies of artistic activity linked with Indian tradition allow a clear differentiation of this dual relationship. On the one side we have the sculpted entrance ornamentation of the Lomas Rishi rock temple in the Barabar hills (3rd century B.C.), while on the other there are the petrified ensigns, these free pillars bearing an animal motive which appeared a little earlier in Ganges valley around the 4th century B.C. (Dagens 1993). However later on – and this is what concerns us – both go together: the art of the temple is usually an expression of a power which may be political – see state temples and kings' pious foundations – or socio-economic as in the case of the silk-weaver guild from Mandasor and in many others.

From Worship to Door Artistic Arrangement

The rock-monument of Lomas Rishi just mentioned presents an interesting case, for this first known manifestation of temple-art in the Indian world is also the first testimony of a constant feature of that art, namely, the importance given to the arrangement of the door - of the sanctum or of the temple itself – which, later on was often the only ornamented part of the whole temple. The artistic celebration of the temple entrance is only a counterpart of the worship presented to the door every morning by the officiating priest, on opening it to enter the temple to wake the god. At this time, he honours the various deities who are around the door and on its frame (doorkeepers and others) and then the ones who rule the door-leaves, sill, lintel, and even the lock, in other words a small pantheon which, while being part of the non-visible iconography, are however indispensable for the regular working of temple.

The Lomas Rishi door arrangement is not very sophisticated, even if it comprises the most important elements for temple doors staging. Some centuries later during the Gupta period, a full-fledged and what we may call a final model was worked out which would later experience some variations and adaptations in India. In contrast, this model was masterfully re-invented in South-East Asia. In Cambodia, for instance, if we put aside the infrequent walls with bas-reliefs, the meaningful iconography is for the most part concentrated on the door and its framings: the decorative lintel, pediment, anta pilasters, shaft dadoes, or even door-post panels are used for this purpose. This concerns

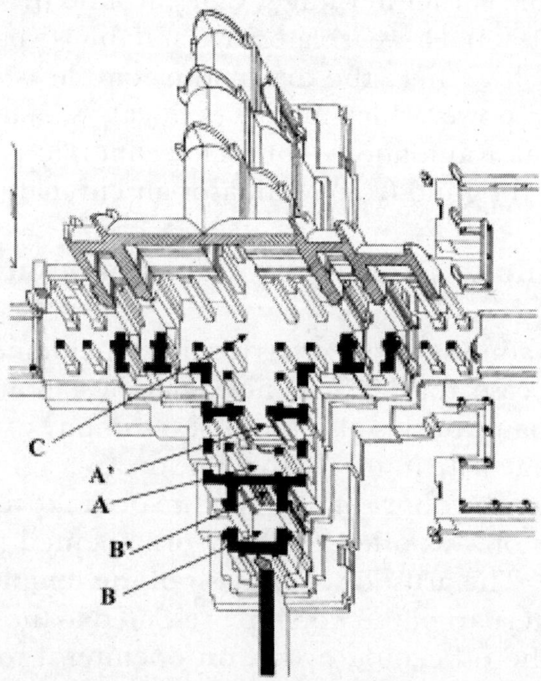

*Fig.51. Banteay Kdei (Angkor, end of 12th c.): Eastern entrance pavilion of the 3rd enclosure (Dumarçay 1988). The room **A** may be reached from the central room **C** only (by using door **A'**). However the architectural arrangement assumes that one is to pass from room **B** (which is a fore-part of **A**) using the (false) door **B'**, then from that room **A** (which is a forepart of **C**) to room **C** by using door **A'**. According to this theoretical arrangement, the false-door **B'** has been provided with a decorative lintel and shafts facing room **B**, and in the same way door **A'** gets the same decorative elements facing room **A**.*

functional doors as well as false ones, which are numerous. Moreover, excessive adornment for the sake of logical consistency may result in placing narrative elements in positions which pertain to non-visible matter. A fine instance is found in an entrance pavilion of a monument from the end of the 12th century (Fig.51). As the axonometric drawing shows, the ornamentation of the doors corresponds to the arrangement of the architecture and movement as are *assumed*, but goes against the sense of the only possible practical movement.

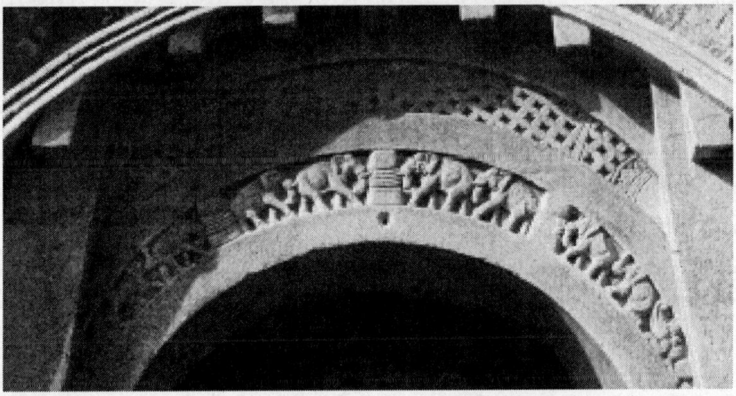

Fig.52. Entrance of Lomas Rishi rock temple (Barabar Hills, Bihar, 3rd c. B.C.). At the top there is a mock sliced bamboo latticed window (with lotus at the ends) while below it is a mock latticed window with passing elephants and, at the each end, a makara.

To go back to the Lomas Rishi door, this initial manifestation of temple art in India also marks the beginning of using the artistic possibilities of the plant kingdom as well as of the animal world and also the use of light, as it is a double curved latticed window which fills the upper part of door frame. We have already dealt with plants, principally with the lotus, which appears in Lomas Rishi at the ends of the door's superior latticed window, and which would henceforth be omnipresent on temple façades through numerous doucine mouldings (see also below regarding festivals). Here, we shall stress on the part played in the show by the animal kingdom and plays of light, adding to them the water mirrors which were invented later and which will lead us to the temple's *mise en abyme.*

Animals in the Temple

The animal kingdom shown at the Lomas Rishi temple by means of a procession of elephants between two *makaras* had first made its appearance through a set of samples on Ganges valley pillars and, from then on, would be seen in all temples (Dagens 2009c). The early apparition of the *makara* – the marine monster based on a crocodile, elephant, and lion – is all the more noticeable, since one of its most frequent positions is on the top of doors (see below). As regards the elephant, it is now seen living in several sanctuaries where that kingly mount often takes part in daily or more formal processions. Such regular performances probably explain why some life-size statues in full round are shown as stationary in the courtyard of the Kailāsanātha rock-temple at Ellora, and also, a little earlier, in the midst of the Mahabalipuram monolith rock-temples (*ratha*). In the latter case, the stone elephant is very near an apsidal temple which refers to its part in the realm of metaphors (see above p.18$ and 71$).

However, the elephant also plays other parts. Thus, as it is well known, mythology puts it in charge of the main and intermediate directions and also depicts it as supporting the universe. It is most probably this two-fold function that is the reason for the lavish troop of elephants in quasi-full round which ornate the base of the Kailāsanātha temple at Ellora mentioned earlier and in counterpoint of which is the famous sculpted composition nearby, where the *asura* Rāvaṇa tries in vain to displace the Kailāsa mountain where Śiva sits enthroned. Created a little earlier, similar but more serene elephants in high relief punctuate the façade of the ground floor at the Kailāsanātha temple in Kancipuram. They are also found in Cambodia where, sculpted in the round and hieratic, they watch over the intermediate directions on several mountain-temples (Eastern Mebon, Phiméanakas, etc.). Thus they lose a part of the chthonian character suggested by their position in India, which they more or less recover in the 14th and 15th century Buddhist monuments in Thailand (Dagens 2009c: Fig.8).

The lion, which is another royal animal that appeared on the top of some Ganges valley pillars, is to be found in all temples. Everywhere, it looks heraldic. Standing up, squatting, being a part of the pillar-shaft or else reduced to an apotropaic mask, possibly of good size (Indonesia), it is the indispensable guard of doors and other open parts throughout the whole Indian world. While the elephants look as if they are following with their eyes the circumambulatory processions, the lions which top or frame the doors are always staring at visitors when they cross these doors while proceeding to the god. . From early times they were also used as supporting figures, without losing their terrifying look. This supporting role is probably linked to the important place given to the lion in the arrangement and symbolism of the king's throne. The latter is designated in Sanskrit as the "lion seat" (*siṃhāsana*), this name being practically rendered to that piece of furniture which has the look of a seat with lion's feet or with feet in form of lions. On cult images, the "lion throne" is often the seat given to divinities, especially the Buddha; it is however also found as one of the levels of the mystical throne built by meditation in order to receive a mystical Śiva's image produced by the same process.

To the elephant which supports the universe and to the lion which guards it, the Indian world adds the bird *Garuḍa*. Sworn enemy of serpents and the regular mount of Viṣṇu whom it helps in battle, this bird of prey is the "Master of the Sky" even if in a practical way it shares the sky with *haṃsa*. Scarcely individualised, the *haṃsa* is a wild goose, even if Westerners tend to see it as a more prestigious swan. Far more ethereal than the *garuḍa*, it is also identified with the soul, this identification being supported by a classical, even if phonetically paradoxical pun upon expiration (HAB-) and inspiration (-SA). In the temple show, these two kinds of birds which seem to be opposed in every way are often given the same role. Sculpted in long rows on the quarter-round moulding placed below cornices of entablatures, they transform the upper part of the temple into

Fig.53. Prah Thkol (Prah Khan of Kompong Svay, Cambodia; end of 12th c.) (DELAPORTE 1880). The faces figured on all the porch pediments are an improper restoration by DELAPORTE. B.-P. GROSLIER and myself have been able to observe that on each of the main pediments of the four cardinal porches was sculpted the mask of a man, a lion, a horse and an elephant respectively, which correspond to the four gargoyles of Neak Pean, one of the nilometer-temples at Angkor [DAGENS 2003, p. 120-121]. The Prah Thkol, built like Neak Pean in the centre of a large reservoir and under the rule of the same king, thus appears as an image displaying the nilometer built in the capital-city.

a flying palace, similar to the "flying chariots" used by the gods to travel through the skies, and of which the generic name (*vimāna*) is very commonly used to designate a temple.

Once more, Cambodia under the rule of Jayavarman VII best uses these animal themes. The outward face of the enclosure wall of the Prah Khan temple at Angkor is regularly punctuated by huge images of *garuḍaṣ* with spread wings, which make the whole sanctuary a flying palace (e.g. Dagens 2003, p.205). As regards the *haṃsas* sculpted on the bases of causeways crossing one of the moats of Prah Khan temple at Kompong Svay, they change such causeways in aerial ways leading to a god's house.

Most of the animals we have mentioned above are found in the Prah Thkol temple which comprises a part of the Kompong Svay compound (Fig.53). The four corners of its tower are occupied by a composition where one above the other are arranged a three-headed elephant, a lion-mask, a *garuḍa* with spread wings and a frieze of *haṃsas*, again with spread wings. This composition is a part of complex Buddhist symbolism, but it suggests at the same time and in a more visible way that the temple solidly supported by elephants, is guarded by lions while its tower is taken over in a flight by the inhabitants of the sky.

Shade and Light upon the Temple

The performing art in architecture also includes the mastery of light when it plays with shade every day. In this field, the Indian world like the Western one has used the many possibilities provided by horizontal moulding compositions, especially as regards bases where lotus-like doucines and torus get an important place. This may be found in compositions with very deeply sculpted mouldings – see for instance the base of some Hoycala temples in Karnataka - where deep grooves are inserted between narrative friezes (*e.g.* Halebid, 12th c.). In a different way, more classical moulded sets are found in South India or in Cambodia, which are marked simultaneously by a stupendous strength and simplicity which in Cambodia is only slightly tempered by the sculpted ornamentation of some mouldings. See, for instance, the base of the Thanjavur temple or that of the first floor of the Baphuon pyramid (11th c.) to say nothing of the enormous base of the third floor at Angkor Wat (12th c.).

Similar plays of light appear on some curvilinear superstructures, especially in the 11th century. Examples are the towers with many slim levels of some Orissan temples (Bhubaneshwar) or the far more complex web-like ornamentation of Madhya Pradesh temples (Khajuraho). In Tamil Nadu and elsewhere in South India, such plays of light are combined with pseudo-hypostyle façades marked by deep recesses, especially on the ground floor. There, the directrix lines able to catch the light of the sun and to create moving shadows are vertical. The play is based less on the generally high position of the sun in the sky than on its daily rotation around the monument. The show is amplified by the sub-tropical position of that region, which allows that for some months the light comes from the North, catching one unawares. Such vertical plays of shade are seen also in the bas-reliefs gallery bordering the first floor of Angkor Wat. Its double rows of pillars as well as its deepness and the presence of bas-reliefs are like many elements of a continuously performing show.

The changing light of the temple is also that which enters it through a latticed window[2]. In Indian treatises of architecture this is often mentioned in a surprising context: it is then a matter of defining the basic measuring unit, that is to say the smallest speck of dust, which only a very capable *yogin* may perceive in a ray of light entering a dark room through a latticed window. This being the case, there are many types of such windows in the Indian world and most of the time they are provided with

2. Designated in Sanskrit by the words *jāla* or *jālaka* ("web"), this kind of window is generally made up of a fixed stone slab regularly pierced in a decorative way.

geometrically arranged piercing, as different from Cambodia where it is an arrangement with vertical turned bars. There also exists, at least in India, some instances of "narrative" piercing. It could be seen as a pierced stone version of Western stained-glass windows if Indian stone pierced images were not aimed at being seen from *outside* the building, and thus to be a part of the staging of its façades. The most ancient of these narrative latticed windows is found in Lomas Rishi (Fig.52). Others are found, for instance, in the bays of Nivṛttisaṅgameśvara temple in Andhra Pradesh (end of 8th c., Dagens 1984a). The pavilion which is in front of the sanctum of that temple comprises, in addition to its normal axial door, two lateral mock entrances provided with false doors of which the "leaves" are made up of stone slabs pierced according to a geometrical pattern. However, on the outside face of these slabs is applied a Dancing Śiva image sculpted on another slab and pierced in the same way. This image fills up the whole frame of the false-door; thus, one may say that the god is dancing to the daily rhythm in front of the door of his temple. A similar arrangement with two pierced slabs is also set in the side window of the covered passage linking the pavilion and the sanctum: there the image is that of Śiva Tripurāntaka standing on his fighting-chariot and heading towards the city of the Asuras, which he is to destroy. There again, it is an image of the god in movement which has been chosen, most probably for it was well suited to the marked play of shade and light. It is a kind of confirmation of the recurrent impression that ideology is not the only factor when arranging the iconography of a temple.

In place of the Indian latticed window that we have just talked about, the arrangement found in Cambodia shows the frame of a window occupied by a row of vertical bars (sometimes there are two parallel rows). The bars, made of sandstone, have been turned, and are sometimes ornamented with a thin relief decoration which combined with a slim mouldering helps a very fine catching of light. It is obvious that the motif is borrowed from local wooden architecture. The use of stone logically leads to enlarging the diameter of the bars, which results in a decrease of the space between them as well as of the light flow entering through the window, which enforces the analogy of Indian windows. It exists also as false-windows provided with bars. The most sophisticated ones are provided with a real frame and real turned bars, the shadows of which move against the wall, filling up the false bay: this gives a remarkable play of light, of which the best example probably is to be found at Angkor Wat, with the false windows placed upon the blind back façades of the bas-reliefs gallery of the first floor or of the second floor gallery. Later on, at the time of Jayavarman VII, the false windows with turned bars multiply but they are then just sculpted in bas-relief on the stone wall; this practically results in suppressing any play of light. However, the arrangement keeps its interest elsewhere. As a matter of fact, while the false window comprises just sculpted bars, its upper part sometimes is "concealed" by the image of a cloth curtain which may be half lowered or half raised, as one prefers, but which in any case is a fine representation of an interrupted time (see below p.105$).

Water-plays and *Mise en Abyme*

Indispensable as regards a temple's daily life, reservoirs, tanks, ponds, moats and the like also have an important part in its staging. Leaving aside for the moment the special case of Cambodian moats, we are to deal here with reservoirs. Sometimes very big and generally of oblong form, they constitute permanent water reserves which may be used in various ways. Thus, they are sometimes used for the aquatic procession of the god on a raft, often a part of the Grand festival. Sometimes they are also given a sophisticated look such as the one attached to the Sun temple at Modhera (Gujarat, 11th c.). They may also be part of very complex arrangements, as in the nilometer-temples at Angkor. Lastly they may play a role in the display of mythology throughout the sanctuary. A good example of this is provided by some large reservoirs appended to Śiva's temples (for instance at Thanjavur or Cidambaram) and designated by the compound *śivagaṅgā* (literally "Ganges [being on] Śiva"). These fine images of, once again, an 'interrupted time' figure the Ganges (*alias* Gaṅgā goddess) when he/she stayed on the head of Śiva during his/her coming down from heaven to the human world. Let us recall that Śiva then had to intervene in order to prevent the violent fall of the river destroying the Earth.

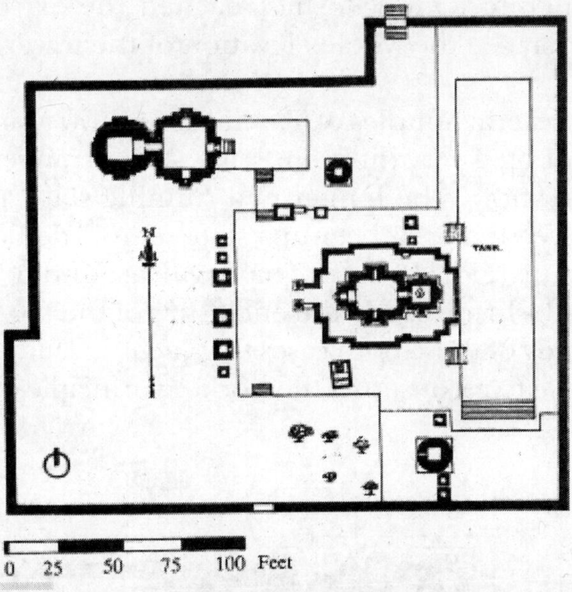

Fig.54. Śiva Mukteśvara Temple (Bhubaneshwar, 9th- 10th c.) ground plan, (SMITH 1994).

These reservoirs sometimes may also be mirrors aimed to reflect the temple itself. At Angkor Wat two tanks are placed at some distance in front the pyramid on both sides of its axis (see ground plan above Fig.44, p.64$). Both of them reflect a nearly complete – even if upside down – image of the mountain-temple in such a way that anyone approaching the temple has in front of him a full representation of a mountain which is to be identified as Mount Meru. This mythic mountain is the *axis mundi* and is supposed to sink below the ground as much as it rises above it. The upside down image reflected by each of the two reservoirs is a perfect representation of the subterranean part of the mountain and perfectly confirms the identity of the temple with Mount Meru and that of the sanctuary which surrounds it with the universe (Dagens 2000). At Bhubaneshwar (Orissa), the Śiva Mukteśvara Temple presents a slightly different case but its aim seems to be the same. Here the oblong tank extends at the back of the temple, just beside the tower which tops its sanctum. One who has reached the extremity of the tank thus may see the whole elevation of the tower reflected in it.

Lastly, several temples of Tamil Nadu show a similar play of mirrors, but on a very different scale. The arrangement which as far as we know is no longer in a running state, may be seen well-preserved in the 12th century state temple dedicated to Śiva at Darasuram (Fig.54) or at Thanjavur around a 17th century Skanda's sub-shrine inside the enclosure of the big Śiva temple. It is on a study of these both cases that Jacques Dumarçay (1996) has been able to reconstitute the working principle of such water-mirrors.

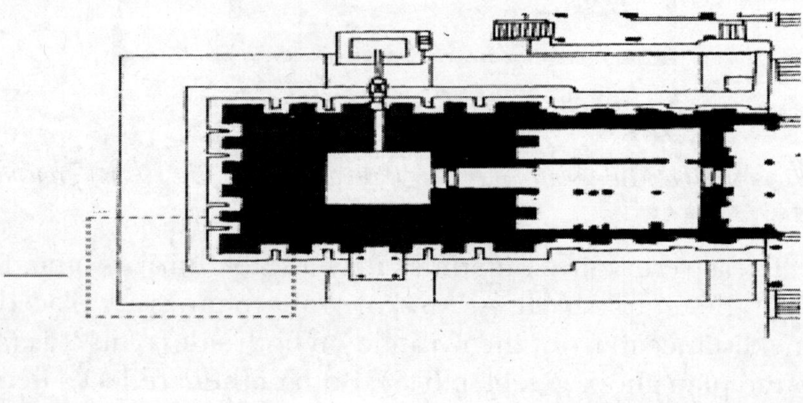

Fig.55. Darasuram: Tower of the main temple as reflected in a water-mirror (Dumarçay 1996 and 2001).

Here it is no more the question of a wide reservoir, but it is just a thin basin of which the bottom is made up by the stone coping of the temple courtyard, while it is bordered by low stone walls around 20 centimetres high. This basin runs around the temple base with two parallel low walls: one juts near the foot of the base while the other makes up the outward limit of the basin, of which the width is no more than ca. 2.5 metres. The outside border is a miniature representation of a temple enclosure wall with a coping bearing regularly spaced images of the god's mount (bulls at Darasuram, but peacocks around Skanda sub-shrine at Thanjavur).

The mock enclosure wall thus figured on the periphery of the mirror transforms the basin and the temple reflection it contains into an extraordinary *mise en abyme* of the full god's sanctuary. This *mise en abyme* supplements as well as enriches the omnipresent one made up by the temple, ornamented by numerous images of itself. However, while in that case the spectators were outside the composition, now it is from the quasi-centre of the sanctuary that they may contemplate a fairly complete image of it. The miniature enclosure bordering the mirror marks the boundaries of the god's estate while the reduced size of the same mirror results in a partial reflection of the building, which naturally gives the illusion of a gigantic temple rising inside the border wall. Various factors were added, such as the lights which probably were surroundings the mirror, thus extending the phenomenon throughout the night, or the basic instability of a water-mirror which suggest an ornamentation of garlands, flags and the like moving in the wind, resulting in a continuously changing performance well described by Jacques Dumarçay in his analysis. Let us add that the spectator is at the same time at the centre of the arrangement – being at the foot of temple – as well as outside of it – being beyond the temple walls. This is to say that – in practice – the devotee is at the start and at the end of the mystical but very real itinerary, which leads him from the border of god's domain marked by the door of the sanctuary entrance-pavilion to the door of the sanctum of the temple itself.

Temple and Space: An Image of the Universe

The temple gives birth to several concentric spaces which fit into each other, with the first of them – the sanctuary – being the only one to be precisely designed and limited. At the same time, numerous details produce an image of a wider ensemble which is more or less consubstantial with the universe. However, such an image is ambiguous, for the majestic greatness of the god requires at the same time that such space extends to the limits of the universe and that it may be contemplated from outside. The fact is that the performance starts before crossing the sanctuary boundaries, sometimes even long before that; from a practical viewpoint, it begins as soon as the presence of the temple is made perceptible either through its tower or through that of an entrance pavilion, which in this case plays the part of a visual substitute.

Reaching the Border

Seen from faraway and, for the time being, from any direction, this first landmark – the tower of the temple or its entrance pavilion – acts as a guide leading to the outermost limit of the sanctuary. However, the first sight changes and becomes more precise as one goes nearer and nearer that limit. In some rare cases, it is the shape of the temple itself which comes into play as learnt from the experience of those who see from faraway the Gangaikondacolapuram temple towering above the Kaveri plain; slowly, its pyramidal mass gets more precise and the extraordinary Liṅga profile looms up and finally suffices to display, by itself, the identity of the god.

Other forms are more anonymous – for instance, that of the Thanjavur temple which, however gigantic the size, limits the options and reduces the doubts . Such a seeming anonymity also concerns huge tower-like entrance pavilions as their fame, more than their aspect or form, allows the attribution from a distance to a particular deity. Dealing with them we have already said that the identification which they convey from a distance is less that of a god than of their patron. On this aspect, the enterprise of King Kṛṣṇadevarāya was an unqualified success. Today, it is without any difficulty that one may pinpoint the temples which he had made the landmarks of his power in Tamil country by providing them with huge towered entrance pavilions.

Other features may suggest the definition of a temple when one nears its sanctuary, as for instance the presence of the god's mount, or of any other mark on the coping of the enclosure wall, or that of large images of his specific door keepers at the door or in the front of the entrance pavilions. More rarely, these are narrative reliefs or images on the outside face of enclosure walls or on the outward façades of entrance-pavilions. Lastly, we are not to forget that an entrance pavilion may reflect the temple itself, as has been already mentioned about Cambodia (see for instance Angkor Wat).

Rites of Passage

The entrance pavilion of the outermost wall which we now reach has a multiple function. First, it is a compulsory passage and viewpoint, but crossing it also corresponds to what may be called a "change of world". Up to there, the progression towards the temple could have been meandering, let us say disorderly. Now the entrance pavilion places the devotee (or the pilgrim) onto the very axis of the temple and the god and thus arranges the passage to a world which is orientated and therefore in line with the universe.

This is important as may be shown in different ways, but we shall once more refer to Cambodia which has, at the same time, both affirmed its own interpretation as well as materialised and made obvious some elements left unsaid in the Indian tradition. In this field, Cambodian architects have made use of the moat with which they duplicate the enclosure wall from outside. While being in its origin a feature pertaining to a non-Indian tradition proper to South-East Asia, the moat has been applied to the rendering of Indian cosmology in a remarkable way.

Being a perfect representation of the ring-shaped ocean which surrounds the universe (or at least its central continent, depending on the cosmological arrangement followed), the moat testifies to the central and special position of the sanctuary the character of which as a divine realm is underlined by a series of metaphors and equivalences which go along with the crossing of the ocean through causeways, and which Paul Mus had splendidly brought to the fore (see above p.54$). Lastly, it must be said that thanks to such causeways, the devotee, even before reaching the entrance-pavilion, is already placed on the axis of the sanctum and that his eyes are then ready to cross the enclosure wall.

At Angkor Wat, where the combination of crossings and viewpoints is perfectly arranged, one progresses on the causeway crossing the moat with the outermost entrance pavilion in front which, as told before, is a perfect representation of the whole pyramid including the towers and gallery with bas-reliefs (p.79-80$). Reaching the end of the causeway at the foot of the entrance pavilion, and through the door of the latter, one perceives the pyramid itself before emerging out of its image and then getting the full view of its magnificence.

According to Indian daily practice, just before entering the door of the sanctuary, the faithful prepares himself for entrance to the god's estate by removing the shoes he possibly wears or, if not, by shaking his feet in order to make them free from road dust. Having performed this act of reverence, he will be able to enjoy the view of the sanctuary.

The Dust upon Pilgrims' Feet

According to tradition some holy places are given the right to receive pilgrims without their needing to perform the basic purification of shaking the dust from their feet. Most such holy places are located in remote places and can be reached only after a long walk; they are defined as *dhūldarśana,* that is to say where one "can see (the god)" (*darśana*) with "(road) dust" (*dhūli*) upon his feet. We were given this explanation at Śrīśailam: the Andhra Pradesh mountain sanctuary dedicated to Śiva, having an enclosure wall of which the gate may be crossed without shaking the road dust. However, according to a tradition attested at least since the 11th century, this temple possesses four cardinal "doors" located far away, the best known of them being the "western door" which would be the sacred city of Alampur located more than 80 kilometres west of Śrīśailam. These four "doors" are since long deemed as the starting places of pilgrims *en route* to Śrīśailam (thus it is from Alampur that King Someśvara 1st started in the 11th c.). One may wonder if the exemption granted to pilgrims at the entrance of the sanctuary was itself not originally justified by the fact that the sanctuary was supposed to extend up to its four "doors", in which case the crossing of the material enclosure wall at Śrīśailam itself would be just the crossing of an inner sub-division of the god's estate.

This being the case, some arrangements have been made in the middle of the 20th c. to bring the temple back to more classical rules. One of them was the organizing of a device for discreetly watering the feet of pilgrims crossing the sill of the door and without their taking any part in the process (Dagens 1984a Vol. I, p.3,33, and 632).

An Infinite or Quasi-Infinite Universe

Once inside the sanctuary precincts, it may take a certain amount of time to reach the temple itself. It all depends upon the size of the sanctuary, the number of concentric enclosures, as well as the stops the devotee may make to honour the deities installed on the way. The foremost of these deities is probably the mount of the god, which is always installed facing its lord on the sanctum axis, and of which the image is often multiplied in order to punctuate various levels on the route to the god.

Various processes are used in order to make the sanctuary an image of a relatively infinite space and thus to extend – visually, at least – the path leading to the god. All such processes are in one way or another based upon perspective effects. Some concern the temple itself and exploit the dimensions of some parts of its tower and/or of some elements of the pyramid on which it rises. Thus, if they are applied to the pyramid they make the temple appear further away in height that it really is, and they do the same for the image of the temple crowning the tower, if they are applied to the latter (see p.36-37$).

Another process concerns the sanctuary more precisely as it is based upon its potential organisation into concentric enclosures. In a centripetal view of the design used in South India, the enclosures and their corresponding tower-like entrance pavilions are of a diminishing height when one proceeds from the entrance of the sanctuary to the door of the central sanctum. To the eyes of the devotee, this progressive reduction makes each of the successive courtyards wider than it really is and thus shows the temple as being further away from the sanctuary entrance that it actually is. Such an illusion is itself reinforced by other perspective effects applied to the tower-like entrance pavilions, as they are to the temple tower.

In both cases, the aim is to show that the centre is farther away from the periphery than it really is, and not the converse. This is important as it reiterates that the main temple performance is at the centre. The lengthening of the approach of the temple in the sanctuary is therefore just an extension of the long pilgrimage which has led the devotee to the entrance of the sanctuary. Now he is guided through the sanctuary to the temple, thus going back to the source of the god's eyes which are his beacon since he entered the sanctuary. As a matter of fact, the itinerary has since long been punctuated by landmarks showing to each devotee, according to his rank, the limit of his approach of the god and his progressive entrance to the performance.

Human Kingdom and the Divine One

When dealing with state temples we had an opportunity to recall how architects cum sculptors of some monuments in Tamil Nadu and Cambodia had been able to transform such state temples into a living image of the real kingdom, of which they were the centre. At Thanjavur, it was the periphery of the kingdom which seemed to have been displayed through the numerous Tripurāntaka statues located on the ground floor façades; provided with arms and ready to fight but at the same time serene, they guard the temple and the kingdom and, at the same time, get ready for the conquest of the surrounding universe. To the contrary, at Angkor Wat it is the kingdom itself which is displayed under the guise of numerous young women who were perhaps shown during a festival. Whichever the case, they certainly illustrate through their diversity and their attire, the provinces of the kingdom. Their images may appear to be haphazardly arranged on the wall but that gives a forceful impression of a life free of worries in a peaceful kingdom.

At Bayon temple, the towers with faces seem to be more hieratic and more regular, but there are various plays of light which liven up those guardians watching in all directions, each over his province, and at the same time over the whole kingdom. Here, it is other parts of the temple – the ground floor galleries – which have been put in charge of showing in a detailed way the peaceful kingdom and the victorious wars of its lord. The whole composition as seen from outside is at the same time supplemented and précised by the sophisticated arrangement of the pantheon housed in the sanctums of face-towered chapels – gods of the kingdom, divinised ancestors of the King, etc. – a pantheon which makes up a court respectfully surrounding the two protagonists: the Buddha housed in the main sanctum and King Jayavarman VII whose statue was in the vestibule of that sanctum and most probably facing the Buddha.

In counterpoint to such sophisticated presentations which, in the case of the Bayon, could even look overloaded, the architect of Kaṇḍarīya Mahādeva Temple at Khajuraho has been able to suggest to the outside world, by just an architectural composition, that the attendants of the god were surrounding him (Fig.29). It is remarkable to see that such simplicity only concerns the divine world and contrasts strongly with the exuberance – which is an understatement – of the human world, for which were reserved the most conspicuous parts of the temple façades. Michael Meister has shown that behind this exuberance was to be seen an elaborate play of equivalence between human unions and articulation of architectural parts of the temple, the vocabulary of human passion meeting that of architectural forms (Meister 1979).

Performance and Time

When speaking about plays of light connected with daily or annual courses of the sun or about various rhythms marking rites, we had noted that the temple performance was able to follow the course of natural time. Thereafter, in this chapter as in the preceding ones, we have alluded to historical time and to the many ways it may intervene in the temple life. It may do so naturally in the temple's rise or possibly its decline, but also in the definition of its titular god, or even its obedience or its political exploitation, etc. We must also add that to speak of its "necessary beauty" (see above) is just a reminder that the temple is contingent in this field, like in others, to the "fashions" which are just an obvious manifestation of historic time.

Here we shall lay stress on the idea of duration, which is to be seen at various levels. First, it will be about the festive time and the possibility of making it permanent by "petrifying" the celebration and thus setting it up for the long run. Thereafter we shall shift to the historical time by underlining the constructive role of a "time-keeper" often played by the temple in the Indian world. On this point it may be useful to recall that the temple can play its role because it is by essence a building, simple or complex, but made up of materials which are, in principle, durable and in any case more durable than most of the surrounding constructions of civil architecture.

Petrified Festival or the Interrupted Time[3]

We have already underlined the metaphorical importance of plants in the temple founding rites as well as in its ornamentation. Sown as a plant, the temple is to grow like a gigantic lotus made up of many piled up layers of doucines and covered by numerous long scroll-works running on the walls and sometimes spreading out as magnificent volutes, for instance at corners of dripstones. If plants are thus not dissociable from temple ornamentation, it is because they are also integral parts of its daily or festive life.

- Plants, from Daily Rites to Festival

Every morning the priest, once he has entered the sanctum, is to expertly renew the flower which must permanently stay on top of the Liṅga. He removes the old flower and places the new one with a single motion and in such a way that the Liṅga's head is never "void", as is said in treatises. Every day, the numerous garlands which so completely cover the god that they almost fully conceal him are to be changed. However, every time some ceremony that is out of the ordinary is to be performed,

3. Here again I am indebted to Jacques Dumarçay for this notion of the time being switched off by the petrifaction of the festival (see especially his *Babel ruinée* [1996], p.36 and following).

and naturally at the time of great festivals, it is the temple itself which is to be ornamented. This concerns at least the doors, those of the temple itself as well as of the pavilion(s) which is or are to be used, whether they are permanent features or just light temporary sheds built for the occasion. Each time, the door is to be framed by an arch made up of palms or foliage or sometimes by two plantain tree trunks. To these are to be added garlands either made up only of leaves tied to a string or far more sophisticated, the main thing being – as in the case of the flower on the Liṅga – that fresh plants still full of sap are to be used to render the temple festive and lively.

- *Petrified Plants, Makara, and Curtain*

In India, it is from very early times that temporary and perishable festive ornamentation was petrified on temple walls without, however, getting out of the habit of fresh ornaments. This phenomenon is most conspicuous above the doors – these being real as well as "false". The decorative arch made of plants already mentioned is thus rendered by a more or less curved and sophisticated cross-piece – just a beam or a kind of foliage torus – from which hang all kinds of garlands and pendants. Due to a strange blend of categories, this cross-piece sprouts from the mouths of two monsters standing on tops of door posts: they are those *makaras* derived from crocodiles, of which we have mentioned the first apparition on precisely the door of the Loma Ṛishi cave temple and of which the tail often becomes a magnificent plant scroll. We find this composition in one form or another throughout India and also in South East Asia, where it is submitted to an interesting development under the guise of "ornamental lintel", the evolution of which is one of the guidelines of the art history of ancient Cambodia.

If we give a special place to Cambodia, it is that the stopping of time, which may be suggested through the petrifaction of festive ornaments of doors, is also implied through another image already mentioned, which appears on façades at the end of 12th century. It concerns the false-windows which are provided with vertical sculpted bars and which are partially closed by a sculpted cloth curtain half unfurled or half furled. If the unchanging freshness of petrified plants which ornaments the door nicely underlines that time has been stopped and that the festival is thus permanent, the curtain comes just to specify which moment has been chosen for that stop: not too early and not too late, in the middle of the morning or the afternoon. Thus the image suggests the permanence of a privileged instant which may concerns several types of time – festive, but also daily, or even cosmic as is proposed by Jacques Dumarçay who sees it as an opening on a new creation, thus linking the Cambodian window to the main Indian cyclical rhythm.

- *Festive Elephants and Chariots*

Coming back to India, we may see that placing the temple in a period through the stopping of time does not uniquely concern the plant realm and the glorification of the temple by its festive ornamentation. In the courtyard of the Kailāsanātha Temple at Ellora we have mentioned elephants stopped in their procession around the temple while in the Vaithala Temple at Vijayanagar there is the Garuḍa chariot, ready to move in procession in front of the temple of Viṣṇu.

However it is at Thanjavur that the phenomenon is most evident, and if we have a late example there, it concerns the Skanda chapel built in the 17th century in the north-west corner of the temple precincts and which we have already mentioned when dealing with water-mirrors. The open porch of the pavilion which is in front of that chapel is designed as a chariot drawn by two horses which would move towards the east, as would be the case of a vehicle going right around the Śiva temple. Thus here the chariot, ready to start, is just waiting the placing on it of Skanda's statue. Then, the suggestion is that it will go in a procession and move around the temple of Śiva, father of Ṣkanda. Here we are at the limit between a "petrified festival"

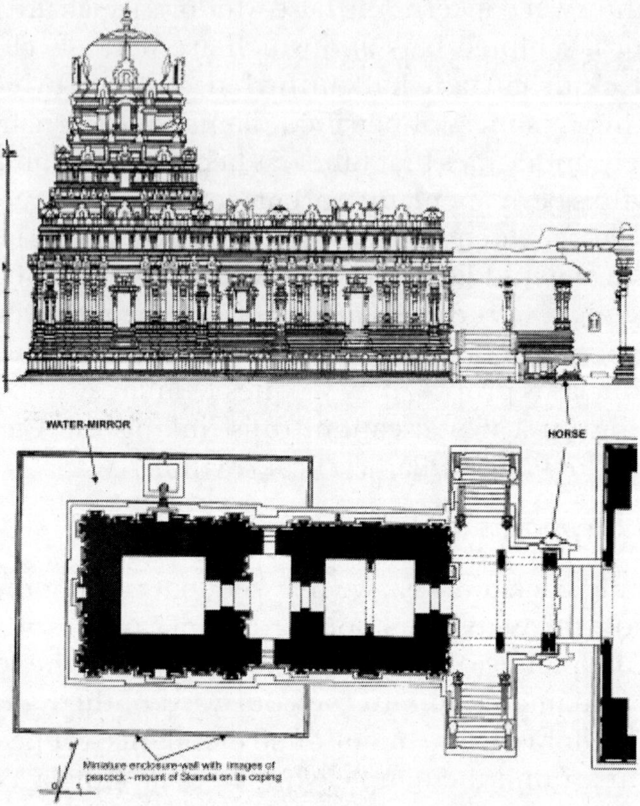

Fig.56. Thanjavur: Skanda's chapel (17th c., north-west corner of Śiva's temple courtyard) (PICHARD 1995). Behind images of horses, may be seen toothing stones which correspond to the place where the chariot wheels were sculpted. As regards the water-mirrors, see above.

and the staging of mythology as mentioned earlier about Tripurāntaka's chariot at Darasuram (see p.45-46$), but also very similar to what is represented by the famous seven horse chariot of the Sun at Konarak (see Dagens 2009c, Fig.9). As a matter of fact, it would be possible to imagine that Skanda in the Thanjavur chapel plays his role of head of the gods' army and which is just entering the battle. This would be all the more so since some Skanda images are inspired by those of Śiva Tripurāntaka (L'Hernault 1978, p.160). Lastly, the choice between the festive and mythological interpretation is of little importance, for in both cases the time is stopped, the main difference being that this stop is very common in iconography but far less when it is a question of stopping the real time and not the mythological one.

Temple as Time-keeper

- About the Value of Architectural Testimony

Its construction with heavy and everlasting materials makes the temple a perfect witness of its time. It brings evidence of its religious choices, aesthetic tastes, or technical capacities. Its evidence may be distorted in many ways at the level of interpretation – the examples are numerous – but as far as we are concerned it may be said *a priori* that the witness is never deliberately lying, as was the case with the Goanese temples, of which we have seen that they were meant to be deceptive.

What possibly could be similar to fabricated evidence would be the "return to the antique" which is however most often an emphatic reference to the past, deemed as better. It is a common case in Indian the world, for instance the adoption of Gupta forms again in India at the end of 1st millenary or the use of Cālukya, Pallava, and Cola formal lexicons later by Vijayanagar builders. In South-East Asia, where the phenomenon is more obvious, its interpretation may lead to questions. Thus Cambodian architects of the second half of the10th century built the mountain-temples of Pre Rup or Ta Kèv with clear reference to a model belonging to the very beginning of the same century (Phnom Bakheng, above p.57$, Fig.37); while doing so, they brushed aside the original creations of the intermediary period (called as "Koh Ker period", ca. 921-944) during which a so-called "usurper" left Angkor in order to build a new capital one hundred kilometres away. As a result the very original state temple built at Koh Ker was to remain as a *hapax* without any issue in the quite coherent lineage of these kinds of monuments.

Like in Goa, we would be faced with an eminently political phenomenon, which in the present case would consist of a rewriting of history with omissions, and that by the order of the King cum patron!

- *A Dynamic Testimony*

While being a witness from the time of its foundation, the temple also reports – we may say in its flesh – its own architectural history and through that the history of architecture as well as that of the sculpture which naturally goes with it. We have already mentioned that in this field the richness of the testimony is not necessarily at the level of the complex life of the temple. We shall not go back to Angkor Wat and the poverty of its architectural history other than to link that poverty with a testimony of the powerful perfection of the foundation by King Sūryavarman II; the 16th century Buddhist inscriptions found at Angkor Wat designate the temple, which at that time had become a Buddhist one, with the extremely Vaishnavite name of its Vaishnavite founder ("the Saint [who after his death has gone to] Viṣṇu's world"). Things are obviously very different at Tiruvannamalai, the architectural history of which looks like a catalogue of all the forms which have been successively favoured by temple builders in Tamil Nadu from the 11th c. up to now (even if the monument as it appears now was practically already existing in the 17th c., with however some supplementary works being done nearly every year since then). There is nothing exceptional in that. Srirangam temple for instance was founded around the 11th or 12th c. but the construction work of its tallest entrance pavilion (ca. 72 m. in height) ended only in 1987, when it was inaugurated. In the mean time construction works in the temple were never stopped for a long period, some of these testifying that the history of this temple was not always a religious one. In the 18th century, during the Franco-English wars in South India, the temple was for a time a fortress which enemies were alternately occupying...

- *Temple and Epigraphy*

In India, like elsewhere, a temple is again a time-keeper through its epigraphy. Here again the fact that it is built with lasting materials evidently drives it to be used to ensure the protection of important texts. Beside those which are engraved on its walls, there are often found inscribed steles which however may be quite easily separated from the architectural context to which they were connected at the start; thus, we shall not deal with them, any more than with the copper-plates and other mobile archives which may be entrusted to temple safekeeping or more precisely to its staff, for which the uncertainty is even more blatant.

Therefore, only the texts inscribed on the temple walls remain, most of which were the temple archives. As regards the construction works, it is noticeable that such inscriptions deal less with them than with the restoration and addition operations performed afterwards. Thus, at Thanjavur, none of the inscriptions has for their main object the commemoration of the temple's founding by Rājarāja I,. while a text from 1801-1802 underlines the repairs and building of some pavilions at that time. In fact, archive inscriptions of the Thanjavur temple mainly commemorate the gifts bestowed to the temple itself (objects, lands, funds). Sometimes the records are organised in a very systematic way: thus, in the year following the inauguration of the Thanjavur temple, an order of its founder rules that all gifts offered to the temple by him or others are to be commemorated on the wall of the temple. This results in a long summary statement with precise dates and followed by a supplementary summary engraved some years later (*S.I.I.* Vol. II).

These archives, which were more often written in the local vernacular than in Sanskrit, are good testimonies to the popularity of a temple and what we have already mentioned about state temples may also be said for others. Thus, if the corpus of the Thanjavur temple inscriptions amounts to around one hundred texts, it looks slim when compared with those of Tiruvannamalai (around 500 texts) or Tirupati (around 700). Concerning the Tirupati temple which is deemed since several centuries to be the richest temple in India, the publication of its epigraphic corpus in the year 1930 was partly meant to help the reconstitution of an inventory of the temple's land properties.

However, a temple is not only its own time keeper. There is no ambiguity when it so happens that some texts are inscribed on its walls which are not directly linked to it, but to which one may wish to give someseriousness and authenticity. Thus, in the 13th century, three feudatory dependants of the King inscribed a text on the Thanjavur temple wall in which, while proclaiming their fidelity to the King, they also asserted their perfect harmony, using terms which the author of "The Three Musketeers" would have much appreciated ("who becomes enemy to one of us be the enemy of us three, who becomes the friend of one of us, be the friend of us three", *S.I.I.* Vol. II). Let us add that the celebration of temple benefactors or sometimes the very minute presentation of the circumstances in which some gifts were offered, are as much occasions to place the temple's performance in its history.

- *Troubled Times*

We have already alluded to the fact that a temple is an excellent archivist of the misfortunes that have taken place, or is the witness, or which it has itself endured. For instance, we may mention that recurring theme in numerous Hindu temples of Tamil Nadu, which is the impaling of 8000 Jains at Madurai around the end of first millenary. The fact that this event's historicity has been debated does not detract from the realism of the bloody frescoes celebrating the victory of Hinduism upon a heterodox religion. We shall not go back here to the savage conversion to Śaivism of Bayon, the state temple of Jayavarman VII, and of other Buddhist temples built by the same sovereign.

However, it shall be reminded that it is due to their complete destruction that some temples give evidence of History and – it may be said – makes History. Thus, the destruction of the Rāma temple at Ayodhya (Uttar Pradesh) by Babur in 1528 led to putting a part of India to fire and sword in the nineties. The "Ayodhya Affair", as it was called, has brought to memory similar events and particularly one of the most famous, the plundering and destruction of the Śiva Somanātha Temple in Gujarat by Mahmud of Ghazni in 1026. A research work authored by Romila Thapar (2004) has brought to light interesting and sometimes surprising results. Systematically using the entirety of ancient sources, she has first noted that the event itself is in reality described only in Turco-Iranian sources, that is to say in Moslem ones. On the other side it is obvious, according to Sanskrit inscriptions, that the Somnath temple which was a highly popular pilgrimage before 1026, was again the same some years later and in the following century. Lastly, at the beginning of 19th century, the colonial power using Moslem sources affirms what would become the official doctrine on the subject, which is that the Somnath destruction had provoked a visceral hatred of the Moslems amongst the Hindus. If the colonial power then presented the 19th century Afghan wars as a revenge for Mahmud's raid, Hindu nationalism made use of that raid which led in 1951 to the rebuilding of the Somnath temple (see above). Romila Thapar ends her study by a tentative history of the political exploitation of the temple – possibly through its plundering or its destruction – a history of which the last episode is, for the time being, the "Ayodhya Affair"

Chapter VIII

Temple's Travels or the Indian Temple Throughout the World

Introduction

The Indian temple has travelled throughout India and outside India, and it still does. In India itself, this has been a continuous process since the time of its invention, when it resulted in multiplication of regional models and when that already appeared which, one and a half decade ago, I had called "Brownian movement", a characteristic of temple architecture history in India, a kind of intense intermixing which insured the continuity of truly Indian architecture and sculpture and the mutual enrichment of those regional models (Dagens 1993). More recently, these travels possibly led to the out of context transfer of some rather typical regional models; thus, the Pan-Indian attraction of the holy city of Varanasi results in the rather exhaustive panorama of Indian temple architecture which may be seen there and which is parallel to the diversity of pilgrims who converge there.

Travels of the temple outside India are both an old and recent phenomenon, for the Indian diaspora has always travelled with its gods and for whom it has built temples, even if some characteristics of this phenomenon have changed since ancient times. In the past, this dissemination of the temple quickly and nearly everywhere combined with an implantation of Indian religions in native societies, which resulted in the appearance of powerful "national" schools with well established independence, not however concealing the underlying presence of an "Indian model". This is obvious in South-East Asia with some exceptions, while it is perhaps a little softened in Central Asia, reached through Afghanistan and Northern Pakistan passes. This being the case, Indian religions – except Buddhism - break off at the doors of China and the Indian temple as such does not enter into the Chinese world, any more than in the Sinicized Far-East, throughout Central Asia or South-East Asia. On the whole, Asian countries which had adopted Indian religions abandoned them all around the 15th century – again apart from Buddhism.

In modern times, new implantations of Indian temple in foreign societies occur in the narrow framework of a diaspora which now covers the five continents, without however arousing an attraction similar to that which in the past had drastically changed the religious and cultural scenery of a big part of Asia. As in the old times, travellers arrive with their gods to whom they build temples which – whenever it is possible – are similar to those they were attending in India. Sometimes, a temple is fully imported as was the case some decades ago of a temple built in Great Britain, but all the stones of which had been cut, dressed, and sculpted at Mahabalipuram. The work of assembling or building on the spot is then generally directed by a traditional architect brought from India for the occasion (see for instance the Goddess temple at Bangkok). This being the case, it happens that for want of anything better the worship is organised – at least for some time - in some building where a room is said to be the sanctum and arranged as such, which may however amount to very little (see for instance the former Gaṇeśa temple in Paris near Porte de la Chapelle).

Here we shall not attempt to follow the temple in all its travels, nor present in details the various forms it might have, or may still take, throughout the world. Rather, we shall try to see which are the whys and wherefores of its travels, and especially which vectors played a part in the process and how this has been adapted to various cultural and geographical contexts.

Prolegomena

Temple's Continuity

It seems that throughout all its travels the Indian temple has remained itself and, we may say, true to the functional definition we have given it at the start of this work. Speaking thus, we mean that it has not undergone basic changes nor given birth to non-religious architectural forms. On these points it differs from the stūpa, another architectural manifestation of an Indian religion. Specific to Buddhism, this monument is a massive structure derived from tumulus which in the Sinicized world has become the "pagoda", a slender tower provided with multiple storeys and an internal stairway, an architectural feature perfectly fit for Buddhist meditation techniques. Nothing similar exists as regards the temple, which has always remained centred on its sanctum, in spite of various garbs given to it. Amongst very few noticeable exceptions is the Thai Buddhist *prang* which however is more a stūpa variation based on the temple than a derivation from the temple. The temple has been able to inspire some civilian monuments like parts of the cultural patchwork that is Lutyens' NewDelhi, or various world-fair pavilions, or, even, the Independence Monument at Phnom Penh which is just a modern variation of the Banteay Srei 10th century temple. However, things stop here and the temple has not given birth to any architectural model as perfectly non-religious as the pagoda, when it spread through Western countries in the 18th century as an ornament for pleasure gardens.

As a matter of fact, the Indian temple has always been strongly related to the practice of the religion for which it was created, even if Buddhism may look as a special case as we shall see below. We have already said that attempts to adapt the temple to Christianity always pertained to the domain of disguise. As regards Islam, it discovered how to create its own Indian architecture and lexicon of forms, as is well proved by the funerary mosques or the palaces, but this was without any relation to the temple even if some technical details may connect them. An example is the vaulted covering which is used mainly for temple annexes but not for the temple itself as was noticed by James Prinsep at the beginning of the 19th century (see below p.119$).

Buddhism and Temple

Buddhism appeared at the very time when the establishment of necessary conditions for the invention of the temple was forthcoming. Atheistic at the start, the Buddhist movement has known a rapid evolution and therefore has, from very early times, shared the use of the temple with the other main Indian religious trends, once it had invented the stūpa. We must look again at this aspect, for it is most probably behind the origin of an important characteristic of the arrangement of the sanctuary, that is to say the implicit or practical concentric pattern, the guiding role of which we have been able to underline several times.

As regards the stūpa, it is well known that an early usage was to surround the monumental ones, especially the most important and most prestigious ones, with smaller votive stūpas sometimes housed in chapels (in which they may possibly be replaced by images). A good example may be found at Taxila around the Dharmarājika stūpa, the construction of which is ascribed to Aśoka (see the ground plan given in Marshall 1960). Later, this pattern took the shape of a cloister-like row of chapels surrounding a stūpa, as may be seen in several monastic compounds at Taxila or in the well known monastery of Takht-i Bahi near Peshawar. This last composition itself is probably derived from the arrangement of the living quarters in monasteries, where a row of cells borders an inner courtyard, an arrangement which most probably goes back to the beginnings of Buddhism. Transferred from the surrounding of stūpas to that of temples, such cloister-like compositions were to meet great success in Brahmanical as well as Buddhist monuments, be it in India or in South-East Asia (above p.59$).

While Buddhism thus introduced the pattern of concentric radiance in the sanctuary and outside it, it also became more theistic and ritualistic. This led it to adopt the temple and there the images of the Buddha started to replace stūpas as cult-objects in elongated two-function sanctums (for some time in the beginning, the statue was standing against the stūpa) as well as in ordinary regular ones. Together with the temple, Buddhism adopted practices very similar to those followed in Brahmanical institutions. This trend which originally was favoured mainly in Mahayanistic circles has become general. Nowadays, the visitor to the temple at Kandy where a tooth of Buddha is kept is surprised to attend ceremonies very difficult to distinguish from those performed in the nearby Hindu temple.

In India proper, the best known example of this kind of Buddhist monument is the so-called Mahābodhi temple built around the 6th c. A.D. at Bodhgaya, the place where Buddha received his awakening. This temple had replaced a former hypaethral monument (p.12-13$) and has, since then, been rebuilt and transformed several times. The present-day building has a height of more than 50 metres and its truncated pyramid-like tower is endowed with typical vertical directrix lines. Rough copies of it exist in Thailand and in Burma and some ruined temples at the main Buddhist site of Nalanda (Bihar) were probably following the same model (see Krishnā Dev in Meister & Dhaky 1988).

When the Indian temple travelled to Central Asia (3rd c. A.D.) and to South-East Asia (ca 5th-6th c.) it had already been adopted by Buddhism. In Central Asia it often houses a stūpa and is characterized by Iranian and regional technical practices. To the Iranian heritage is owed a frequent use of vaults or cupolas, while the regional influence is marked by a systematic use of adobe and unbaked bricks which results in very thick walls, as well as by a recourse to wooden frameworks and, lastly, by a major importance given to earthen statues and wall paintings (Franz 1979).

Things are different in South-East Asia where important variations exist from one region to the other. Thus Cambodia and Champa had, so to speak, ignored the stūpa up to the 15th century and until that period their Buddhist architecture is limited to temples which may be distinguished from the Brahmanical ones only through their iconography. Indonesia, which did not ignore the stūpa – see the magnificent one at Borobudur – united it with the temple in regard to roofing; see Candi Sewu, Candi Kalasan, Candi Plaosan, etc. As for Burma, in a systematic way it used the combination of temple and stūpa, especially at Pagan, and always in a Theravādin context, contrary to Indonesia where it was Mahayanistic. In Thailand, during the post-Angkorean period were developed huge worship halls with a double function, but also some new shapes, the most common of them being the already mentioned *prang*, which gives to the stūpa a form derived from the Cambodian version of the Indian temple (see above p.42$). Other temples such as that of Wat Si Chum at Sukhotai are provided with a sanctum topped by a slender tower-like roof with false-storeys which bring it all the more closer to the Chinese pagoda, since it is provided with an internal stairway, a fine upward meditation itinerary as its ceiling is ornamented with pious images.[1]

Temple Travels throughout India

Having appeared in Northern India around the 4th century B.C., the temple, a little less than half a millenary later is firmly

1. See in Skilling 2008, the Wat Si Chum restitution proposed by Pierre Pichard and our remarks on the subject in *Aséanie*, Vol.23 (2009).

established in the whole Indian sub-continent where it is framed into well defined regional schools. This phenomenon may be deemed as achieved around the 5th century A.D., but the temple by then had already started to spread in the same way beyond the seas. Let us add that this chronology regarding temple travels is approximate and that it concerns the appearance of clearly defined architectural forms but not the previous arrival of the religious faith which gave birth to them. However, the spread of the temple throughout India is far from being a linear process, for while following the religious doctrines it falls within the scope of many different regional contexts, accompanied by several factors which may be political, technical, etc.

Regional Exchanges

We shall examine here again one of the best characterized exchange areas in the historical geography of India, namely the axis made up by the Krishnā and Tungabhadra rivers and crossing the Indian peninsula in its middle from West to East (Dagens 1993). Around 540-550, the Western Cālukya kings had installed their capital at Badami (Karnataka) between the two rivers; then, from the beginning of 7th century they collide (in every sense of the word) with the Pallavas of Kancipuram who were ruling the area south of the Krishnā. The Cālukya architecture is singular, as it uses both the curvilinear tower which will never go further to the South and the false-storeys which it shares with the Pallava school. However, it is clear that the bond behind their initial rendering of the false-storey type is more at the level of cousinhood than of filiation, and that it is more the result of descent from the same ancestor. Things become more complex when a Cālukya king, having for a time occupied Kancipuram, the capital city of the Pallavas, makes one of his queens build in his own capital, Pattadakal, a state temple which was clearly inspired by the Kailāsanātha state temple at Kancipuram, while being bigger. More than that and this is probably more important, that Virūpākṣa temple at Pattadakal is marked by changes regarding the proportions of the false storeys and arrangement of façade pilasters. Both are nearer to the Pallava model than to the previous Cālukya buildings. Such a transformation is an interesting symbol, as it underlines a real annexation of the Pallava model and does so in a conclusive way, for the new characteristics will now be found in all creations having a false-storey option. This was due to the successors of the Cālukya dynasty either at the end of 8th century to the north of the Krishnā-Tungabhadra axis (see for instance Kailāsanātha temple at Ellora), or later within that axis itself in Andhra Pradesh during the Vijayanagar period, when the Hindu tradition would be asserted in front of a rising Islam.

Interesting though it is, this meeting of the two regional traditions however does not allow finding out the source of the false-storey tower, any more than that of the hypostyle option, both of which at that time went together, even if less systematically structured in the Cālukya area than in the Pallava model. We had previously been interested by the fact that the Pallava architects cum sculptors seemingly wanted to conceal the stone under the wood; one may wonder if the reason for this is not to be found in the closeness of the assumed wooden model, but this is no more than a hypothesis. As for the arrangement of false storeys, the idea that it first appeared in some buildings (now ruined) of Central India (see p.39$) is again no more than a hypothesis and, as a matter of fact, does not offer any hint to explain why its success exclusively remains a southern and overseas phenomenon.

Adaptation to Environment

Adaptation of the temple to a particular geographical environment is another noteworthy phenomenon, for which fine testimonies are found in Kerala and Nepal. In Kerala, where the rains are torrential and forests rich in wood for timberwork, wood is introduced into an architecture which pretends to be built with that material and which will not renounce that pretence even after such an introduction. Thus, the temple in Kerala follows the pseudo-hypostyle and false storey option borrowed from nearby Tamil Nadu but combines it either with a timber-work roof which envelops the whole structure (Fig.57) or with a similar roof above the attic (or the upper false storey) supplemented with a lean-to roof at the level of entablature (see a similar Nepalese arrangement in Fig.58). Inside the temple, the sanctum may be provided with a stone or wooden ceiling, or else just covered by the intrados of a timber-work roof. Lastly, a curtain-wall or a wooden partition generally bears the eaves of the enveloping roof and thus delimits the outwork ambulatory.

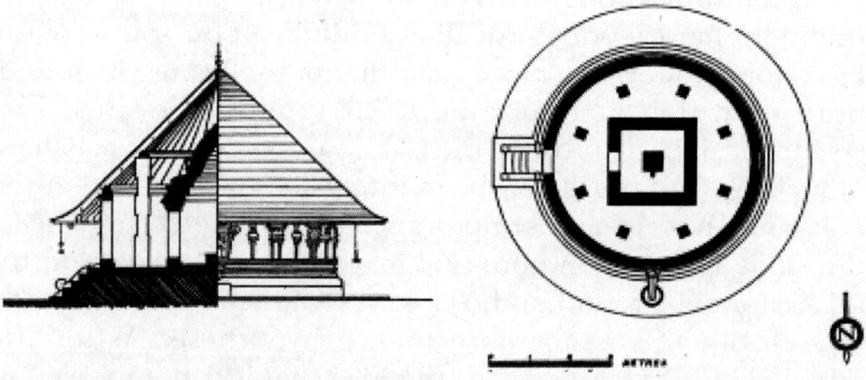

Fig.57. Śiva Temple at Mitranandapuram (Trivandrum, Kerala, 12th c.) (RAJAN 1974). An intermediary row of pillars bears the middle of the rafters of an enveloping roof and their eaves are supported by the peripheral curtain wall.

The interpretation of the false-storey option in Nepal is quite similar to that found in Kerala. However, wooden parts are far more important on the façades and while the arrangement of the outwork ambulatory is not very sophisticated, the use of widely overhanging roofs has led to placing of struts which also make fine iconographic supports (Juramie 2001). Another singularity of the Nepal architecture is seen in the many forms which are given to the Indian temple (*ibidem*, Vol. 2, *passim*). Variations regarding curvilinear towers are especially noteworthy since they are based upon a common North India model, possibly singularised by a timber-work roof crowning the tower.

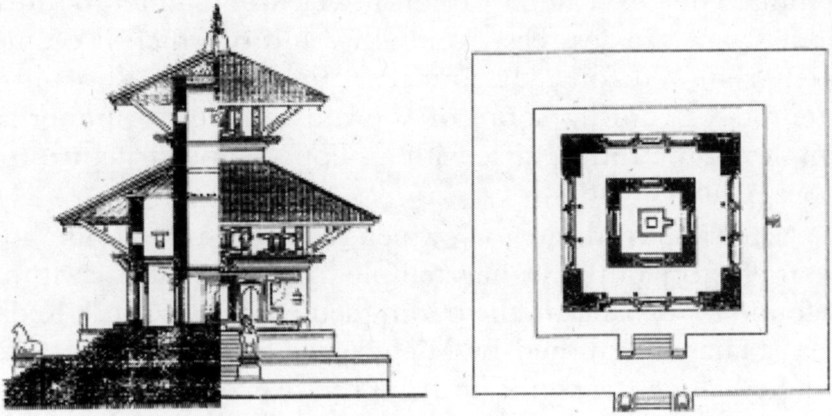

Fig.58. Car Narayan Temple at Patan (Nepal) (according to JURAMIE *2001). The long struts bearing the eaves of roofs are noteworthy.*

Travels outside India and Vectors' Problem

In ancient times, temple travels outside India were mainly headed toward Central and South-East Asia. Central Asia has already been dealt with when looking at Buddhist temples and we shall not look at it again. On the contrary, we shall go through some details regarding South-East Asia where native versions of the Indian temple appear from the 6th century A.D. in various countries. These countries were producing original interpretations, which however presuppose a prehistory for which direct testimonies are lacking.

What Could Become the Indian temple in South-East Asia?

In ancient South-East Asia, there appear three main categories of "Indian" temples, which however are unevenly present. The most frequent category concerns well determined productions of the various native schools, which can be said to be at the same time in perfect harmony with the Indian normative tradition and, simultaneously, absolutely unthinkable in India. The next category refers in a clearer manner to Indian models more or less easy to identify and of which it offers a partly renewed form. It concerns, for instance, short-lived attempts of roofing some of the most ancient Cambodian temples in the Indian style with a stepped superstructure (see above p.40$).

As for the third category, which can offer some hints about the prehistory of the Indian temple in South-East Asia, it may be found for instance in the trading settlements of South-Kedah area (Malaysia) studied by Michel Jacq-Hergoualc'h (1992). Installed along rivers not far from the sea coast, these trading points were ruled by a native and non-Indianized elite and were frequented by foreign traders, comprising Hindu or Buddhist Indians. The "Indian" temples intended for such Indian traders and often installed at out of the way places, were basic buildings of which the only remains are usually moulded (or not) bases in bricks or lateritic stone. Various pieces of evidence lead us to believe that such bases were supporting rough walling or similar masonry work maintained by a wooden framework. As for the Hindu or Buddhist religious persuasion of each temple, it may be asserted only through the archaeological context (statues, inscriptions, etc.). It has been suggested that some technicians in charge of the worship also looked at the construction of these temples (*ibidem*), which is possible. However these monuments look more like the result of orders placed with native builders by foreign patrons settled in the area since some time and anxious to practice their faith in appropriate buildings of worship. Their requirements were most probably limited to accordance with some rules which made the buildings fit for worship, which possibly needed the presence of a qualified priest. However, there is no indication of the presence of any

Indian builder who would have given instructions for using Indian forms, which appear to be very scarce if not nonexistent.

The main interest of the third category of temple is to show what the Indian temple in South-East Asia would have been if it had remained as just the product of an order passed to a native craftsman by a foreigner – an Indian - if that magnificent alchemy had not occurred through which an "Indian model" arrived in South-East Asia, and was re-invented there through its contact with each of the various cultural idioms which were accommodating it. One of the factors of this re-invention was that the patron was not an Indian trader but a native who had made an Indian religion his own by integrating it in his own way of thinking. Such a patron needed a temple which complied with a model proper to the Indian religion he had adopted and, at the same time, was "beautiful" in his own eyes, a necessity *per se* as we have seen.

We shall not here attempt to explain in detail how that alchemy was working but only examine how the requirements for its functioning were met, that is to say which the vectors of the model were, on which the re-invention was based. In thus doing, we shall re-use with complements and rectifications the results of a previous study dealing mainly with entrance pavilions (Dagens 1994).

Travelling Architects or Travelling Treatises?

When one wonders about the origin of Indian temples found in South-East Asia, the simplest answer is that their architecture is based upon that of temples built by Indian architects. We have already emphasized that nowadays the Indian diaspora often calls upon metropolitan architects and we may surmise that in the past also, during the first centuries A.D., Indian traders acted similarly as soon as their numbers increased and their stay overseas tended to continue. The temples which were built thus would have been used as basic models by the native architects engaged to build "Indian temples", which had progressively known a kind of emancipation by taking into account several regional data – religious, aesthetic, and technical. As a matter of fact, the phenomenon would have been the same as the one which occurred in the case of palaeography: all the "native" scripts used in South-East Asia were derived from Indian scripts which have been transformed and modified in order to be in a position to transcribe Sanskrit as well as the local vernacular, the last never being a part of the Indo-Aryan family.

If a similar process seems perfectly possible, it appeared to us that it was not sufficient to account for some characteristics of Indian temples from South-East Asia, the characteristics which we had identified when dealing with Cambodia and found again elsewhere. It was obvious that in the background of these Cambodian (or other) temples was a kind of model made idealistic by its perfection and which could not simply be the fruit of a local adaptation of a temple built by an Indian. This being the case, that model possibly could be found in those normative treatises which we presented in the first pages of this book. The theory of the temple which they enunciate is both simplifying and unifying, which makes it a fine basis for the idealistic model we were looking after.

Launched on this hypothesis, the study of the specific case of entrance pavilions has shown that an apparently nonsensical option followed by the Cambodians by turning these monumental gateways into chapels could be explained by a literal interpretation of theoretical data found in Indian normative treatises. As a matter of fact, these texts use in a very systematic way the nomenclature usually applied to temples when they describe the entrance-pavilions, regarding which it is ruled that they are to be "like temples". Thus, the terms which usually designate the sanctum of the temple (*garbhagṛha*, *nālīgṛha*) are here applied to the passage going through the pavilion. Such polysemy combined with the ruling we have just mentioned have led Cambodian architects to convert the passage into a sanctum and then to create in the entrance pavilion itself two lateral corridors in order, most certainly to create new passages for crossing the enclosure wall by circumventing the one which has been made a sanctum (see for instance the Thommanon entrance pavilion in Fig.59/B). Sometimes, the bypassing of the sanctum goes through a simple door pierced in the wall beside the entrance pavilion (but that door does not exist in most of the cases).

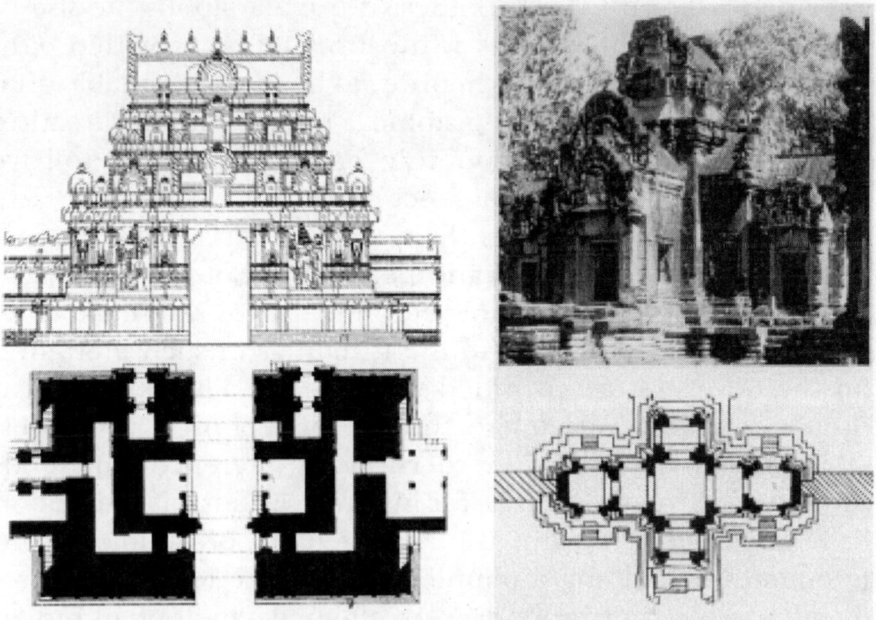

Fig.59. Entrance pavilions at Thanjavur (left) and Thommanon (right) (Pichard 1995, Dumarçay 1988). The central passage of the Thanjavur entrance pavilion is closed by an only door while that of Thommanon (Angkor, 12th c.) is provided with a door and a porch at each of its two extremities and with two side doors leading to the wings where are located the lateral passages bypassing the sanctum. The superstructure of the Thommanon pavilion is a simple arrangement with a two-slopped roof while at Thanjavur it is "alike that of a temple", which temple would be an oblong one.

This literal interpretation is not surprising for it was well in line with the tendency of rendering in a very concrete way abstract Indian concepts, a tendency which is very widespread in South-East Asia. Several examples of this have been already given in preceding chapters; we may add here that of the openwork stūpas housing a statue of Buddha at Borobudur, an arrangement which is nothing other than a physical rendering of the identity of Buddha and the stūpa. Lastly, in our opinion this idea of a literal transfer from the abstract to the concrete goes perfectly with the hypothesis we make about the use of such treatises: these texts while not being provided with illustrations however need, in order to be understandable, that their reader proceed to a graphical interpretation (treatises themselves often insist strenuously that the architect is to have a good knowledge of drawing technicalities).[2]

Our hypothesis naturally assumes that such technical treatises have been known and perused in South-East Asia. If on the one hand we have not yet found a clear reference to an identified treatise or even to the teachings of such literature, on the other we are provided with precise allusions (even if they are often abstruse) to the use of technical processes, allusions which can only be understood by reference to methods presented in treatises. Thus, for instance, a Sanskrit inscription from Cambodia explains the arrangement of a plot of land intended for building a temple by reference to an 81 square diagram, which corresponds to a well-known method in Indian normative tradition.[3]

It is obvious that treatises cannot explain all the direct links which exist between temples in India and Indian temples found overseas. It is highly probable that some updating of these

2. Manuscripts provided with drawings (elevations and the like) which appeared in the year 1960 in Orissa are recent and even more recent are the texts which they contain (*Śilpaprakāśa*, etc.); they cannot be considered as representative of a tradition of illustrated treatises of which they would be the only testimonies.
3. See above p.XXXX$ and for the interpretation of inscription K.567, Provost-Roche 2009 (chapter 2).

overseas Indian temples results from the arrival of one of those "Brahmins coming from India" sometimes mentioned in inscriptions. This seems to be the case for the innovations which mark the Banteay Srei temple and which concern iconography as well as arrangement of the sanctuary (see p.56-57$). There is also the case of some construction techniques which, even if little mentioned in treatises, have however travelled throughout Asia. Some years ago, Jacques Dumarçay gave a convincing demonstration when dealing with the use of a wedge-stone to tighten a layer of freestone masonry. Such techniques started to travel in the middle of the 8th century A.D. from Sri Lanka and went to Java where, due to contacts with processes imported from South India, it was modified. Then it went from Java to Cambodia and South India where its renewed form was used in a systematic way by the builders of big 11th c. temples such as Thanjavur or Gangaikondacolapuram (Dumarçay 1976). One may wonder if the corbelling construction technique, the universal use of which goes hand in hand with the universal absence of any reference to it, had not travelled in the same way all over Asia.

In some cases, such travels of ideas, forms, or techniques fully bypass India. Such is the case for those which correspond to exchanges between Indonesia and continental South-East Asia. However things are not always clear about them, especially when it concerns Java and Cambodia at the end of 8th century and beginning of the 9th. While it is probable that the evolution of water storage in Cambodia as well as creation of the basic pattern of pyramid based state temples resort to Javanese models, the historical context in which such transfers occurred remains very doubtful. As regards Java and Champa, some of their exchanges are most probably linked to the fact that the maritime traffic connecting Indonesia and China used to call at various places on the Champa coast.

Imaginary Travels and the Like

Archaeological Fantasies

While the Indian temple has truly travelled a lot, some imaginary travels have also been attributed to it as well to some of its presumed models. The presuppositions which are at the basis of such hypothesis are not always sincere, while the scientific side of the demonstration, even when loudly asserted, are unconfirmed due to the insignificant value of the documents used or due to unsolved chronological problems.

One of the most classic of these imaginary travels bring the Indian temple to Central America, sometimes including even pyramid based temples from South-East Asia (which for some nationalist cultural circles is nothing other than "Greater India"!) which South-East Asian temples are said to be "Indian" models of Mexican pyramids. Less distant and less ambitious, another hypothesis that is attributed to a well-known scholar wanted to identify two small rock-monuments of Petra as Indian temples. As has been shown by G.R.H. Wright, this so-called demonstration was bringing together Indian models from the 6th or 7th centuries and their alleged Nabataean copies dating from the 3rd century; moreover, it was resting on extremely fuzzy photographs of these Nabataean monuments which, as matter of fact, pertain to a monument series well-known in the Middle-East (Wright 1978).

Hermann Goetz, inventor of these Indian temples at Petra, had some years before published a long paper where, mixing cautious reserve and peremptory affirmations, he developed the idea that Hellenistico-Roman art had been imitated and absorbed by India (Goetz 1959). Without entering into the details of his demonstration, we may note that about architecture he was relying on the so-called flat-roofed temple hypothesis (see above p.35$), his idea being that the break with the "Greco-Roman model" occurred in the 5th century A.D. when the curvilinear towers appeared, about which he added that "it is again a foreign idea: the Babylonian ziggurat interpreted in Indian way". That paper marks a shift – even if Goetz denied it – toward what we would call the "axiomatic travels". As a matter of fact, such imaginary travels are linked with a systematic search for an out-of-India origin of Indian forms, which starts from the premise that India as well as South-East Asia are unable to produce any original forms. Such an attitude has been a common one for a long time when dealing with India. Some years ago I had the opportunity to recall how John Irwin had ruled out axiomatic models – either Achaemenid or Hellenistic – of the free standing pillars (so called "Ashokean pillars") of the Ganges Valley, which are the first architectural manifestations inspired by Indian tradition and of which he had proved, by the same way, that their Indian origin was obvious (Dagens 1993). As regards South-East Asia, the prehistory of its knowledge brings some fine examples of such axiomatic models with several origins proposed for Angkorean architecture by 16th and 17th century travellers, be it Alexandrian, Roman, Jewish, from China, etc. Later, the questions dealt with evaluation of links with India, for which the evidence, given as early as 1860 by Bastian, a geographer, and soon taken up again by Ferguson (Dagens 2005b), brings up other questions (see above).

Gustave Moreau and the Eyes of the God

There is a last category of imaginary travel of the Indian temple which would be better placed in the realm of dreams. One such travel is the one that would have done some pieces of a Goanese Indian temple if Giuliano de' Medici had answered to the proposal to send them to Europe, proposal made by a Florentine trader who seems to have been a man of taste and who was visiting India (Mitter 1977, p. 34).

Another and more recent dream-like travel is the one organised by the French painter Gustave Moreau in his *Triumph of Alexander*. In line with Alexandrian tradition, India is given the central place in this painting and is depicted by a complex pyramidal assembly of temples; in another famous painting, two centuries earlier, Charles Le Brun had figured the meeting of Alexander with Porus and India appeared there merely in the guise of the wounded king's elephant! In Moreau's work, the choice of images and their arrangement are fine. The selected temples and statues pertain to North India and to Karṇataka; a Khajuraho tower temple dominates the whole composition

Fig.60. Gustave Moreau: The Triumph of Alexander (detail of central part, sketch by Jacques Dumarçay). The possible mirror basin which we mention in our text is at the foot of the stairs (first plan). The first door (that of the sanctuary) gets a very classical ornamentation, most probably borrowed from a photograph.

where a rock-stūpa from Ajanta is seen halfway up, while the Sravanabelgola Jain colossus stands on the side. The most extraordinary part is however to be seen in the centre. There Gustave Moreau has drawn a temple door in front of which is, at the foot of some stairs, what seems to be a mirror basin. In the frame of the door may be seen at the far end and in full light, a second door, in the doorway of which appears a statue. We have thus a startling image of temple performance with an axis that goes straight through the door of the sanctuary, then through that of the sanctum and up to the god whose eyes it crosses. Gustave Moreau seems to have grasped – but how? – a very important feature of the Indian temple which he knew through some photographs only.

Dream and Politics

To conclude, I would be inclined to link to the realm of dreams the political travels of Indian temples which have been organized by various colonial powers since the end of the 19th century and up to the Second World War. Angkor Wat, as rebuilt for the Paris Colonial Exhibition of 1931 (but used first at the Marseilles Exhibition some years before) is well known, but the India Pavilion at the Paris Universal Exhibition of 1900 is as significant with its enormous curvilinear superstructure inspired by the Khajuraho towers (Mitter 1977: Fig.119). In both cases, all this has been done in order that the "colony" of which the products are presented inside the "temple" will be identified with the latter, a fine poster encouraging visitors to travel or at least to dream.

Conclusion

Indian Temple's Discovery

As already noted, the Indian temple in some parts has remained very unfamiliar to the West. Possibly the subject of an admiring curiosity or of studies which for Christian missions often had a motivation of self-interest, it has never been a model to which one refers and its Western descent may said to be nonexistent if one puts aside the few temples built by the Indian diaspora for its own use. Oddly enough, in those coffee table books which were so very popular in 19th century Europe, India appeared more often in the guise of its mosques than of its temples. The approach to the Indian temple by the Western world has been very slow and it really started only when the temple began to be seen, in the course of the 19th century, through a bilingual perspective helped by those treatises we have used as guides here. Once it had been admitted that the Indian temple was the fruit of a fully mature architectural art, the next important stage was to replace it in its ideological context. The last stage was to extend this replacement to the social field in order that the Indian temple eventually became a kind of global mirror.

From Philostratus to Nikitin

Amongst the oldest Western so-called descriptions of Indian temples is the one given by Philostratus (2nd-3rd c. A.D.) in his account of the visit that Apollonius of Tyana had paid to Taxila in the first century A.D. All is uncertain as regards this record, its historicity as well as the precise identification of the "described" temple which is far less certain than had been told in the past. In the event, this temple would have been one hundred feet long, it would have comprised of a small sanctum (νεώς) and its walls would have been ornamented with bronze panels illustrating the feats of Alexander and Porus (see *The Life of Apollonius of Tyana,* II.20.2). Philostratus also mentions another temple dedicated to the Sun and where the cult-image is made up of mother-of-pearl and provided with the "symbolic shape" (ξνμβόλικον τρόπν) "that all barbarians use for their holy objects" (*ibidem* II.24.1). All this makes very little, but two details possibly may be of interest as they concern the smallness of the sanctum and the symbolic shape of the cult object.

At the end of Antiquity and during the Middle-Ages, travellers were seemingly less interested in temples of Indian gods than in their statues, which they deemed monstrous –that is to say 'diabolic' – and by some religious practices considered as 'fanatic' (see Odoric of Pordenone about the chariot festival). However, the Elephanta and other rock temples of Mumbai area arouse attention; hence the descriptions which multiply in the 16th century (Mitter, 1977) but concern more such deserted rock-monuments than living and active temples attended by crowds of pilgrims. There are however some exceptions like the Portuguese visitors to Vijayanagar who, at the beginning of 16th century, mention polychrome temples in that capital city, then reaching its peak. In the same way, it was a temple in full activity which was visited by the Russian Athanasius Nikitin at Śrīśailam. He called the place "Parvata"("Mount", a common synonym of *śailam*) and when designating the temple itself, he used a Persian word - *butkhāna* ("house of idols") – a derogatory expression often applied by Moslems for deserted or still active Hindu or Buddhist monuments.

Missionaries and Architects

In the 17th century, Abraham Roger, a Dutch missionary based to the North of Madras has provided us with what is most probably one of the oldest reasoned presentations of the Indian temple (which, like many other travellers of that time, he often designates as a "pagoda") and of its functioning (Roger 1670):

> According to Brahmins, temples are "houses of God where they believe that he inhabits". Located inside a courtyard enclosed by a wall provided with towers (Roger certainly alludes to entrance pavilions), the temple is surrounded by "small pagodas" (that we call "chapels" or "sub-shrines") about which Roger lists the attendant deities of Viṣṇu and Śiva. He

> tells us that the temple itself is organised in three parts, the first being an open pavilion where "all people" can enter, the second a closed pavilion reserved by Brahmins to their own use, and the last a sanctum housing a statue of Viṇṇu or a Liṅga of Śiva. Out of respect, people must be barefooted and with covered shoulders when they enter temple precincts; however that entry is forbidden to outcasts who "by their own impurity would pollute as well Brahmins as the temple itself". Social hierarchy found also expression through the value of gifts which each caste is supposed to offer to temple.

However, such studies where architecture is only a utilitarian accessory of religious practice only got a limited success. To the contrary, during the 18th century, images and descriptions multiply and the same period is marked by the picturesque, which paves the way for romantic views and reaches its peak with the Daniell brothers and their magnificent aquatints published during the end of the century (see for instance Archer 1980).

Around 1830, temple architecture really becomes a subject for research and the first two authors to involve themselves in such studies do it by perusing Indian treatises of architecture. The first published work in the field – *Benares Illustrated*, Calcutta 1831 – is owed to James Prinsep, who was working at the Calcutta Mint and whose famous epigraphic studies released some years later eclipsed his researches on Indian architecture. which were brought back to light only at the end of the 20th century, thanks to a paper of M.C. Joshi (1983) which we are using here. In his pioneering work dealing with Varanasi monuments, often of Bengali inspiration, Prinsep mentions some normative treatises ("Silp-Shastra") and states that the craftsmen in charge of building ("Head Masons") had in a general way inherited the drawings – ground-plans and elevations – and quotations of treatises, both kinds of documents being very difficult to understand. Prinsep also notes that some of these craftsmen were making use of elements pertaining to Moslem architecture. Lastly, he insists on the use of a diagram for locating on the site

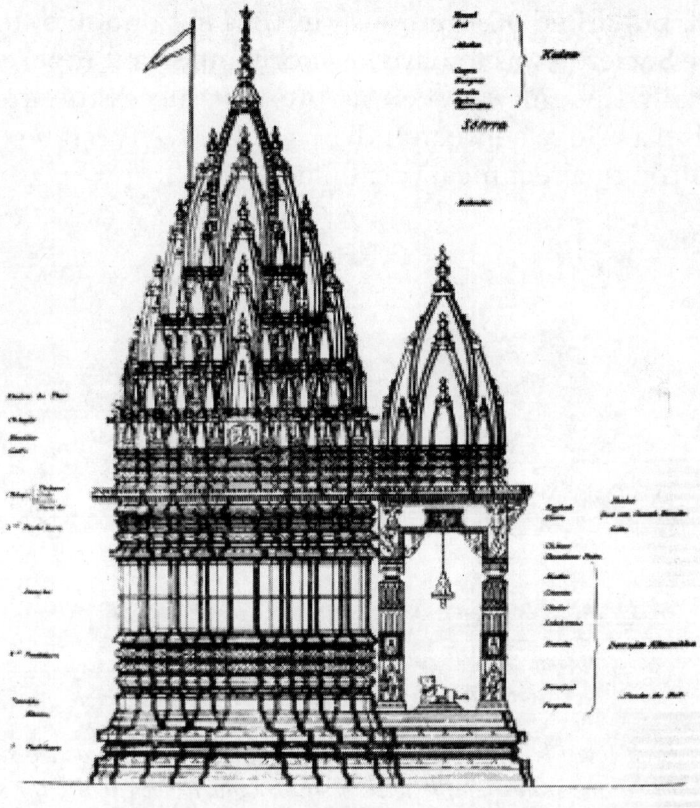

Fig.61. James PRINSEP *(1831): Drawing inspired by Viśveśvara Temple at Varanaṣi (*JOSHI *1983) (about this kind of representation of curvilinear towers inspired by Gothic art, see above p.41$)*

the building-to-be. His work is illustrated by drawings of contemporary temples, some architectural elements there being designated with a Sanskrit-Bengalese nomenclature which he had collected from local practitioners (Fig.61).

Ram Raz, Towards a Bridge between Architectures

The work of Prinsep, which was quickly forgotten, relied on a limited collection of technical texts without possible comparison with the one used – roughly at the same time – by

Ram Raz. The work of the latter – *Essay on the Architecture of the Hindus* published posthumously in 1834 in London by the Royal Asiatic Society – was to have far more important repercussions, especially since it was seen as the first successful attempt to establish a bridge between Indian and Western architecture and that through a technical vocabulary.

Fig. 62. Ram Raz (1834): Drawings of temples with one and two storeys. To the left is a one-storey temple with a square main body while the summit arrangement (attic-roof-finial) is circular. To the right is represented the main temple of the Viṣṇu sanctuary at Srirangam: an elliptic roof bears four finials put in a line on a pseudo-ridge beam (the sanctum which houses an image of reclining Viṣṇu being itself of circular plan).

Ram Raz was a clerk and had been in charge of various administrative functions, the last one being that of "native judge" at Bangalore. He knew Sanskrit and Tamil languages and also English; on this last point it is however possible that the role of his British friends in the writing of his book (and in the references to Western classical architecture) had been more important than is told in the Preface. This remark however does not diminish the value of his work, which is the first bilingual study on Indian temple architecture and which, on some points, may be deemed as conclusive. Ram Raz had perused several Sanskrit treatises – all from South India – amongst which was the *Mānasāra,* a copious treatise most probably pertaining to the Vijayanagar period and from which he translates long excerpts (a complete translation was to be prepared and published by P.K. Acharya in the 20th century). Ram Raz also sought advice from traditional architects as did Prinsep during the same time. His work is illustrated with drawings of moulded sets based upon descriptions with figures provided by the *Mānasāra,* but clearly inspired by existing monuments (see Fig.63); other illustrations represent edifices which are sometimes identified in captions such as the central temple of Srirangam (our Figure 62) or the full compound of Tiruvarur sanctuary (located to the east of Thanjavur) about which are given the ground plans and more important a fine bird's eye view (see above Fig.40, p.60$).

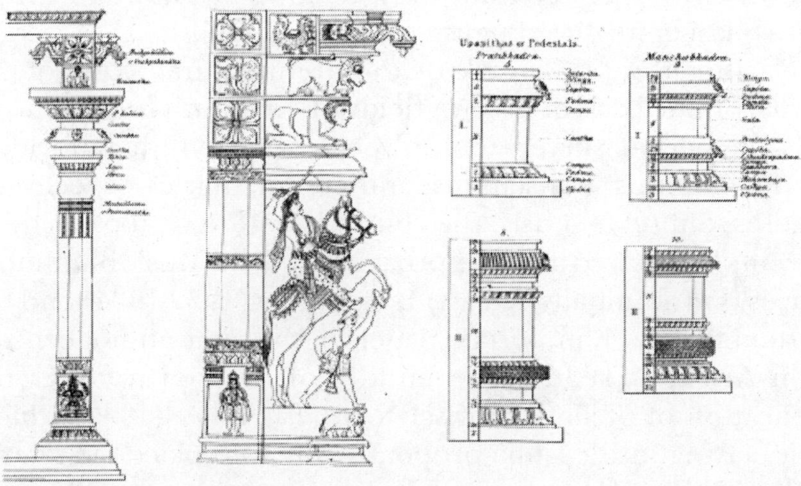

Fig.63. Ram Raz (1834): Drawings of moulded sets. The proportions as well as Sanskrit names of mouldings are most probably borrowed from the Mānasāra, but the drawings are inspired by Post-Vijayanagar tradition which was very much in vogue in South India in 18th c.-19th c. The pillar with the horseman (centre) corresponds to a very common type (especially at Srirangam).

The results of Ram Raz's work were very important for improving the knowledge of Indian temple architecture. Combining drawings and texts, he was able to put at our disposal the first bilingual reference vocabulary which, as a result of progressive additions, is at the base of the great descriptive surveys which were launched across India in the second half of the 19th century and which also use Sanskrit or English nomenclatures according to the equivalence system provided by Ram Raz.

Towards a Global Study

As early as 1867, James Fergusson who took an active interest in Indian architecture since the year 1840, completed his general presentation of world architecture by introducing the monuments of South-East Asia, besides those of India (Dagens 2005b). In the 20th century work of Jouveau-Dubreuil (1914, with a quasi-immediate English translation published at Madras), he clarifies the framework of the architectural study of the temple on the basis of his own fieldwork in South India. During the same period, surveys multiply in the entire Indian world, as also for editions, translations, and commentaries of technical treatises. Simultaneously, the research on the symbolic side of the temple received a new approach with Paul Mus' voluminous articles on (nominally at least) Borobudur (1932-1934) and the shorter but equally important papers by the same author centred upon Angkor (1936). The middle of the century sees the publication of Stella Kramrisch's *Hindu Temple* (1946) which, while staying inside India proper, is able to replace the temple in the ideological mould of Indian tradition. In her work, references to Indian treatises of architecture are omnipresent, as also to ancient sources. Some affirmations may look questionable – regarding dolmens for instance – but the book is marked by an acute sense of values for architectural elements (see for instance about the "higher temple" which Kramrisch identifies as the temple summit group made up of attic, roof and finial).

Stella Kramrisch's work remains a theoretical study which does not concern the temple's functioning or its connection with its human environment. As a matter of fact, it lacks what Abraham Roger had initiated on this point three centuries earlier. Only a few years after Kramrisch's publication, there appeared what may be considered – if I am not mistaken – the first "global" study of an Indian temple. Written by a historian, K.K. Pillai (1953) and marked by constant switching between present observations and epigraphic data, it deals with the big Śiva's temple at Suchindram, a city located in the far south of India near Cape Comorin (now Kanyakumari) in Tamil Nadu, but in an area culturally linked to neighbouring Kerala.

The studies which came afterwards are collective and multidisciplinary works where historians, architects, philologists, anthropologists, demographers, etc. intervene, the teams being a mix of Indian and Western scholars and engaged in long periods of field-work. We shall mention here two such enterprises. The first, launched by Heidelberg University for the study of the Jagannātha Temple at Puri had to be interrupted before completion, but the published results make this project a kind of model. The other study is the one devoted to Tiruvannamalai by a team of scholars from Pondicherry who succeeded in bringing it to completion. At several places in the present work we have already underlined the interest and importance of this collective study in the field of methodology as well as in the results which were published between 1990 and 1999 (see in our bibliography *Tiruvannamalai* 1 to 5).

New Temples

Temple attendance continues these days and new temples are being built. The daily attendance is of devotees from the neighbourhood who on their way pay their respect to the god, often at the end of the day and especially in the cities. But there are also pilgrims coming from far away, often their very long trips being marked by regular stops in various holy places. It is thus very common to see buses arriving from Rajasthan or Uttar Pradesh at Srirangam, Tirupati, or Cidambaram. Festivals also often attract big crowds and temple officials do not hesitate to announce them widely through illuminations and the like, not forgetting the huge billboards and other road-signs on nearby highways.

New temples are of various types and sizes. There are small ones built for and by a small village community, most often in the right of succession of those built centuries ago and more or less sophisticated according to the means of the patrons. Besides, the building costs of some important temples are frequently taken on by various foundations (namely "trusts" see below). Some of these foundations are created for the occasion and they deal with the building of a specific temple and then with its daily running as well as with the launching of charity projects. But there are also more widespread and concerted projects which can relate to many parts of India and for which national level involvement is important. Fine examples of such endeavours are provided by the Birla Foundation, or the Tirupati Tirumala Devasthanam, the first one for its connection with a generous social policy and the other for its non-sectarian defence of Hinduism. There also exist other concerted projects which are instruments of an aggressive and intolerant policy – see regarding Ayodhya – but we will not deal with them here.

Social Minded Views and Projects for Safeguarding the Faith

The Birla Foundation, created by one of the big families which have long dominated the Indian economy, has organised the building of prestigious new temples in several important cities of North India since the year 1930. It was a means to implement the support given by the Birla family to Mahatma Gandhi, especially for his actions regarding "untouchables". The first of such temples was built in New Delhi (1938) and on the day of its opening it was proclaimed with great ceremony that it would be open to all without any exception, a clause which was to apply to all "Birla temples" as they are usually called. Generally dedicated to one or the other of Viṣṇu's forms, they follow architectural models of Rajasthan, where the Birla family comes from, and are most of the time built in white marble found in the same area. The use of this material as well as their frequent position on hilltops – see for instance at Hyderabad – make them especially conspicuous evidences of the piety of the founding family and of its social commitments.

The Tirupati Tirumala Devasthanam (T.T.D.) is in charge of the administration of Viṣṇu Veṅkateśvara Temple at Tirupati and the many charities it finances. One of its main projects concerns the building and renovation of temples pertaining to all the branches of contemporary Hinduism. One interesting form of its activity is what we had called "shared temples", when making a systematic regional survey in Andhra Pradesh; such temples are buildings where several gods are installed together without any clear hierarchical order, their most common list comprising Śiva, Viṣṇu, the Goddess, Hanuman and Gaṇeśa. In Andhra Pradesh, such foundations are especially found in villages where there is an influential Moslem community which dominates the local economy. They provide less economically favoured Hindu groups with cult places that each of them would be unable to finance by themselves (Dagens: 1984 p.625-627 and 701). As regards renovation of temples in a bad condition, T.T.D. pays careful attention to entrance pavilions; they are considered most important to ensure to the temple a popularity which goes beyond its immediate surroundings, thus ensuring its financial independence as was told to us around 1980 by a T.T.D. officer in charge of such a renovation not far from Madras. It is also important to underline that T.T.D. activities, if non-sectarian at the level of Hinduism, is readily tolerant as regards other religious faiths existing in India, a policy which may lead to unkind reactions from Hindu quarters. This was the case in the eighties when the T.T.D. had to abandon a publication project of sacred Christian and Moslem texts translated into various Indian vernaculars, a project which was oriented to promote mutual understanding among the many Indian religious groups.

Expected Success of a Hanuman Temple

We have already mentioned an Āñjaneya-Hanuman temple built sometime ago at Pancavati (Tamil Nadu), not far from

Fig.64. Āñjaneya-Hanuman Temple at Pancavati (Tamil Nadu, 21th c.; author's photo).

Pondicherry, where the cult image was so big that it had to be installed before the building of the sanctum walls. However, this temple affords other points of interest, especially the conditions of its founding and of its building, as well as what is planned for its future, for in all such matters it offers a good example of what occurs nowadays.

As to the origin of this temple, a devotee of Āñjaneya had a vision around 1999 when he entered the plot of land where the temple was later built. Following the vision, and in accordance with the advice and technical instructions of a holy man, the devotee started to build the temple, after however seeking encouragement from the highest ranking religious authorities of the region. The building itself was financed by an *ad hoc* foundation getting funds through private donations; it comprised two successive stages, with the installation of an enormous statue in the interim (2003) as already mentioned, and the inauguration of the temple in 2007.

The building (Fig.64) appears to be more like a free copy of the great Thanjavur Bṛhadīśvara Temple. The height is around 29 metres, which is *grosso modo* half that of Thanjavur temple (60 metres), but there is an important change in the proportions: the ground floor of the new temple makes up ca. 15 metres which is roughly half of the total height, while this ratio is far less than a third at Thanjavur. Such a change is probably due to taking into account the big size of Hanuman's statue (ca. 9.20 metres, while it is 4.5 metres for the Thanjavur Liṅga) and to the desire to make it easy to see. Moreover, it is to be noted that the sanctum is illuminated by large glass windows which makes the light shine on the statue and which allows devotees to contemplate the god and focus on several acts of reverence performed by the priest and his aides, especially the baths and the "flowers rains", for which a complex arrangement of gangways has been installed.

The image shows the god standing with eight arms and five faces which are those of Āñjaneya itself (main face), the three Avatars of Viṣṇu (Narasiṃha, Hayagrīva, and Vāraha) and lastly that of Garuḍa, Viṣṇu's mount; the name of the gods is accompanied by various epithets, amongst which one emphasizes on his forms being a "cosmic one" (*viśvarūpa,* see above p.80-81$). Lastly, the temple is surrounded by two sub-shrines which house Gaṇapati (very popular in the area) and Rāma respectively.

The construction is "modern", which is rendered by marble pavements and by stainless-steel handrails aimed at channelling devotees, helping them to climb stairs, and allowing priests to bathe the statue from gangways without risking a fall – a very "modern" concern, but typical of the industrialists who are the important patrons of the temple.

The identity of the god himself is interesting; Hanuman the faithful friend of Rāma in the *Rāmāyaṇa* is very popular in many regions of India. He has many temples, especially in Andhra Pradesh and Maharashtra he which are present in all villages (as is the case in more northern areas). In all these places he is shown in various forms, but always as a familiar and protective deity. His popularity is less in Tamil Nadu where it is Gaṇeśa who is usually associated with the daily life of Hindus. Therefore, its geographical position results in the Pancavati temple getting quite a regular and substantial attendance. Moreover, the temple is located next to a national highway leading to that pan-Indian and cosmopolitan meeting place which is Pondicherry, which is 150 kilometres from Chennai (earlier called Madras), another cosmopolitan city which has many links with Andhra Pradesh, from where a huge part of its high middle class devotees originate. In point of fact, most of the officials of both foundations in charge of the Pancavati temple have their homes at Chennai.

The works at Pancavati have not ended with the temple inauguration, and officials of the temple have great ambitions which they display in the booklets handed to visitors, as also on the website of the temple. They plan to launch pious and charitable programs for the welfare of disadvantaged sections of the population as well as for disabled persons or for spiritually minded ones. They also want to create a "centre of excellence" for education and research, which would be provided with a matching library and a multi-media centre. While looking at such programmes and also at the present state of the temple area, one may visualise all this as an accumulation of pious hopes, aiming to give a *modern and productive aura* to a plan that appears to be sanctimonious and hollow. However, such a pessimistic view is entirely tentative, as is shown by our next example, a temple of the Goddess located 100 kilometres from the one we were just talking about and founded less than half a century before it.

The Networked Goddess temple

Located at less than 110 kilometres from Chennai and dedicated in 1971 to the Ādiparaśakti Goddess – the Primordial Supreme Power – the temple of Melmaruvathur has a pre-history which seems to go back to 1966 and has witnessed since then a historical development seen by all those who have been commuting for the last 40 years or so on the highway linking Chennai to the south of Tamil Nadu (Tiruchirapalli, Madurai, etc.). Its history tells us of the continuous growth of a small road-side temple which has become a complex compound, of which our Fig.65 gives just a faint idea, as this ensemble is only the central part of a network which now covers Asia, Europe, North America, and Australia.

The tale regarding the origin of the temple is interesting. It starts in 1966 when a tempest uprooted a holy tree and, doing thus, extricated a stone which was a "Liṅga by itself" (above p.7-8$). The power of Śiva (*śakti*) which was embedded in the Liṅga then entered a holy man who from this time pronounced oracles. The first time it was to announce that the Power had come down to Earth as "Mother" (*Amma* in Tamil) and that she was to be worshipped as the Goddess Ādiparaśakti (see above). However, the term "Mother" used thus to designate the temple deity is also the one used by devotees when addressing the holy man in whom that Goddess has entered! This holy man who is celebrated as a virtuous father of a family presents himself as a devotee amongst others as well as an "avatar" of the Goddess, that is to say an incarnation of Ādiparaśakti. He pronounces oracles on fixed days in a room near the temple sanctum.

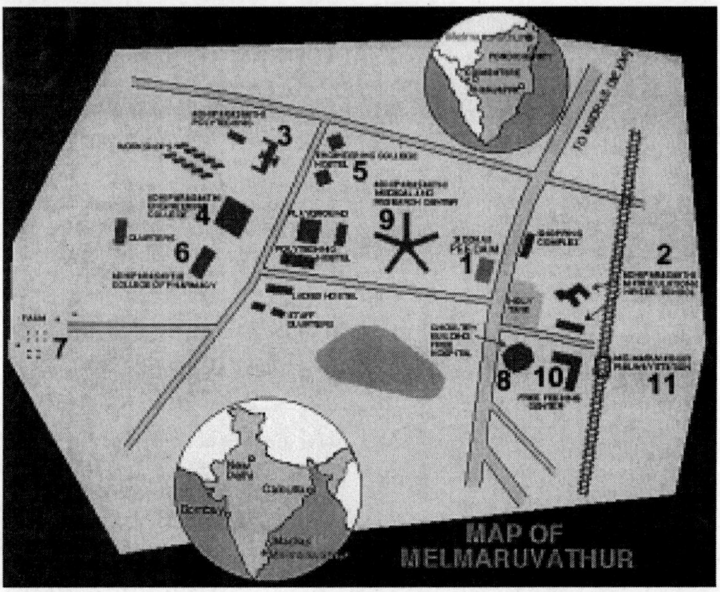

*Fig.65. Ādiparaśakti Temple at Melmaruvathur (Tamil Nadu, 20th -21th c.): Sketch of the site. On the side of the highway is the Goddess Temple (**1**) where the master pronounces his oracles in a room located on the side of the sanctum; the secondary school (**2**) and the colleges (which each gets its own student-hostel) (**3-7**) have been created from the eighties; the free hospital (**8**) founded in 1986 has been supplemented with a research centre (**9**) of which the five branch starred plan figures the five elements. The free refectory (**10**) where pilgrims and others are fed is one of the oldest creations. The highway now crosses the compound through a fly-over and the simple railway halt has been converted into a full-fledged station (**11**) served regularly by special trains during the pilgrimage period.*

As for the temple, it is defined as a "throne of the Goddess" (*śaktipīṭha*) according to an expression borrowed from the ancient tradition where it is connected with the Goddess' Śaivite cycle (see below). It houses in its sanctum a statue of the Goddess, in front of which the "Liṅga by itself" miraculously appeared in 1966, and to which the Goddess is supposed to have offered worship. However, against all Indian traditions there is no officiating priest attached to the temple and worship to the deity is offered by devotees themselves. Furthermore, the sanctum is open to all, of whichever caste, faith, religious sect, or sex. Thus, anybody can worship there, including women, who get an important place. They are in fact numerous amongst the devotees of Amma – at the same time the Goddess and the holy man – and they are often seen, clad in bright red, when they travel in dense and enthusiastic troops through Tamil Nadu on their way to the oracle.

It seems that the temple met with an early success. What began as just a stop on the highway, it progressively became the aim of the journey and its popularity seems to have gathered pace after a happy prophecy about an election. With visitors have come donations which are managed by a trust and have allowed for a progressive growth of the temple and its annexes (Fig.65). Simultaneously it has become the centre of a network of what truly look like "branches". According to classical Śaivite tradition, it is well-known that Śiva, after the death of the Goddess, went through India bearing her corpse on his shoulders and that her limbs fell to the ground one after the other. They were thus giving birth each time to a "throne of the Goddess" (*śaktipīṭha*), that is to say a holy place dedicated to her. It is this ancient mythological pattern that the officials of Melmaruvathur temple have used, to establish temples of Ādiparaśakti in several places. These modern *śaktipīṭhas* are also designated as collective centres of worship (*mandram*); each of them houses a statue which is a faithful copy of the one in the original temple; like the latter, it runs without an officiating priest, being under the charge of a local association of devotees which manages it and organizes the worship. These relays in fund raising as well as launching of charities have been mainly created in Tamil speaking contexts, first in South India and then throughout the Tamil diaspora across the world, especially where it is significant, as in Singapore and Australia. The Internet is widely used and a central website disseminates reports on the various centres and even offers a virtual *pūjā* room.

Back to the Mirror

In spite of appearances, the Hanuman temple through its expectations and the one of the Goddess through its successes are good representatives of the Indian temple. Based upon tradition, they claim to follow it even if they happen to take a differing view such as running the Goddess temple without an officiating priest. At the start, they rest on an act of faith – connected to a vision or a revelation – but their doctrinal foundation is slim and on this side tradition provides a convenient reference. This being the case, the spiritual need to see the deity – to get *darshan* according to a modern expression used in all languages – remains as powerful as when the right to have it fulfilled was dependent on social rank.

On this last point, the two examples we have chosen are both marked by an extraordinary social conformism, which is very generous as it is fully from the present time. The fact that temples are to be open to all is no more a mark of political commitment like when the first Birla temples were built, for that has become the rule, even if the term "all" has been shifted from the social to the religious field, implying that henceforth it concerns only believers. Moreover, one may see that the idea of "opening" has sometimes been enriched and twice the officiating priest's role has been given without any distinction to all faithful, including women.

As for the three centres of social activity of the temple – generosity towards the needy, care of public health, and commitment to education – these are the normal charges of the affluent concerned with their salute and it cannot be said that uniting them with the temple is a real innovation. The continuity which is not always a material one and which is ascribed to the temple results in this which has always been seen – most probably since it exists – as the best guardian of its three activities. What is new is that in the cases we are dealing with here, such a function has been introduced in the initial plan of the temple and thus justifies that this temple is considered and even designed to be a profit centre from the beginning. The reference to Thanjavur temple, the big size of the image – it was announced that the one of Hanuman was the biggest in the world - or the re-use of the old myth of the dismembering of the Goddess' corpse in order to justify the multiplication of the temple, all these are instruments to ensure the coming of pious crowds and benefactors.

These new temples are however to be seen as complements to the existing ones – this is sometimes made very clear. Thus, before the commencement of the building works, Hanuman in the symbolic guise of a sacred diagram which had been engraved on a golden leaf made a ceremonial tour of all the main temples of South India in order to announce his forthcoming installation at Pancavati. The already existent religious infrastructure is immeasurable, to put it properly, for India is a land where gods or their temples never die. I In the eighties, when we were surveying on the Krishnā river banks temples that were isolated and apparently deserted since long, we were surprised to learn that most of them were coming alive annually for the Śivarātri festival: then, for a few days they were ornamented and worship was resumed. On another side, it is well known that when an old temple consigned to be a historical monument is subject to conservation works, it very often happens that worship is resumed here, first in a discreet way and then with more and more visibility, as for instance at Gangaikondacolapuram. However, most temples have a long life with a quiet history marked regularly by renovations, of which the most obvious are those of the painted stucco or mortar statues of the façades (and especially those of entrance pavilions towers); a renovation which is marked, at the same time, by a respect of tradition and updating to the day's fashion.

Old or new, all these temples have no other raison d'être than divine service and the aim of their direct charitable activities is ostensibly to make the accommodation of devotees easier. The case of T.T.D. of Tirupati is a little different, in the sense that its multiple activities are justified by the necessity to use the enormous income of that sanctuary and to prevent the political power from being tempted to take its cut, as it has done several times in the past or to take control of things, an intention it has regularly shown since long.

Glossary of Main Architectural Expressions

Definitions, often based upon *Vocabulaire de l'architecture*, are adapted to the use made of the expressions in the present work.

Aedicule: decorative piece looking like a miniature temple and placed upon the peripheral *platform topping the *entablature of real or false *storeys (see p.38$). In Cambodia, from the end of 10th century such aedicules were replaced by **pieces d'accent.*

Ambulatory: covered passage surrounding the *sanctum. When it is an *in-work one it is pierced lengthways in the (thick) wall of the main *body encasing the sanctum (Fig.12) while an *outwork one is inside a structure built against that main body (Fig.16).

Apsidal plan: an oblong plan of which one of the small sides is replaced by a semi-circular one; this plan also may be based on a square plan.

Attic: a *level of the temple elevation; it looks like a *false-storey placed just below the *roof and recessed in regard to the roof as well as to the element on which it rests; hence its Sanskrit name of "neck" (see Fig.6 and 7).

Barrel vault: expression used to designate a double slope *corbelled roofing provided with a more or less curved profile.

Base: massive element on which rests a *building. The same word designates a *level of elevation which looks like a moulded set placed at the bottom of the *elevation but of which the vertical extent does not necessarily correspond with that of the base, technically speaking.

Blind: qualifier applied to an architectural element provided with false openings (doors or windows).

Body: see *Building.

Building: separate edifice; generally it comprises several *bodies amongst which one is the "main body" and other ones said to be "secondary bodies" are attached to it. It may also comprise one body only.

Causeway: elevated passage crossing a *moat surrounding a temple (Cambodia).

Ceiling: flat *covering of a room.

Chapel: secondary temple housing an attendant deity of the god, lord of the main temple of the *sanctuary.

Cloister-like gallery: gallery surrounding the courtyard of the *temple toward which it opens.

Corbelled: qualifier applied to a *roofing made by piling up stone layers (sometimes brick layers) one above the other with, each time, the upper one overhanging the one below (see also *superstructure). The intrados of such a roofing may take the form of a *barrel vault (when covering a gallery or a pavilion, see for instance Fig.55) or that of a chimney shaft, this last being more or less a square, or round, or even octagonal section shaft (Fig.16, 48) (the technical expression for such corbelled structures is "tas de charge").

Cornice: moulding crowning an *entablature or a *base and often playing the part of a *dripstone. In Indian temple architecture it often gets the look of *eaves. Its profile most often is rounded; however, when straight it is oblique (see Fig.23) or vertical and then looks like a *string-course.

Covering: device which bounds an interior volume towards the top; it may be a flat *ceiling, etc. or its part may be played by the intrados of the roofing device.

Curtain-wall: a kind of *partition wall and closing, for instance an *outwork *ambulatory.

Doorjambs: upright elements of a door frame.

Doucine: composite moulding with an S-shaped profile; in Indian tradition it is designated as a "lotus" and often consequently decorated.

Dripstone: a projecting element meant to avoid rainwater flowing down a wall; its part is played by a *cornice arranged like *eaves.

Eaves: overhanging bottom part of a *roof.

Elevation: drawing of a façade of an edifice and by extension real or decorative architectural arrangement of that façade.

Enclosure: area bordered by a continuous surrounding (enclosure-) wall and making up a ring-shaped courtyard around the temple or around another enclosure when the temple is at the centre of several concentric enclosures arrangement. The only or outermost enclosure marks the border of the *sanctuary and thus corresponds to the *peribolos* of Western classical tradition.

Entablature: moulded set which corresponds to the top part of the order and which constitutes the third *level of elevation. It crowns a row of pillars as well as a wall that may or may not be ornamented with *pilasters. Its bottom part is made up by the architrave and its top by the *cornice above, which can possibly be a *stereobate.

Entrance pavilion: monumental *building of large or small size making up a gateway crossing an *enclosure-wall.

False-dormer window: a décor element imitating a dormer window set on a *roof. These false-dormer windows are set either on false-roofs (most often curved ones) or on extrados of the *cornice topping an entablature or a *base. Their *pediment is frequently decorated by an image (often just a face) or a vegetal motive. In art history books they are often designated by their Tamil name *kuḍu* ("bird-nest");.

False-storey: an image of a *storey made up by that of an *entablature topping that of a *level of pillars. False-storeys ornament the façades of tower-like *superstructures and they do not correspond to any structural division of it.

Finial: moulded and pointed element making the uppermost *level of elevation of a temple (Fig.6 and 19). There is one finial above centred *roofs and several above oblong or elliptic ones. A row of similar but less elaborate finials may also also be found on the coping of *enclosure walls.

Flat-roof (*alias* "terrace"): a horizontally flat or slightly convex *roofing.

Forepart: a secondary structure built against a *body of a building; it may be a *porch, a *chapel, etc.

Groove: narrow recessed moulding generally with a semicircular profile.

Hip: *roofing of the rounded part of an apsidal building and of the rounded sides of an elliptical *roof.

Hipped: see *Hip.

Hypaethral temple: temple without *roofing,

In-work: expression applied to an element integrated in the structure to which it pertains (see for instance Fig.12).

Latticed window: stone slab provided with an arranged piercing and filling up the frame of a window or, possibly, a door.

Lean-to roof: used to cover an *outwork element such as an ambulatory built against the main body of an edifice.

Levels of elevation: horizontal divisions of the temple façade decoration; they do not necessarily correspond to the structural horizontal divisions of the edifice (See Fig.6 and 7)

Library (pseudo-): a temple annexe specific to Cambodia. It probably played the part of a chapel and/or a sacrificial pavilion; its modern name comes from an inscription where such a building is designated in Sanskrit as a 'library' *(pustakāśrama)*.

Mise en abyme: process using mirrors facing each other to make an image multiply *ad infinitum*. By extension this expression is applied to processes tending to similar multiplication, such as placing aedicules on temple façades, which are to be seen as many images of that temple itself.

Moat: a ring-shaped reservoir twinning from outside the *enclosure wall of a *sanctuary (Cambodia only).

Mountain-like (temple): a composition where a temple stands on a stepped pyramid and which is specific to Cambodian state-temples.

Outwork: expression applied to an element which is built against the building to which it pertains.

Partition wall: a wall without any structural load, used to divide an interior volume.

Pavilion: edifice which generally (but not necessarily) is hypostyle and provided with a flat roof. It may be a separate *building or a *body being part of a more or less complex building.

Pediment: decorative element being the closing piece of the gable of a two-sloped roof or of a *false dormer-window. In Cambodia it is specially used when such a two-sloped roof is that of a *forepart housing a *porch which results in the pediment being conspicuously above a door: in that case it is more or less triangular, surrounded by a row of rising leaves, and decorated with an image of a god or of a mythological scene.

Pièce d'accent: A feature found only in Cambodia where, from the 10th century, it is used to replace *aedicules upon the platform topping the entablature of false-storeys (see for instance Fig.21A or Fig.27). It looks like a vertical slab or corner piece with a more or less ogival contour. It is bordered by a row of rising leaves surrounding an image of a deity or an aniconic decorative motive.

Platform (peripheral -): flat terraced space left empty at the top of a *(false-) storey by the recessed position of the one built above. On such platforms are often found aedicules, *pieces d'accent*, and other decorative elements.

Pilaster: sculpted image of a pillar sculpted on a wall.

Porch: *forepart built in front of a real or false entrance-door.

Rafter: straight or curved piece of timber used to support roof-slopes of real carpentry-work roofs. It leans at its top on the ridge beam and near its lower end upon the top of a wall or upon an architrave. See also *Screed.

Roof: element of *roofing which may be real and supported by a wooden carpentry-work, or false and then sculpted in a stone masonry assembly or sometimes in a monolith piece. It makes up the 5th *level of temple elevation.

Roofing: more or less complex device which closes an edifice at its top (see *Roof, *Terrace, *Hip, *Superstructure).

Rough walling: masonry made of rubble and generally assembled between two faces of ashlar.

Sanctuary: bounded plot of ground on which is built the *temple (and its annexes) and which may be considered as the god's estate. It is bordered by an *enclosure wall, but it may be divided in concentric courtyards by intermediary enclosure walls.

Sanctum: room of the temple where is housed the cult object representing the god, lord of the temple.

Screed: curved *rafter used in the making of *wagon roofs and similar timber work bulged roofs.

State-temple: category of royal foundation temples which embody in one way or another their founder king's power for the duration of his rule (see especially chapter VI).

Stereobate: a moulded set inserted between two main levels of elevation and playing the part of a secondary one. It is commonly seen at the base of the *attic and looks then as the *base of the summit-aedicule made up by *attic, *roof, and *finial (see Fig.19).

Storey: in Indian architecture it corresponds to several Sanskrit words (*tala*, etc.) which all designate an "inhabitable" level of an edifice which may be real or *false. Thus, in temple architecture, it is the ground-floor – usually real – and the upper ones which are most often false. This being the case, the *attic is never accounted for as one of the "storeys", even if it is again the image of an "inhabitable" level.

String-course: flat projecting thick moulding. When it is at the top of a moulded composition it plays the part of a cornice. In Cambodia may be seen vertical string-courses which are just simplified forms of pilasters.

Strut: piece of carpentry placed in an oblique position and supporting the *eaves when these are real and largely overhanging (Kerala, Nepal). In false architecture, it is a purely decorative element which is supposed to support a *cornice arranged like overhanging eaves (Karṇataka).

Superstructure: a complex *roofing most generally assembled according to *corbelling technique. It looks somewhat like a pyramidal tower and its façades are made up of horizontal divisions which may be more or less definite and numerous (*false-storeys, steps, and the like).

Temple: separate *building or main *body of such a building encasing the *sanctum in which is installed the representation of the god, lord of that temple.

Torus: projecting moulding with a semicircular or semi-octagonal profile.

Trussing (roof-): upper part of the inner volume of an edifice, encased in carpentry-work or vaulted roofing.

Wagon roof: real or false roof provided by two curved-slopes.

Bibliography

ARCHER (M.) – 1980: *Early Views of India. The Picturesque Journeys of Thomas and Williams Daniell,* London.

BARAZER-BILLORET (M.-L.) – 1993-1994 : « Les cérémonies d'installation selon les āgama śivaïtes », *Bulletin d'Etudes Indiennes,* vol. 11-12, p. 39-69.

— 1999: *La grande fête du temple* (mahotsava) *d'après les āgama śivaïtes,* Thèse, Université Paris III – Sorbonne nouvelle, Paris.

— 2009C: « Le bestiaire de Śiva: de Paśupati à Śarabha », in N. Balbir et G.-J. Pinault (éd.), *Penser, dire et représenter l'animal dans le monde indien,* Paris, p.499-515.

BARAZER-BILLORET (M.-L.) ET AL. – 2004-2009 see *Dīptāgama.*

BAREAU (A.) – 1987: « Lumbini et la naissance du futur Buddha », *B.E.F.E.O.,* t. 76, p. 69-81 [and in BAREAU (A.), *Recherches sur la biographie du Buddha dans les Sūtrapimaka et le Vnayapiṭaka anciens III. Articles complémentaires,* Paris 1995, p. 1-13].

BARRE (V.), BERFER (P.), FEVEILE (L.), TOFFIN (G.) – 1981, *Panauti - une ville au Népal,* Paris.

BASHAM (A.L.) – 1983 « The Mandasor Inscription of the Silk-weavers », Bardwell L. SMITH (ed.), *Essays on Gupta Culture,* Delhi, p.93 et suiv.

BAÜMER (B.) & DAS (R.P.) – 1994: *Śilparatnakośa – a glossary of Orissan Temple Architecture,* New Delhi (I.G.N.C.A.).

BIZOT (F.) – 1994 : « La consécration des statues et le culte des morts », in F. BIZOT, *Recherches nouvelles sur le Cambodge,* Paris (PEFEO), p.101-139.

BOISSELIER (Jean) – 1966 : *Le Cambodge,* Paris.

BRUNNER-LACHAUX (H.) – 1963 = *Somaśambhupaddhati,* text, transl. and notes, vol.I: *Rituel quotidien,* Pondichéry (PIFI 25-1).

BRUNNER (H.) – 1969 : « De la consommation du *nirmālya* de Śiva », *Journal Asiatique* p.213-262.

CHOCKALINGAM (K.) – 1981 : *Chidambaram* (Census of India 1971, Series 19: Tamil Nadu, Part VI-B Socio-Economic Survey of Selected Towns).

COEDES (G.) – 1956 : « Nouvelles données sur les origines du royaume khmèr: la stèle de Vat Luong Kau près de Vat Phu », *B.E.F.E.O.* t. 48, p.209-220 [and in G. COEDES, *Articles sur le pays khmer*, 1989 [t. I], p. 367-378].

COLAS (G.) – 1986: *Le temple selon Marīci,* extraits de la *Marīci-saṃhitā* étudiés, ed. and transl., Pondichéry (PIFI n° 71).

DAGENS (B.) – 1969 : « Etude sur l'iconographie du Bayon (frontons et linteaux) », *Arts Asiatiques*, t.XIX p. 123-167.

— 1979 : *Le florilège de la doctrine Śivaïte: Śaivāgamaparibhāṣāmañjarī de Vedajñāna*, crit. ed. and transl., Pondichéry (PIFI n°60).

— 1984a : *Entre Alampur et Srisailam, recherches archéologiques en Andhra Pradesh*, 2 vol., Pondichéry (PIFI n° 67).

—1984b *Architecture in the Ajitāgama and the Rauravāgama - a study of two south indian texts*, New-Delhi.

— 1991 : Centralisme et architecture : les hôpitaux de Jayavarman VII en Thaïlande, dans *Récentes recherches en archéologie en Thaïlande* (Bangkok), p.24-35 [and in DAGENS 2005: 251-267].

— 1993: « L'Asie du Sud et du Sud-Est » dans *Le grand atlas de l'Art* (2 vol., Paris, Encyclopaedia Universalis), t. II, p.292-293, 296-307, 310-315 [and in DAGENS 2005 : 1-36].

— 1994: « Le temple indien en Asie du Sud-Est. Archéologie d'une forme », dans F. BIZOT, *Recherches nouvelles sur le Cambodge,* Paris (PEFEO), p. 259-272 [and in DAGENS 2005: 205-220].

— 1996: « Le temple corps du dieu », dans N. BALBIR et G.J. PINAULT (éd.), *Langue, style et structure dans le monde indien,* Paris (Bib.EPHE IV n°334) p. 353-383. [and in DAGENS 2005:125-149].

— 2000: « Le temple et le miroir à travers le monde indien », in M.-L. BARAZER-BILLORET et J. FEZAS (éd.), *La norme et son application dans le monde indien* , Paris (E.F.E.O, Etudes Thématiques n°11), p. 175-191 [and in DAGENS 2005: 181-201].

— 2000b: « Architecture, espace et temps dans le Cambodge ancien », in H. MULTZER O'NAGHTEN, *Architecture et espace sacré dans les temples du Cambodge,* Paris, Geuthner.

— 2003: *Les Khmers,* Paris (Les Belles Lettres).

— 2005: *Traités, temples et images du monde indien – études d'histoire et d'archéologie,* papers collected by M.-L. BARAZER-BILLORET & Vincent

LEFEVRE, Pondichéry-Paris.

— 2005b: « La découverte scientifique d'Angkor », in BACQUE-GRAMMONT (J.-L.) et al. (éds.), *D'un Orient à l'autre – Actes des troisièmes journées de l'Orient (Bordeaux, 2-4 octobre 2002)*, Paris-Louvain, p. 217-236.

— 2009a: « Temple indien et milieu naturel: l'exemple du Dīptāgama », *Bulletin d'Etudes Indiennes*, t.24-25, 2006-2007 [pub. in 2009]Amiens p.45-58.

— 2009b: « Mythologie indienne et pouvoir royal dans le Monde indien: l'exemple du Cambodge ancien », *Mythes et mythologies. Actes du Colloque d'Amiens, 6, 7 et 8 mars 2008*, Amiens, p.76-84.

— 2009c: « Les animaux dans l'architecture du temple indien. Images et métaphores », in N. BALBIR & G.-J. PINAULT (ed.), *Penser, dire et représenter l'animal dans le monde indien*, Paris, p.333-362.

DAGENS (B.) & BARAZER-BILLORET (M.-L.) – 2000: see *Rauravāgama.*

DATTA (B.M.) – 1975 : *Bengal Temples*, New Delhi.

DEHEJIA (V.) – 1972 : *Early Buddhist Rock Temples. A Chronology*, Ithaca-New York.

— 1986 : *Yogini Cult and Temples, a Tantric Tradition*, New Delhi.

DELAPORTE (L.) – 1880 : *Voyage au Cambodge. L'architecture khmer*, Paris.

DELARUELLE (M.) – 1999 : *L'iconographie des pavillons d'entrée des sanctuaires au Tamilnad (Inde du sud) à partir du VIIe de notre ère*, Thèse, Université de Paris III.

DERRETT (J.D.M.) – 1968 : *Religion, Law and the State in India*, London.

DHAKY (M.A.) – 1970 : « Caṇḍeśa in North Indian Tradition », *Journal of the Asiatic Society* (vol.12).

— 1982 : « The praṇāla in Indian and South-Asian sacred Architecture », *Rūpa-Pratirūpa - Alice Boner Commemoration Volume* (New Delhi), p.119-166.

Dīptāgama : BARAZER-BILLORET (M.-L.) ET AL. – 2004-2009: *Dīptāgama*, crit. ed. by M.-L. BARAZER-BILLORET, B. DAGENS & V. LEFVRE with collaboration de S. SAMBANDHA SIVĀCARYA and participation de C. BAROIS, 3 vol., Pondichéry (Publications du Département d'Indologie n° 81.1-3).

DONALDSON (T.E.) – 1985-87 : *Hindu Temple Art of Orissa*, 3 vol., Leiden.

DUCHEMIN (Vanessa) – 2001: *L'architecture de Pagan (Birmanie): ses sources et ses particularités*, Thèse, Université Paris III – Sorbonne nouvelle, Paris

DUMARÇAY (J.) – 1967-1973 : *Le Bayon. Histoire architecturale du temple:*[I]

Atlas et notice des planches, [II] *Texte*, Paris (Mém.Archéol.EFEO n°III/1 et 2).

-- 1971: *Ta Kèv, Etude architecturale du temple*, Paris (Mém.Archéol.EFEO n°VI).

-- 1972: *Phnom Bakheng, Etude architecturale du temple*, Paris (Mém.Archéol.EFEO n°VII).

— 1976: « La Stéréotomie de l'Asie Méridionale du VIIIème au XIVème siècle », *B.E.F.E.O.*, t .63, p.397-445.

— 1981 : *Candi Sewu et l'architecture bouddhique du centre de Java*, Paris. (Mém.Archéol. EFEO, n°XIV).

— 1983 : *Les effets perspectifs dans l'architecture de l'Asie méridionale*, Paris. (Mém.Archéol. EFEO n°XV).

— 1986 : *The temples of Java*, Singapour (O.U.P.).

— 1988 : *Documents graphiques de la Conservation d'Angkor 1963-1973*, Paris (Mém. Archéol. EFEO n°XVII).

— 1993 : *Histoire de l'architecture de Java*, Paris (Mém. Archéol. EFEO n°XIX).

— 1996 : *Babel ruinée. Petit traité du regard porté sur l'architecture en Asie méridionale*, Paris (Librairie Oriens).

— 1998 : *L'architecture et ses modèles en Asie du sud-est*, Paris (Librairie Oriens).

— 2001 : *Métaphores littéraires et architecturales*, Paris (Librairie Oriens).

DUMARÇAY (J.) & L'HERNAULT (F.) – 1975 : *Temples Pallava construits*, Paris, (Mém.Archéol.EFEO n°IX).

DUMARÇAY (J.) & ROYERE (P.) – 2001: *Cambodian Architecture: eight to thirteenth centuries*, Leiden 2001.

ESCHMANN (A.), KULKE (H.) & TRIPATHI (G.C.), Eds. – 1978: *The Cult of Jagannath and the Regional Tradition of Orissa*, New Delhi.

FISCHER (K.) – 1974 : *Dächer, Decken und Gewölbe indischer Kultstätten und Nutzbauten*, Wiesbaden.

FILLIOZAT (J.) – 1954 : « Le symbolisme du monument du Phnom Bakheng », *B.E.F.E.O.*, t.44, pp.527-554 [and in J. Filliozat, *Laghu-prabandhāḥ*, Leyden, 1974, p. 425-453].

— 1959: « Gopura 'porte de ville' », *Journal Asiatique* (1959) p. 251-255.

FILLIOZAT (P.S.) – 1975 : « Le droit d'entrer dans les temples de Śiva au XIème siècle », *Journal Asiatique* (1976), p 103-117 [text, transl. and comm. of the treatise said to be by Rāmakaṇṭha].

FRANZ (H.G.) – 1979 : *Von Gandhara bis Pagan - Kultbauten des Buddhismus und Hinduismus in Süd- und Zentralasien*, Graz.

GALEY (J.-C.) – 1985-86 : *L'espace du temple I: Les sanctuaires dans le royaume* (= *Purusartha* n°8) et *II : Espaces, itinéraires, médiations* (= *Purusartha* n°10), Paris.

GILL (S.) – 2000 : *Phantasmic Anatomy of the Statues of Mathurā*, New Delhi.

GOETZ (H.) – 1959 : « Imperial Rome and the Genesis of Classic Indian Art », reproduit dans H. GOETZ, *Studies in the History, Religion and Art of Classical and Mediaeval India* (Wiesbaden 1974), p. 3-48.

GUILMOTO (C.), REINICHE (M.-L.) et PICHARD (P.) – 1990: see *Tiruvannamalai* 5.

HARDY (A.) – 2007 : *The Temple Architecture of India*, [Chichester], John Wiley & Sons Ltd.

HARLE (J.C.) – 1963 : *Temple Gateways in South India (The Architecture and Iconography of Cidambaram Gopuras)*, Londres.

–– 1986 : *The Art and Architecture of the Indian Subcontinent*, Harmondsworth (The Pelican History of Art).

HOECKVELD-MEIJER (G.) – 1981 : *Koyils in the Colamandalam...*, Amsterdam.

JACQ-HERGOUALC'H (M.) – 1992 : *La civilisation des ports-entrepôts du Sud-Kedah (Malaysia) Ve-XIVe siècle*, Paris.

JOSHI (M.C.) – 1983 : « James Prinsep on Temple Architecture », *Śrīnidhiḥ. Perspective in Indian Archaeology, Art and Culture. Shri K.R. Srinivasan Festschrift*, Madras, p. 422-429.

JOSHI (N.P.) – 1973 : « Some Kusana passages in the Harivamsa », *Indologen Tagung 1971*, Wiesbaden p.238-252.

JOSHI (Rasik Vihari) – 1959, *Le rituel de la dévotion kṛṣṇaïte*, Pondichéry (PIFI n° 17).

JOUVEAU-DUBREUIL (G.) – 1914 : *L'Archéologie du Sud de l'Inde*, 2 vol., Paris.

JURAMIE (Anne-Claire) – 2001 : *Architecture et iconographie des temples de Viṣṇu dans la Vallée de Kāṭhmāṇḍu, Népal*, Thèse, Université Paris III – Sorbonne nouvelle, Paris.

KOSAMBI (D.D.) – 1962 : *Myth and reality, studies in the formation of Indian culture*, Bombay.

KNOX (R.) – 1992 : *Amaravati. Buddhist Sculpture from the Great Stūpa*, London.

KRAMRISCH (S.) – 1946 : *The Hindu Temple,* 2 vol., Calcutta.

KREISEL (G.) – 1986 : *Die Śiva-Bildwerke der Mathura-Kunst: ein Beitrag zur frḷhhinduistichen Ikonographie,* Stuttgart.

KULKE (H.) – 1979 : *Jagannātha und Gajapati-Königtum,* Wiesbaden.

LEFEVRE (V.) – 2006 : *Commanditaires et artistes en Inde du Sud. Des Pallava aux Nāyak (VIe-XVIIIe siècle),* Paris.

LEGRAND (B.) – 1987 : *Kilaiyur-Melappaluvur: Epanouissement d'une dynastie princière en Inde à l'époque Cola,* Paris.

L'HERNAULT (F.) – 1978 : *L'iconographie de Subrahmanya au Tamilnad,* Pondichéry (PIFI n° 59).

L'HERNAULT (F.) – 1987 : (avec P.Srinivasan et J.Dumarçay), *Darasuram,* Paris (Mém.Archéol.EFEO n°XVI).

L'HERNAULT (F.), PICHARD (P.) et DELOCHE (J.) – 1990; voir *Tiruvannamalai* 2.

L'HERNAULT (F.) et REINICHE (M.-L.) – 1999 : voir *Tiruvannamalai* 3.

MALAMOUD (C.) – 1972 : « Observations sur la notion de reste dans le brahmanisme ancien », *Wiener Zeitschrift für die Kunde Südasiens,* t. XVI p.5-26 [and in C. MALAMOUD, *Cuire le monde - rite et pensée dans l'Inde ancienne,* Paris 1989].

Mānasāra : ACHARYA (P.K.), *Mānasāra on Architecture and Sculpture* [Sanskrit text], Oxford..., 1933, et *Architecture of Mānasāra* [translation], Oxford..., 1933 [+ rééditions].

MARSHALL (J.) – 1960 : *A guide to Taxila,* Cambridge.

Mayamata : Dagens (B.) – 1994: *The Mayamata - an Indian Treatise of Housing, Architecture and Iconography,* Sanskrit text edited and translated, 2 vol., New-Delhi (I.G.N.C.A. and Motilal Banarsidass Publishers).

MEISTER (M.W.) – 1979 : « Juncture and Conjuncture : Punning and temple architecture », *Artibus Asiae,* t. 41, p. 226-234.

MEISTER (M.W.) & DHAKY (M.A.) – 1983 : *Encyclopaedia of Indian Temple Architecture,* ed. by. - and - ,Vol.I.part 1: *South India Lower Dravidadesa,* 2 tomes, New Delhi.

— 1986 : *idem,* Vol I. Part 2: *South India Upper Dravidadesa, Early Phase A.D.550-1075,* 2 tomes, New Delhi.

— 1988 : *idem,* Vol.II.part 1:*North India : Foundations of North-Indian styles,* 2 tomes New Delhi.

MEVISSEN (G.) – 1996 : « The Suggestion of Movement. A Contribution to the Study of Chariot-shaped Structures in Indian Temple-architecture », D. MITRA (ed.), *Explorations in Art and Archaeology of South Asia. Essays dedicated to N.G. Majumdar,* Calcutta, p.477-512.

MICHELL (G.) – 1975 : *An Architectural Description and Analysis of the Early Western Calukyan Temples,* 2 vol., AARP, Londres.

— 1989 : *The Penguins Guide to the Monuments of India,* Vol. I *Buddhist, Juin, Hindu,* London.

— 1995 : *Architecture and art of Southern India, Vijayanagara and the successor states,* Cambridge University Press, Cambridge (The New Cambridge History of India, I:6).

MITTER (P.) – 1977 : *Much Maligned Monsters – History of European Reactions to Indian Art,* Oxford.

MITRA (D.) – 1980 : *Buddhist Monuments,* Calcutta (= reed.).

MUS (P.) – 1932-1934 : « Barabudur. Les origines du stupa et la transmigration. Essai d'archéologie religieuse comparée », *B.E.F.E.O.* t. 32 (p. 269-439), t. 33 (p. 577-980) et t.34 (p. 175-400).

— 1936 : « Le symbolisme à Angkor-Thom: le Grand Miracle du Bayon », *C.R.A.I.B.L,* 1936, p.57 et suiv.

NAFILYAN (G.) – 1969 : *Angkor Vat, Description graphique du temple,* Paris (Mém.Arch.EFEO n°IV).

NANAVATI (J.M.) & DHAKY (M.A.) – 1969 : *The Maitraka and the Saindhava Temples of Gujarat,* Ascona.

NIKITINE (Athanase), *Voyage au delá des trois mers,* trad. C. Malamoud, Paris 1982.

PARLIER-RENAULT (Edith) – 2006 : *Temples de l'Inde méridionale (VIe-VIIIe siècles) – La mise en scène des mythes,* PUPS, Paris.

PARMENTIER (H.) – 1927 : *L'art Khmèr primitif,* 2 vols., Pub.EFEO, Paris.

PEROUSE DE MONTCLOS (J. M.) – 1989 : *Architecture - Vocabulaire, Principes d'analyse scientifique,* 2e éd., Paris Imprimerie Nationale [1st ed. in 1972 without author's name: *Architecture - Principes d'analyse scientifique.* Méthode et Vocabulaire, 2 vol.].

PICHARD (P.) – 1976 : *Pimay, Etude architecturale du temple,* Paris (Mém.Arch.EFEO n°X).

— 1985 : « Les monuments sur plan pentagone à Pagan », *B.E.F.E.O.* vol.74, p. 305-368.

— 1992-2001 : *Inventory of monuments at Pagan / Inventaire des monuments,* 8 volumes, Paris-Gartmore.

— 1995 : *Tanjavur Bṛhadīśvara,* New Delhi (I.G.N.C.A.) / Pondicherry (E.F.E.O.).

PICHARD (P.), L'HERNAULT (F.), BOUDIGNON (F.), THYAGARAJAN (L.) - 1994: *Vingt après Tanjavur, Gangaikondacholapuram*, 2 vol., Paris (Mém. Archéol. EFEO n° XX).

PILLAY (K.K.) – 1953 : *The Sucindram Temple*, Madras.

PROVOST-ROCHE (L.) – 2009 : *Les derniers siècles de l'époque angkorienne au Cambodge*, Thèse en cours, Université de Paris III –Sorbonne nouvelle.

RAJAN (K.V. Soundara) – 1974 : *Temple Architecture in Kerala*, Trivandrum.

— 1981 : *Cave Temples of the Deccan*, New Delhi (ASI).

RAM RAZ - 1834 : *Essay on the Architecture of the Hindus*, Londres [reed. Varanasi-Delhi, 1972].

RAO (V.N. Hari) – 1967 : *The Srirangam Temple.Art and Architecture*, Tirupati.

Rauravāgama (edit.) = BHATT (N.R.) (ed.) – 1961-1988 : *Rauravāgama*, crit. ed., 3 vol., Pondichéry (PIFI n°18:1-3).

Rauravāgama (transl.) = DAGENS (B.) et BARAZER-BILLORET (L.)- 2000: *Le Rauravāgama*, trad. et note, Pondichéry (PIFI n°89.1-2).

REINICHE (M.-L.) – 1989 : *Tiruvannamalai* 4.

RENOU (L.) – 1939 [1997] : « La maison védique », *Journal Asiatique* (1939) [and in L. RENOU, *Choix d'études indiennes* réunies par N. BALBIR, G. PINAULT et J. FEZAS, 2 vol., Paris 1997, p. 819-842].

ROGER (Abraham) – 1670 : *Le théâtre de l'idolâtrie ou la Porte ouverte pour parvenir à la cognaisssance du paganisme caché...*, transl. by Thomas La Grue, Amsterdam.

SANGAVE (Vilas A.) – 1981 : *The sacred Shravanabelagola, a Socio-Religious Study*, New Delhi.

SARKAR (H.) – 1978 : *An architectural survey of temples of Kerala*, ASI, New-Delhi.

SARKAR (H.) & MITRA (D.) 1966 – : *Nagarjunakoṇda*, ASI, New Delhi.

SCHILDT (H.) – (in the press) : « The application of the so-called āyādi formulae in Kerala », dans B. Dagens et G. Flood (eds.), *Further Tantric Studies*, New Delhi.

S.I.I. vol. II = *South Indian Inscriptions*, Vol.II. *Tamil Inscriptions of Rajaraja, Rajendra, Rajendra-Chola and others in the Rajarajesvara temple at Tanjore*, ed. and transl. by E. Hultzsch and R.B.V. Venkayya, 1891-1913, Madras.

SIRCAR (D.C.) – 1965 : *Select Inscriptions bearing on Indian History and Civilization*, Vol.I : *From the 6th cenury B.C to the 6th century AD*, 2nd ed., Delhi (Motilal Banarsidass).

SKILLING (P.) – 2008, *Past Lives of the Buddha – Wat Si Chum – Art, Architecture and Inscriptions,* with contributions of PATTARATORN CHIRAPRAVATI, P. PICHARD, PRAPOD ASSAVAVIRULHAKARN, SANTI PAKDEEKHAM, P. SKILLING, Bangkok (River Books), 2008.

SMITH (Walter) – 1994 : *The Mukteśvara Temple in Bhubaneswar,* Delhi.

SRINIVASAN (K. R.) – 1964 : *Cave Temples of the Pallavas,* New Delhi (ASI).

SRINIVASAN (P.R.) – 1990 : see *Tiruvannamalai* 1.

STAAL (F.) – 1992 : Māna – Vedic, in *Kalatattvakośa* vol.II *Concepts of Space and time* (New Delhi), p.355-357.

THAPAR (Romila) – 2004: *Somanatha. The many voices of history,* New Delhi.

Tiruvannamalai 1 = P.R. SRINIVASAN, ed. and transl. – 1990 : *Tiruvannamalai - a Śaiva sacred complex of South India* : 1. *The Inscriptions,* 2 vol., Pondichéry (Institut Français).

Tiruvannamalai 2 = F. L'HERNAULT, P. PICHARD et J. DELOCHE – 1990 : *Tiruvannamalai - un lieu saint śivaïte du sud de l'Inde* : 2. *L'archéologie du Site,* Paris (E.F.E.O.).

Tiruvannamalai 3 = F. L'HERNAULT et M.-L. REINICHE – 1999: *Tiruvannamalai - un lieu saint śivaïte du sud de l'Inde* : 3. *Rites et fêtes,* Paris (E.F.E.O.).

Tiruvannamalai 4 = M.-L. REINICHE – 1989 *Tiruvannamalai - un lieu saint śivaïte du sud de l'Inde* : 4. *La configuration sociologique du temple hindou,* Paris (E.F.E.O.).

Tiruvannamalai 5 = C. GUILMOTO, M.-L. REINICHE et P. PICHARD – 1990: *Tiruvannamalai - un lieu saint śivaïte du sud de l'Inde* : 5. *La ville,* Paris (E.F.E.O.).

VIENNOT (O.) – 1968 : « Le problème des temples à toit plat dans l'Inde du Nord », *Arts Asiatiques,* t.18, p.23-84.

VIENNOT (O.) – 1976 : *Temples de l'Inde centrale et occidentale,* Paris (Mém. Archéol. EFEO n° XI).

Vocabulaire de l'Architecture : see PEROUSE DE MONTCLOS (J. M.).

VIRAMMA et RACINE (Josiane et Jean) – 1994 : *Une vie paria. Le rire des asservis en Inde du Sud,* Paris (Collection Terre humaine).

WILLIS (Michael D.) – 1997 : *Temples of Gopakcetra. A Regional History of Architecture and Sculpture in Central India* AD *600-900,* London.

WRIGHT (G.R.H.) 1978 : « Indian summer at Petra », in R. NAGASWAMY (ed.), *South Indian Studies* , Madras, p. 79-81.

Topographic and Geographic Index

Each name is followed by its localisation according to the code below and by possibly a date

Abbreviations:

- Indian states: AP (Andhra Pradesh), BI (Bihar), CA (Kashmir), GU (Gujarat), KA (Karnataka), KE (Kerala), MA (Maharastra), MP (Madhya Pradesh), OR (Orisssa), RA (Rajasthan) TN (Tamilnadu), UP (Uttar Pradesh).
- Other countries: AF (Afghanistan), BU (Burma/Myanmar), IN (Indonesia) KH (Cambodia), LA (Laos), TH (Thailand).

T

U-V

General Index

E

F

G-H

I-J

K-L

M

N

O

P

R

S